ACTING WHITE

The Ironic
Legacy of
Desegregation

Stuart Buck

Yale UNIVERSITY PRESS

New Haven & London

Published with assistance from the foundation established in memory of Amasa Stone Mather of the Class of 1907, Yale College.

Set in Galliard type by The Composing Room of Michigan, Inc.
Printed in the United States of America.

Library of Congress Cataloging-in-Publication Data
Buck, Stuart
   Acting white : the ironic legacy of desegregation / Stuart Buck.
      p. cm.
   Includes bibliographic references and index.
   ISBN 978-0-300-12391-3 (cloth : alk. paper)

A catalogue record for this book is available from the British Library.

This paper meets the requirements of ANSI/NISO Z39.48-1992 (Permanence of Paper).

10 9 8 7 6 5 4 3 2 1

CONTENTS

ACKNOWLEDGMENTS

This book is dedicated to Vester Hughes, a dear friend and mentor.

My wife and children deserve a great deal of thanks for putting up with me over the past several years. They are a blessing to me every day.

Thanks to all of the people who experienced desegregation and agreed to talk to me.

For helpful comments, criticisms, and answers to my questions, thanks to Stephan Thernstrom of the Harvard History Department; Roland Fryer of the Harvard Economics Department; John McWhorter of the Manhattan Institute; Jay Greene of the University of Arkansas and the Manhattan Institute; Laurence Steinberg of Temple University; Seymour Spilerman of Columbia University; Randall Kennedy of Harvard Law School; Henry Louis Gates of the Harvard Afro-American Studies Department; Hugh Price of the Brookings Institution; and Adrian Piper.

Thanks to the Manuscript Department at the University of North Carolina, the Greensboro Public Library, the Special Collections Department at the University of Virginia, the State Library and Archives of Florida, and the Springdale Public Library for assistance in locating various materials. For being gracious enough to send copies of their scholarly articles to a complete stranger, thanks to David Bergin, Ted Hamann, Deborah Jamiol, Grace Kao, Kelly Navies, Jason Nier, Jason Osborne, James Patton, Meredith Phillips, Tim Sass, and Sabrina Zirkel.

Thanks to the editors at Yale University Press, including Keith Condon,

Christina Tucker, William Frucht, and Philip King; the book is far the better for their meticulous scrutiny and thoughtful suggestions.

Special thanks to Jeremy Beer, publications director and editor in chief of Intercollegiate Studies Institute Books. I had sent out my book proposal to a variety of presses, including ISI. Jeremy Beer called one day, and said that he would like my permission to forward the proposal to a colleague at Yale University Press. Needless to say, I agreed to his generous offer.

INTRODUCTION

"Go into any inner-city neighborhood," Barack Obama said in his address to the Democratic National Convention in 2004, "and folks will tell you that government alone can't teach kids to learn. They know that parents have to parent, that children can't achieve unless we raise their expectations and eradicate the slander that says a black youth with a book is acting white." Michelle Obama, according to a May 2009 report in *Newsweek*, "described the ridicule she faced from neighborhood kids for 'acting white' when she got good grades" as a child.

The Obamas are far from alone in their observations. Many people in recent years—most famously, Bill Cosby—have pointed out that black children often seem to think of schoolwork as a "white" activity. Anecdotal evidence abounds in newspaper articles and on the Internet. One black valedictorian in Virginia, for example, told a newspaper that "as I've gone through my whole school career, people have called me white because I've made good grades and didn't conform to the stereotype."

Along with these reports in the popular press, scholars have had a contentious debate about "acting white" for some twenty years now. On one side, many academic studies have shown that some black children think of doing schoolwork as "acting white," and a study by Roland Fryer—a black Harvard economist—shows that black children nationwide become less popular if their grade-point average rises above 3.5.

On the other side, a few studies have purported to disprove "acting white." But these studies are flawed: they rely on limited anecdotal evidence or on black children's reports of their own popularity (which could be inflated by the perfectly natural desire to brag). Moreover, it is implausible that the "acting white" criticism would not affect children's ability to achieve at high levels in school. We are all less likely to throw ourselves wholeheartedly into anything that might bring the ridicule or even the slight disapproval of our peers. This is true of choosing an occupation or a university, a neighborhood to live in, what clothes to wear, whether or not to take up golf, or countless other examples. Black schoolchildren are surely not immune to such a universal human trait.

The "acting white" thesis is controversial, of course, because of the fear that it lets the rest of us off the hook too easily—that suburban whites will, perhaps regretfully, write off the urban black population as uneducable. But people who are inclined to ignore the problems of poor blacks will always be able to come up with an excuse to do so, regardless of what the scholarly community says. Another perceived problem is that the "acting white" thesis seems to blame black children themselves for failing to achieve in school, rather than blaming only external factors such as poverty, racism, and inadequate schools. No one denies that these other factors have a strong effect on academic achievement, but poverty and inadequate schools cannot be the whole story. There is an achievement gap between black students and white students even in studies that compare children in the same schools, with the same household incomes and family backgrounds. *Something else* has to be a contributing factor as well, and an obvious candidate is the attitude that people have toward education.

So much for the current state of the "acting white" debate. Why this book? For all of the back and forth on "acting white," few scholars have stopped to consider *where* that criticism came from in the first place.

"Acting white" has been discussed so often in the popular press that it no longer comes as a surprise. *But it should.* If we look at the historical record, there is no evidence that black schoolchildren back in the days of slavery or Jim Crow accused a studious schoolmate of "acting white." To the contrary, *white* people occasionally accused educated blacks of trying to be white. As historian Leon Litwack points out, nineteenth-century whites sometimes "equated black success with 'uppityness,' 'impudence,' getting out of place,' and pretensions toward racial equality. 'He think he white' was the expression whites sometimes used to convey that suspicion, or 'He is too smart,' 'He wants to be white and act like white people,' and "He think he somebody.'"[1] A Northerner who had moved to Georgia after the Civil War noted that "in the days of Slavery, the masters ridiculed the negroes' efforts to use good language, and become like the whites."[2] In the 1960s, a black plaintiff in a North Carolina desegregation case testified that she had received threatening telephone calls, many of which "asked me was I trying to get white."[3]

Yet today, the "acting white" criticism that was once occasionally used by racist whites has been adopted by some black schoolchildren. That is the central mystery that this book addresses: what happened between the nineteenth century and today?

The answer, I believe, springs from the complex history of desegregation. Although desegregation arose from noble and necessary impulses, and although desegregation was to the overall benefit of the nation, it was often implemented in a way that was devastating to black communities. It destroyed black schools, reduced the numbers of black principals and teachers who could serve as role models, and brought many black schoolchildren into daily contact with whites who made school a strange and uncomfortable environment that was viewed as quintessentially "white."

Numerous scholars and commentators have observed that the "acting white" criticism arose during the 1960s—precisely the time when desegregation actually happened. Indeed, many black people recall that they were first accused of "acting white" or "trying to be white" during the desegregation experience. For example, Bernice McNair Barnett, who teaches at the University of Illinois at Urbana-Champaign, recalls that she was "isolated and cut off from the world of my former Black peers (who saw my school desegregation choice as 'trying to be White') as well as my new White peers (who were both hate filled bullies and otherwise good hearted but silent bystanders)." As Beverly Daniel Tatum—the president of Spelman College—points out, "An oppositional identity that disdains academic achievement has not always been a characteristic of Black adolescent peer groups. It seems to be a post-desegregation phenomenon."[4]

All of this occurred in part because desegregation undermined one of the traditional centers of the black community: the school. In the segregated schools, black children had consistently seen other blacks succeeding in the academic world. The authority figures and role models—that is, the teachers and principals—were virtually always black. And the best students in black schools were black as well.

This ended with desegregation. Many black schools disappeared altogether: school boards all across the South closed or demolished black schools in pursuit of desegregation (or occasionally kept the school open while changing its name and status, so as to erase its historical connection to the black community). After desegregation, many black children were taught by white teachers who disliked them, did not care about their success, underestimated their capabilities, or—at the opposite extreme—coddled them out of guilt. Even when the white teachers did everything right, the black schoolchildren still, for the first time, faced the possibility of seeing "school" as a place where success equaled seeking the approval of whites.

Black schoolchildren, now dispersed into formerly all-white schools, suddenly had to deal with unfriendly classmates on a day-to-day basis. School was no longer a place where black children could avoid interacting with racist people. As John McWhorter points out, the "demise of segregation" helped "pave the way for the 'acting white' charge. With the closing of black schools after desegregation orders, black students began going to school with white ones in larger numbers than ever before, which meant that whites were available for black students to model themselves against."[5]

Many desegregated schools made greater use of academic "tracking," which kept most of the better-prepared white students in a separate class from the black students. This too reinforced the message that "academic achievement is the province of whites." By contrast, as Beverly Daniel Tatum explains, "in the context of a segregated school, it was a given that the high achieving students would all be Black. Academic achievement did not have to mean separation from one's Black peers."[6]

Thus, as Harvard economist Roland Fryer points out, one's attitude toward education can now function as a *racial signal*. A black student who is too eager in class may be seen as trying to curry favor with the mostly white teachers. And where the advanced classes or academic clubs are predominantly white, the black student who takes advanced classes or joins an academic club is seen as having preferred the company of whites over blacks. In other words, just by the fact that desegregation brought black and white students into contact with one another, it became possible for either blacks *or* whites to view the other race as outsiders in the school environment, and to start punishing children who spent too much time crossing the boundary lines between races.

There is nothing unusual in this: Humans are tribal creatures. It is a universal human trait for group members to expect loyalty to the group, whether the "group" involves employees of a particular corporation; Democrats or Republicans; literally thousands of religious sects and denominations; citizens of a particular country, state, or town; fans of the Yankees or any other sports team; or a nearly infinite range of groups based on all sorts of characteristics. It was an ironic byproduct of desegregation that this universal human expectation—"be loyal to our group, or else"—showed up in schools.

Martin Luther King, Jr., famously wrote, "It is appalling that the most segregated hour of Christian America is eleven o'clock on Sunday morning."[7] Though there are many more integrated church congregations today than there were in 1958, when King wrote those words, there are still many churches that are largely white or largely black.[8]

Imagine that there had been a long governmental history of mandatory church segregation. Now imagine that the government had a change of heart. Church segregation, everyone now agreed, was immoral. Besides, white churches often had superior facilities, heated baptistries, higher steeples, more stained glass windows, newer hymnbooks, bigger parking lots, and padded chairs instead of wooden pews. It was unfair for black people to attend churches with such inadequate resources. Thus, churches would now be integrated.

But how would church integration come about? By forcing whites to attend black churches? No: in this story, one of the very premises of church integration was that white churches were superior, and that the religious training of blacks would improve if only they were admitted to white churches. And besides, few whites would want to attend black churches and be subject to the leadership of black pastors.

So then, imagine that state governments set about shutting down most of the black Baptist and AME churches and demolishing the church buildings (or else commandeering them for another purpose). Imagine that most black churchgoers were forced to go to predominantly white churches scattered across town, in which the style of worship was different from that to which they were accustomed. Imagine that some of these white congregations protested or even rioted over the fact that a few blacks would be allowed in their presence. Imagine that the white churches often refused to give meaningful jobs to black ministers, and that they put many of the blacks in a separate Sunday School class.

In other words, black people would have been taken out of a church that, for better or worse, they could call their own, and would instead have found themselves a mostly unwelcome minority in a white-controlled church.

What would be the result? While no doubt some blacks would benefit from increased opportunities, from a larger network of white friends, or perhaps from improved Sunday School classes, the effect on some other blacks is easy to predict. They would become discontent or disillusioned with their new church. They would resent having been marginalized and excluded from positions of responsibility. They would feel uncomfortable, whether with white peoples' attitudes or with the very notion of being forced to go to a different church. Most importantly, some might begin to see religion as something controlled by and meant for *white people*. Going to church would begin to be viewed as "acting white."

This story of church desegregation makes intuitive sense. As we will see in subsequent chapters, the same story can be told about the field of education. But, with education, the story is true.

Some people might rationally wonder whether I oppose desegregation. Why else would I take the time to highlight problems with desegregation rather than focus on some other aspect of education?

I believe strongly in integration as a moral ideal. The message that I intend to convey is *not* that desegregation was a bad idea, *not* that the people who pursued desegregation were foolish or misguided, *not* that desegregation is something that we should consider reversing. Desegregation was unquestionably the right thing to do, and it benefited many black Americans by bringing them into the mainstream of American society.

At the same time, nothing in life is free. Anything that is valuable and worth achieving comes at a price. Intellectual honesty obligates us to weigh—and consider how to mitigate—the costs imposed by our preferred policies, rather than sweeping the problems under the rug. The costs of desegregation included the destruction of black institutions, the trauma experienced by some black children, and the overall effect on black attitudes toward education. While the benefits of desegregation outweigh the costs, this book is not intended to focus on the benefits (which are amply discussed elsewhere). Rather, it is intended to consider how the costs arose and whether we might reduce or eliminate them.

That is the spirit in which this book is written, and in which I hope it will be received.

Now for a brief outline of the following chapters. Some readers may, at least initially, be skeptical whether "acting white" really occurs, and whether it has any effect on school achievement. The first chapter describes the empirical evidence showing that "acting white" does indeed occur, and the second argues that any attempt to explain the achievement gap should include the role of peers. Both of these chapters are introductory; they explain why this book exists in the first place. If you already agree that "acting white" is a significant phenomenon, feel free to skip ahead.

Chapter 3 takes us back to the era of slavery and Jim Crow, and recounts the ample historical evidence that the black community made great strides in pursuing education during those years. The striking thing is that the "acting white" phenomenon was unknown at that time.

Most of the rest of the chapters then explain why it makes sense that "acting white" would have arisen as an unfortunate byproduct of desegregation. Chapter 4 describes the positive and nurturing academic environment that flourished in many black schools before desegregation. Chapters 5 through 7 explain the devastation that occurred when, as desegregation occurred, many of those black schools were destroyed, black principals lost their jobs, and black children found themselves shunted to lower academic tracks in predominantly white schools. Finally, Chapter 8 addresses the central question: *When* did "acting white" start to become more widespread in schools? After all, if "acting white" arose in the 1940s or the 1990s, it would not make sense to blame desegregation. In fact, however, it is a point of unanimity that the "acting white" attitude in schools first became common in the 1960s, along with desegregation. The book then closes with a few tentative suggestions about how to counteract the psychological forces that give rise to "acting white."

1

DOES "ACTING WHITE" OCCUR?

Courtney Smith figures she heard it nearly every day she was in public school: "Courtney acts white." "Courtney talks white." "Courtney thinks she's all that." Just because she did well in school and spoke proper English. "[Other students] feel they're supposed to be cool, and cool is not supposed to be making good grades in school."

—*Virginian-Pilot,* Norfolk, Virginia, 2006

"All of my life, I've been accused of acting white," [Alexandra] Gray said. "Just because you are articulate or take [Advanced Placement] classes, kids want to say that. But I'm only being me. I'm only being myself." Many students echoed her ideas, saying that taking ballet classes or playing the violin brought accusations that they weren't "acting black enough."

—*East Valley Tribune,* Mesa, Arizona, 2008

Many people think that the "acting white" phenomenon is just a myth. Michael Eric Dyson, for example, the University of Pennsylvania professor and public intellectual, in his book *Is Bill Cosby Right?* claims that "acting white" is the "academic equivalent of an urban legend" that is "rooted in a single 1986 study of a Washington, D.C., high school."

Indeed, some think that the "acting white" thesis is dangerous. Dyson argues that the "social mythology of low black academic desire" serves only to "deprive black students of an equal education."[1] A piece in the *New York Times Magazine* claims that "the idea that failing black kids pull down successful black kids can be used as an excuse by administrators to conceal or justify discrimination in the public education system."[2] Strikingly, a Duke professor who co-authored a study on black academic attitudes (described later in this chapter) has called his own scholarship "warfare in the academy" against the "acting white" thesis.[3]

The "acting white" phenomenon is not a myth. Far from only a "single 1986 study," at least fifteen academic studies (from surveys to ethnographies) have found evidence of the "acting white" phenomenon in education over the past thirty-seven years. In addition, abundant anecdotal evidence shows that accomplished black students are often ridiculed. The "acting white" criticism deserves more than a hand-waving dismissal.

Is It a Myth?
The Scholarly Evidence for "Acting White"

The most solid evidence in support of the "acting white" thesis comes from a study by Harvard economist Roland Fryer, Jr., a thirty-something black man who has already published a ream of important articles on race in America. Fryer found that smart black students are less popular with their peers.

Fryer's finding came from the National Longitudinal Study of Adolescent Health, which collected information about the friends of some ninety thousand students nationwide who entered high school in the mid-1990s. The information was not self-reported (as we shall see, this makes Fryer's study more reliable than the studies that purport to disprove "acting white"). Rather, the students were asked to provide a list of their closest male and female friends. Fryer counted "how often each student's name appeared on peers' lists," and then—just as Google reportedly does with its ranking of Web sites—he weighted the raw counts according to how "frequently a peer is listed by others."[4] He also controlled for factors such as parental education, occupation, and participation in extracurricular activities (including sports, student government, and cheerleading).

The results were striking. Whereas white students' popularity steadily *increased* along with their grade-point average (such that the most accomplished white children were the most popular), black children experienced a drop-off in popularity as their grade-point average rose above 3.5. In Fryer's words, "A black student with a 4.0 has, on average, 1.5 fewer friends of the same ethnicity than a white student with the same GPA. Put differently, a black student with straight As is no more popular than a black student with a 2.9 GPA, but high-achieving whites are at the top of the popularity pyramid."[5]

A skeptic might ask, "Are white kids really more popular when they make higher grades? Isn't there a common stereotype of the friendless nerd in the American high school? Did that stereotype just come from nowhere?"

It is not that smart kids are *always* popular; just on *average*. Children who are wealthy often tend to be smarter, or at least better prepared from having had the sort of parents who put alphabet flashcards above their infants' cribs. Thus, some of the kids who are dominant in the high school scene (because of their wealth and style) are also the same kids who have been pushed to succeed academically from a young age. Another possibility is that some of the smartest kids are eager to build a long résumé to send off for college admissions, and therefore join many clubs or organizations, bringing them into contact with potential friends. Yet another possibility is that the smarter kids are better able to figure out how to navigate the complicated social world of high school.

Tellingly, Fryer found that the "acting white" criticism is unique to integrated schools, while in predominantly black schools, there is *"no evidence at all* that getting good grades adversely affects students' popularity." What's more, when Fryer looked at schools with greater levels of "internal integration"—that is, more friendships between different races in general—he found *much* higher levels of the "acting white" effect. In Fryer's words, "Black males in such schools fare the worst, penalized seven times as harshly as my estimate of the average effect of acting white on all black students!" He then suggests that this effect may be because "racially integrated settings only reinforce pressures to toe the ethnic line."

Fryer's study is an interesting contrast with one performed in the late 1960s on the experiences of around sixty-five hundred children during desegregation. The children were asked to complete questionnaires in which each student gave first, second, and third choices for "whom from among his classmates he would prefer for friends, for schoolwork partners, and for members of a ball team." Among "segregated minority children" in the year preceding desegregation, the black students who ranked in the highest third of achievement were by far the most popular.[6]

Fryer is far from the only scholar to have found an "acting white" effect in schools. Here are just a few others:

- In 1986, Nigerian-American sociologist John Ogbu and Signithia Fordham published what became a famous article describing the "acting white" criticism in a high school in Washington, D.C.[7] Fordham later wrote a book about that high school, reporting that "students had an inordinately long list of ways in which it was possible to act white, many of them directly related to behaviors in and outside the school and some directly related to the pursuit of academic achievement." She briefly suggests a connection to desegregation: "Kaela admits that she and her friend were ashamed to tell their families that they had been down at the Smithsonian because, in this era of integration, 'cozying up' to White Americans brings one's identity into question."[8]

- One case study of 148 black students in an urban school district found the "acting white" criticism to be common, and concluded that "peer pressure and fear of isolation are powerful contributors to underachievement among Black students, and gifted learners in general."[9] The same scholar followed up with another study focusing on black female elementary students. Out of 89 participants, 54 percent reported having been "teased for 'getting good grades,'" and 31 percent had been accused of "acting white."[10] And in March 2008, the same scholar and several colleagues surveyed 166 gifted black students in Ohio, and found that 66 percent reported that they knew someone who was ridiculed for doing well in school, that most students thought of "acting white" as being smart and doing well in school, and (troublingly) that most students thought of "acting black" as being dumb and pretending not to care about school.[11]

- In a 1993 lecture, two professors reported on a survey of 190 black middle and high school students from Michigan, all of whom were enrolled in summer academic programs. They found that a "sizable proportion" of the students (around 21–25 percent) agreed that their friends thought of academic success in terms of "acting white." The professors admitted that theirs was not a random sample but argued that they were probably "underestimating the prevalence" of "acting white," because they looked only at students who already tended to be in smart peer groups.[12]

- In a 1996 book, psychology professor Laurence Steinberg reported on the results of a multiyear study that surveyed some twenty thousand high school students as well as hundreds of parents and teachers. In his words, "we heard variations on the 'acting White' theme many, many times over the course of our interviews with high school students." As a result, many black students "are forced to choose between doing well in school and having friends."[13]

- As reported in a recent book, researchers found strong evidence of "acting white" in a survey of more than one hundred black students in Charlotte, North Carolina. One girl, for example, said, "I was always on the honor roll . . . you know, you get called white, which I think is ridiculous 'cause that's meaning that if you're intelligent, you're white, if you're dumb, then you're black."[14]

- In late 2006, Ronald Ferguson of Harvard released a survey that was part of a broader research project involving twenty high schools in eight states. He found that in integrated schools, almost half of the A students reported that they were "sometimes" or "always" accused of acting white.[15]

There are several other academic papers that found an "acting white" phenomenon in particular schools.[16] Any one of these studies does not prove a nationwide pattern. At the same time, when one ethnography after another keeps finding the same thing—whether in D.C., Michigan, Ohio, or elsewhere—the combined results are difficult to ignore.

Several common themes can be seen in these many studies.

Integrated Schools. Many studies, like Fryer's, suggest that "acting white" is a problem in integrated schools. For example, the first academic study that found "acting white" was a 1970 book about a desegregated school. In that study, sociologists found many examples of the "acting white" criticism. One student was asked, "What pressures do you feel from the fact that you attend a desegregated school?" He responded, "Well, I participate in speech; I'm the only Negro in the whole group. . . . The Negroes accuse me of thinking I'm white. . . . I think it's this kind of pressure from the other Negro kids which causes me the greatest concern."[17]

The book points out that "derogatory attitudes are particularly noticeable toward blacks, who . . . try to compete with white students for academic honors, school offices, and roles in extracurricular activities. . . . The black student who enters these activities is called a 'white nigger' or an 'Uncle Tom' by other blacks."[18] Indeed, the study's authors pointed out that the "acting white" criticism was directly tied to integration: "To do what 'whitey' does is the Negro's right, but once the right becomes a reality, the black is 'playing it white.' *Thus, the Negro who is at the frontiers of integration is doing what his race demands but is, simultaneously, rejected by many other Negroes.*"[19]

Similarly, sociologist Karolyn Tyson—who is otherwise a skeptic on the "acting white" issue—found, based on four ethnographic studies conducted over nine years, that "some black students are indeed accused of 'acting white' by their peers."[20] Tyson points out that students who "attended all-black schools or schools that had more racially balanced classrooms" "rarely recalled ever being accused of acting white."[21] (Racially balanced classrooms avoid the scenario in racially balanced *schools* wherein white students tend to be in the more advanced classes.) As well, a study of the St. Louis desegregation program notes that the "eleventh-grade transfer students participating in the focus group described how they 'hate it' when African-American students talk and act 'all white' when they are at their county schools and then get on the bus and start talking 'black' again."[22]

Finally, David Bergin and Helen Cooks interviewed thirty-eight black students from several different schools in an unidentified "midwestern city."[23] They suggest that the "acting white" syndrome is worst in racially mixed schools: "High-achieving students of color in racially balanced schools appear most likely to be accused of acting white because their enrollment in advanced classes puts them in constant contact with white students, and at the same time, there is a large number of students of color who are in a position to notice and comment on the supposed defection . . . . Students in racially balanced schools seemed to feel more polarization based on race, so they were under more pressure to 'choose sides.'"[24]

The same phenomenon seems not to affect all-black schools. Drawing on his own experience attending predominantly black schools when he was younger, Roland Fryer explains. "We didn't act white—we didn't know what that was," he said. "There were no white kids around."[25]

The Effect on Boys. The second common theme is that "acting white" seems to have a stronger effect on boys, which potentially could help explain why black boys graduate from high school at a lower rate than black girls.[26] Roland Fryer found that the cost of academic success is higher for black males than for black females: "Popularity begins to decrease at lower GPAs for young black men than young black women (3.25 GPA compared with a 3.5), and the rate at which males lose friends after this point is far greater. As a result, black male high achievers have notably fewer friends than do female ones."[27]

Other researchers surveyed 2,730 eighth graders at randomly selected schools in Charlotte, North Carolina (just over 1,000 were black). They asked about "oppositional attitudes"—that is, whether the students agreed with statements such as "my friends at home believe that too much education makes a person give up his or her real identity." They found that "males expressed more cynical oppositional attitudes toward education," that both "male and female students' oppositional attitudes had negative effects on their [test] scores," and that "this finding offers insight into the gender gaps in achievement among Black middle school students."[28]

More anecdotally, one journalist noted in describing a school in Washington, D.C.: "For a girl to be a 'goody' or a 'whitey' by wanting to do well and leave everyone behind is not considered as serious a disrespect to the less fortunate as it is for a boy. A straight-arrow boy who thinks 'he's better than other people' can get taken down with violence. A girl of the same mien can be taken down with sex, making her a prize for a tough guy who can exhibit irresistible charms."[29]

If such social pressures on black boys are widespread, it would not be surprising if they have a harder time succeeding in school. To be sure, there is a gender gap among white students as well, and I am not claiming that "acting white" would be the only factor affecting black boys.

The Middle School Years. We can all remember that awkward and intense time of life when it seemed that the approval of our peers was the most important thing in the world. Perhaps you wore loafers with white socks, or polyester plaid pants, or bouffant bangs (all the girls had this when I was growing up), or whatever now embarrassing thing that was in style when you were a teenager, simply out of a desire to conform to your peers.[30] Psychologists observe that "vulnerability to peer pressure . . . rises as children become teenagers," and "peaks sometime around eighth or ninth grade," because "individuals are easily influenced by their peers" from ages twelve to sixteen.[31]

During the middle and high school years, children not only become more dependent on their peers, they become more conscious of racial issues. As a result, middle school students become much more divided into racial peer groups. To take a specific example, *New York Times* reporters found that in elementary school, "nobody cared about race," but a "racial split" seemed to be "inevitable" in middle school.[32] One white girl's best friend (who was black) said that she could "no longer afford white friends"; a black boy said of a previous white friend of his, "the summer before high school, we just went different ways."[33] A student in Baltimore "shared a similar experience, stating: 'In sixth grade, I remember when I came, everyone was just a happy-go-lucky family, and they wanted me to be the new Black kid in the family.' Yet, by high school, she noted, the Black students tended to separate themselves from the White students insofar as social activities were concerned."[34] Indeed, some children are caught in the middle: at Crete-Monee High School in Illinois, a biracial child named Charles pointed out that "whites who don't know him ask his white friends, 'Why you hang around with Charles? He's black.' And blacks who don't know him ask his black friends, 'Why you hang around with Charles? He's white.'"[35]

This is why "acting white" arises—at least in integrated schools—in the middle school years.[36] As John Ogbu noticed in Shaker Heights, Ohio, "the idea that school success made a Black student less Black was non-existent at the elementary school." In middle school, however, several students admitted that "negative peer pressures were pervasive and led to disengagement from schoolwork." Then in high school, "peer pressures reached their peak," having "much greater influence on student enrollment in honors and AP classes and academic performance."[37]

"Acting white" isn't *only* about academics, to be sure. As many commentators and scholars have pointed out, the "acting white" charge often is targeted at how someone talks or dresses, rather than at academic achievement in itself. Ogbu points out that the black students he studied "did not reject making good grades per se," but rather rejected "attitudes and behaviors that they perceived or interpreted as White, but that were conducive to making good grades."[38] Angela Neal-Barnett says that the students she studied often believed that "acting white" meant a wide variety of activities related to "speech, dress, academic performance, and home training."[39] Ronald Ferguson notes that in his survey, kids who reported having been accused of "acting white" also reported that the most common causes were "their personal styles such as the ways that they speak" or the "music they listen to."[40]

Nonetheless, in a world where black and white students often exhibit an achievement gap, whites will still predominate in the academically challenging classes. Blacks who enter those classes will then be more likely to befriend whites, and to speak more like their white classmates. (Children learn to speak in the accent of their peers; this is why the children of adult immigrants speak with an American accent, rather than the one they hear from their parents at home.) As Karolyn Tyson points out, where high-achieving black students are "racially isolated in high-ability classes," their "chances of forming friendships with and adopting certain preferences and styles of speech, dress, and behavior from white students are greater."[41] As a result, whether or not the "acting white" charge is inherently aimed at academic achievement, it could still deter blacks from participating in the very activities or classes that go along with academic success.

Anecdotal Evidence of "Acting White"

"The plural of anecdote is not data," goes the cliché. That's true in some cases, but it does not apply here. We already have plenty of data, as discussed above, and anecdotes put a human face on it.

This anecdotal evidence is fairly overwhelming. For example, John McWhorter points out that after he wrote his best-selling book *Losing the Race* a few years ago, he received more than a hundred unsolicited testimonials from black people who had personally experienced the "acting white" criticism.[42] After providing a depressingly long list of examples, he makes the obvious point that "we cannot assume that for some reason I have been apprised of the sum total of such events," and there must "have been countless others."[43]

I too have come across many anecdotes of "acting white," whether in conversation, in newspaper accounts, or in Internet postings—enough to fill dozens of pages. Some of these anecdotes are reprinted at the head of various chapters. To list a very few examples here: A 2006 story from Michigan points out, "Sixteen-year-old Antwon Fox, a sophomore at Loy Norrix High School, said he wouldn't call getting good grades 'acting white,' but he did acknowledge that it's not cool among his peers to get good grades. He described himself as a B-minus student. And what would he call an African-American student who gets A's? he was asked. As a sheepish looking grin broke out on his face, he replied quietly, 'Acting white.'"[44] Ellis Cose reported in *Newsweek* on numerous New York youngsters who were accused of acting white: "'Your African identity has to be defined by ignorance,' observed Edad Mercier, a junior at the Dalton School in New York City. 'Caucasians don't have that pressure,' she added." In Florida, Clarence Stephen, the 2004 valedictorian at Seminole High School, heard his black classmates say that he was a "white boy in a black man's body."[45] A Boston news story recounts that "as a top student and the first black female class president at Weston High, [Kandice] Sumner at times battled the notion that she was 'acting white,' or trying to be something she wasn't."[46] From North Carolina, an honor roll tenth grader says of her black peers, "They can get high grades but they don't want to because they'll be considered as acting white, so they put white people down." Another student says, "Black students that are doing well in the classroom or hang out with white friends or have good grammar, talk properly or don't use slang, they get accused of being white a lot."[47]

In New Jersey, a black girl points out, "A lot of people think of the black kids in the top classes, the ones who don't hang out with a lot of African-Americans, as the 'white' black kids. I'd never say it to them, but in my head I call them the white black kids too."[48] In the same school, another girl laments, "I'm too white to be black and I'm too black to be white."[49]

Opponents of "Acting White"

Opponents of the "acting white" thesis are far from rare. At one extreme, some people argue that many of the things learned in school—ways of thinking, writing, or problem-solving, for example—*are* "white" or "Eurocentric." To ask black students to learn a given curriculum, or to sit still in a classroom, *really is* asking them to "act white." The solution, therefore, is to have a curriculum that is "culturally relevant," or "multicultural," or "culturally responsive," or some similar buzzword.

There's a grain of truth here, and I agree that there can be cultural clashes between black students and white teachers, or even between the school environment and the fact that some children (often boys) need more physical activity. In the end, though, I cannot agree that it is unfair to expect children to speak in standard English, to write formal essays, to read Shakespeare, or to learn math.[50] It does black students no favor to argue that they are ill-suited for academic skills that, like it or not, are highly rewarded in America. As John Ogbu pointed out, "The way to help these young people . . . is to show them that following school rules of behavior for achievement . . . does not require them to give up their own minority cultural frame of reference. We do not help these young people by telling them that we admire and encourage their 'resistance' to the system."[51]

Moreover, as Laurence Steinberg and his colleagues found in a study of some twenty thousand students, "foreign-born students—who, incidentally, report significantly more discrimination than American-born youngsters and significantly more difficulty with the English language—nevertheless earn higher grades in school."[52] In Shaker Heights, Ohio, one immigrant from Trinidad criticized his African-American classmates for "insisting that the curriculum should be 'relevant' for them to learn," and told Ogbu that he did not expect the schools to teach him anything that was "based on his native Trinidad culture."[53]

On an empirical level, several studies have purported to disprove "acting white." As I will explain, these studies are less convincing than the studies discussed above—both because they are fewer in number and because they depend on less reliable data.

The first study was done by Karolyn Tyson, Domini Castellino, and William Darity (this is the same study portrayed in the *New York Times Magazine* as having proved that "acting white" is a myth, and Darity is the scholar who describes his research as "warfare in the academy"). This was an ethnographic study, in which the authors or their researchers interviewed a total of 125 students at 11 North Carolina schools.[54]

Notably, a working draft of this paper (which was emailed to me in 2004) pointed out that the researchers did not ask directly about "acting white." This is a red flag. Students are not always eager to bring up racial subjects on their own, which means that one cannot claim to have proved that "acting white" is a myth merely because students failed to *volunteer* that information. As Prudence Carter of the Harvard sociology department found in her study of New York students, they "hesitated to invoke language about race unless I mentioned it first. . . . After a handful of interviews, I decided to ask directly about 'acting ethnic' or acting white. . . . Doing so often resulted in visible signs of relief on the students' part."[55] Similarly, a journalist from Austin, Texas, writes that a group of students "had been a bit reserved at the onset of the interview," but "my question about this 'acting white' business releases them from their shyness, and the room erupts into electrified chatter as they all try to respond at once. Yes, yes, some of them had had that epithet thrown at them, or at least, were familiar with the label."[56]

Tyson and her colleagues claim that there was a "desire to do well academically among all" students that they interviewed. Students cannot always be trusted, however, to give a completely frank answer to such questions. Whether black or white, some children will earnestly assure researchers that they desire academic success—and they may be quite sincere —but that does not mean that, when push comes to shove, they would be willing to study on a Friday night.[57] In fact, the Tyson study provides evidence of this very point: One student, when asked why she was not in the gifted program, straightforwardly admitted that it was "because I'm lazy and you have to do more projects and stuff." The study says that "there was no evidence that she was averse to academic success," because she herself reported earning As and Bs. I suspect, however, that it would be more plausible to take such a student at her word that she disliked hard work— a prerequisite to academic success.

At one high school, Tyson and her colleagues *did* find "a burden of acting white with respect to achievement," from both the students and the teachers. A black counselor whose daughter had graduated a few years earlier reported that "some of the kids felt that if they were in these honors classes, . . . the black kids look at them as if they were acting white, not recognizing that you could be smart and black." One black girl "recalled being called 'white girl' and 'Oreo' by fellow blacks in middle school after being separated from her black peers and placed in an accelerated class with only whites. She described that period as 'hell.'"

What made this high school different from the other schools in the study is that it was well integrated, with lots of both black and white students. But, as is all too common, the white students dominated the advanced classes, more than was the case in other schools in the study. Indeed, the authors noted "evidence of a burden of acting white in another study we conducted involving 65 high-achieving black students at 19 high schools. . . . All were cases of students attending racially mixed schools, and almost all the students were isolated from other blacks in advanced classes."[58]

In short, the Tyson study was small in size, depended on self-reported information that did not include direct questions about "acting white," and still did find the "acting white" charge at the most well-integrated school in the study. On the whole, this study does more to support my theory than to prove it a myth.

Two other empirical studies that purport to disprove "acting white" are both from 1998: a paper in the *American Sociological Review* by James Ainsworth-Darnell and Douglas Downey, and a chapter by Philip Cook and Jens Ludwig in the book *The Black-White Test Score Gap*.[59] Both papers looked at data from the National Education Longitudinal Study (or NELS). As with the Tyson study, I think these studies are less informative, because they depend either on circumstantial evidence or on the fact that blacks in the NELS database *self-reported* that they were popular.

For example, Ainsworth-Darnell and Downey state that "African American students report more positive attitudes toward school than do white students." The basis for this statement is how often the students themselves claim to have a variety of positive attitudes toward school (for example, "that they try hard in class," or that "others view them as a good student . . . but not a troublemaker"). Blacks who claim to be devoted students also claim to be "especially popular."[60]

But this could mean only that some children are inclined to exaggerate across the board—they exaggerate when they claim to work hard, and they exaggerate when they claim to be popular. Self-reports tend to be less reliable where people have an incentive to give a rosy picture of their own lives.[61] Imagine a study purporting to show that racial discrimination had disappeared in the banking industry, because a survey of loan officers revealed that they all described themselves as non-racist.[62]

To be sure, much of the evidence that I cite in this book is self-reported, and a critic might therefore claim that I am contradicting myself. There is a key distinction, however: When people self-report something bad that happened to them (such as the "acting white" accusation), or even when they simply describe the facts of how their schools operate, they are not inclined to exaggerate as much as when they are asked to report on information that reflects *their own self-worth*. Thus, when people say, "I was accused of acting white," or "I thought my teachers in black schools cared about my academic success," that information seems inherently more reliable than when people say, "Sure, I'm a popular guy, I have lots of friends."

Ainsworth-Darnell and Downey concede that "blacks may report working 'very hard' in school but, on average, they may not put forth the same effort as white students who report the same attitude." Indeed, "African American students who reported that they work 'as hard as they can almost every day' in their classes also reported doing an average of 3.9 hours of homework per week. In contrast, Asian American students and white students who reported working 'as hard as they can almost every day' averaged 7.5 and 5.4 hours of homework per week, respectively."[63] Nonetheless, Ainsworth-Darnell and Downey say that "it is unclear whether black students' attitudes are inconsistent with their behaviors," "because there is no definite number of hours students who work 'as hard as they can almost every day' are *supposed* to spend on homework." Thus, perhaps it's just that white students "suffer from negativity bias" rather than that blacks "exhibit positivity bias."[64]

Whatever you call it—white negativity bias or black positivity bias—Ainsworth-Darnell and Downey's own research shows that among students who all claim that they work as hard as possible, the white students are actually doing 38 percent more homework per week, while Asian Americans are doing 92 percent more homework per week. In light of these significant differences, black students and white students do not *really* have identical attitudes toward schoolwork. They may all claim that they are working "hard," but that word must mean something different. Indeed, Ainsworth-Darnell and Downey note that "whether one 'tried hard in school' may mean different things to black students and white students because *they are surrounded by different sets of peers with varying norms and expectations regarding school-related behaviors.*"[65] In other words, black students belong to a peer group that lowers their academic standards, by making them think they are working "as hard as they can" even though whites and especially Asian Americans manage to work quite a bit harder. That is the very quandary here.

Ludwig and Cook report that blacks drop out of high school at similar rates as whites, if you control for socioeconomic background, and also that blacks and whites nationwide have similar rates of skipping class or school altogether.[66] They then claim that this is relevant to "acting white" because "if the African-American adolescent community does discourage academic achievement, one would expect blacks to skip class and miss school more often than whites."[67]

That assumption does not strike me as self-evidently true. Many students may show up at school while still thinking of it as a necessary evil that allows them to socialize with other students, or to participate in sports, cheerleading, or other activities. By the same token, the mere fact that students fail to drop out of school does not prove that they are all passionate about learning. There is a reason that movies like *Ferris Bueller's Day Off* strike a familiar chord—whether or not some students literally drop out of high school, they are not all equally thrilled to be there. As Signithia Fordham reported in her study on Capital High in Washington, D.C., "for some of the students in the sample group, particularly the males, the extracurricular activities appear to be the reason for coming to school."[68] She gives an example of a student who so much "abhors acting white" that he "refuse[s], unconditionally, to complete *any* assigned classwork." Even so, he maintained an "excellent attendance record."[69] This suggests, to my mind, that whether or not "acting white" occurs cannot be determined just by looking at attendance records.

Ludwig and Cook then turn to the question of time spent on homework. Here, their findings are curious: They claim that the statistics are similar, in that 68 percent of whites and 65 percent of blacks "said they spent at least two to three hours a week outside school doing homework."[70] But recall that Ludwig and Cook are examining the exact same data as Ainsworth-Darnell and Downey, who found that blacks who claim to work "as hard as they can" did only 3.9 hours of homework per week, compared to 7.5 hours for Asians and 5.4 hours for whites. The answer becomes plain when you realize that Ludwig and Cook are merely comparing how many blacks and whites cleared a fairly low hurdle—whether they did at least two hours of homework per week—whereas Ainsworth-Darnell and Downey were looking at the higher end of the spectrum, which is where the differences become rather more important.[71]

A fourth study purporting to refute the "acting white" theory comes from Angel Harris, a sociology professor at Princeton.[72] Harris relies on the Maryland Adolescence Development in Context Study, which sampled and collected data on 1,480 teens in Maryland from middle school (starting in 1991) until three years after high school. Harris finds that black Maryland students were slightly more likely than white students to claim that they enjoyed classes and school, and that blacks claimed to "spend the same amount of time on homework and educational activities" as whites.[73] The problem is that, like the other studies mentioned above, self-reported data may be exaggerated.

Notably, Harris finds that 17 percent of black seventh graders directly said that "getting good grades" is "part of 'acting white.'"[74] The reason Harris does not treat this finding as confirmation of the "acting white" theory is that high-achieving and low-achieving seventh graders were equally likely to say that getting good grades was part of "acting white." This means, in Harris's words, that "the fear of appearing white for performing well in school is not the reason for differences in school performance between these groups."[75] That conclusion is a bit too quick, though. The "acting white" theory does not predict that any *one* group of black students (whether high- or low-achieving) would have a greater likelihood of positively responding to such a survey question. Even if all levels of black students are equally likely to say that getting good grades is part of "acting white" in their school, that may just mean that the low-achievers have *been harmed* by that attitude, while the high-achievers have had to *overcome* that attitude.

Moreover, Harris's own analysis finds that "good performing students (top quarter of the GPA distribution pooled across grades 8 and 11) are only 75 percent as likely as students with average school performance to report they have plenty of friends."[76] This finding is, from all appearances, consistent with Roland Fryer's finding that high-achieving black students tend to be less popular. Harris dismisses his own finding, however, on the grounds that "blacks find it easier to make friends than whites at all levels of school performance," and that "good-performing blacks do not have significantly more trouble getting along with their peers than good-performing whites."[77] Again, though, the "acting white" theory does not have anything to say about how popular blacks are *compared to whites*. Perhaps all black students are 50 percent more popular than all white students (or perhaps the black students here are exaggerating their own popularity), but what really matters is how black students' popularity is affected when, as individuals, they move up or down in academic achievement. In other words, no matter how popular a given black student is, the "acting white" problem exists if his popularity would decrease when he starts to do all the things necessary to get good grades.

The evidence supporting the "acting white" thesis is fairly robust: We have over a dozen scholarly studies from the 1970s to 2008 confirming that the "acting white" phenomenon does happen, while the studies that are supposed to disprove "acting white" are fewer and less reliable.

I should emphasize, however, that there are many whites and other ethnicities that criticize nerds and geeks, or that are antagonistic toward the world of school.[78] Close to fifty years ago, the eminent sociologist James Coleman's *The Adolescent Society* looked at several white high schools in Illinois. Even back then, boys were prized for their cars or athletic ability, while girls were valued mainly for their "physical beauty, nice clothes, and an enticing manner."[79] Coleman observes that in no respectable area of adult life are these qualities "as important for performing successfully as they are in high school," and that the typical high school might as well be designed to turn females into "chorus girls" or "call girls" who exist only to "serve as *objects of attention* for men."[80] Instead, the "adolescent subcultures in these schools exert a rather strong deterrent to academic achievement."[81] More recently, psychology professor Laurence Steinberg found in his study of some twenty thousand students that "adolescent peer culture in contemporary America demeans academic success and scorns students who try to do well in school."[82]

Still, the "acting white" accusation seems more devastating than the "nerd" or "geek" labels. As one black scholar pointed out, a student who is accused of acting white is "essentially being told they do not belong in the black race," and acting white "*is* the most negative accusation that can be hurled at black adolescents."[83]

2

WHY SHOULD WE CARE? HOW PEERS AFFECT THE ACHIEVEMENT GAP

"Clarence Bibby, a City of Austin employee who holds a doctorate in psychology, lamented that African American children who excel in school often are belittled for 'acting white.' 'If my son, who is a scholar, tries to be an intelligent boy, some other boys will tell him he is a chump.'"

—*Austin American-Statesman,* Austin, Texas, 2006

The Racial Gap in Achievement

The reason that we might worry about "acting white"—just as we might worry about anything that impedes educational progress—is that there is a disconcertingly large achievement gap between black students and white students. The average black high school senior in America is performing at about the level of white eighth graders.[1] According to recent scores from the National Center for Education Statistics, black students scored around 25–30 points lower on standardized reading tests in the fourth, eighth, and twelfth grades.[2] Similarly, the average black student's SAT score in 2006 was 200 points lower than the average white student's score.[3]

The gap has narrowed considerably between 1978 and 2004, and according to more recent research, the achievement gap may not be as great in the younger generations of blacks and whites.[4] But for now, a substantial gap is still there.

The achievement gap is one of our nation's most pressing social problems. For one thing, if the gap disappeared, the wages earned by blacks in the labor market would likely be much closer to the wages earned by whites.[5] And if not for the achievement gap in high schools and on the SAT, colleges and universities wouldn't even see a need for affirmative action, and society would be spared a rancorous debate.

Moreover, education is like money in the bank. Someone who starts with ten thousand dollars will earn more interest from day one than someone who starts with ten dollars, and the spread between the two accounts will only grow larger as the interest is compounded over time. In education, the achievement gap is present on the first day that kids arrive for kindergarten, and only gets wider as years go by.[6] From then on, it is a vicious cycle: The black children's lack of preparation can create a feeling of frustration and inadequacy, which in turn leads to detachment from school, which makes the lack of achievement even worse. The white and Asian kids, in turn, are often able to enjoy school more—it is always more enjoyable to do something for which you are well prepared. Success breeds more success, and failure more failure.[7]

There are many possible explanations for the achievement gap, and I do *not* believe that "acting white" is the only factor. John Ogbu, the researcher who did the most to put "acting white" on the map, agreed that "there are many other factors that might adversely affect the school performance of Black students."[8]

Nonetheless, the common explanations for the achievement gap do not explain *enough*. No matter *what* researchers take into account—families, schools, income—a substantial black-white achievement gap still remains.[9] As one researcher puts it, "neither socioeconomic differences, nor differences in measurable school characteristics, are sufficient to explain why African American students learn less over time than white students with similar initial levels of achievement."[10]

What follows is a look at a few alternative explanations. Keep in mind that each of these topics has been the subject of many books in itself; my discussion here is necessarily cursory.

Socioeconomic Status

Blacks in America have lower average incomes and much less family wealth than whites. Thus, poorer black families are missing out on many advantages that would increase school performance—more books in the home, fewer stressful family situations that might distract a child from schoolwork, the ability to hire tutors or music teachers, better nutrition, fewer homes with lead paint, and so forth.

This is a lamentable situation that surely affects educational performance. At the same time, black students tend to perform more poorly *across the board,* including middle-class and wealthy blacks. As one group of researchers put it, "Despite the widely held assumption that ethnic differences in achievement are accounted for by group differences on other variables, such as socioeconomic status and family structure, research indicates quite clearly that these patterns of ethnic differences in achievement persist even after important third variables are taken into account."[11] Another group of researchers found that "even after we take into account differences in family background and individual characteristics, blacks and Hispanics achieve substantially *lower* grades than white students."[12]

School Spending

Many people believe that black inner cities are short on money compared with rich white suburbs, and that this lack of money causes the achievement gap.

A spending gap did exist in the past, and may still exist in a few districts today. Nonetheless, as Eric Hanushek and Alfred Lindseth point out in their 2009 book *Schoolhouses, Courthouses, and Statehouses,* comprehensive national data show that "for the last decade or more school districts serving the most disadvantaged populations, on average, have more to spend on each student than more economically advantaged districts."[13]

In any event, it is not clear how much overall spending affects school achievement. The massive Coleman Report in the 1960s found that school spending was much less important in shaping school achievement than family and peer characteristics.[14] In Coleman's words, "the factors that, under all conditions, accounted for more variances than any others were the characteristics of the student's peers; those that accounted for the next highest amount of variance were teachers' characteristics; and finally, other school characteristics, including per pupil expenditure . . . , accounted for very little variance at all."[15] In fact, most of the differences between students exist *within the same school,* as opposed to between schools.[16] This means that there may be individual schools where you find everything from A students to D students, but the difference between School 1 and School 2 is more like the difference between an A-minus student and a B-plus student.

Since the Coleman Report, social scientists have disagreed as to how much educational achievement is affected by variations in spending, if at all.[17] As William Howell and Paul Peterson of Harvard put it, "A handful of studies show clearly positive effects of expenditures on test scores, but others show negative effects, and the vast majority show no effect at all."[18] On the other hand, a few scholars think that spending has at least a small effect.[19] For example, some teachers are much more effective at getting their children to learn the basics of reading and math,[20] but minorities are more likely to be taught by less qualified and experienced teachers.[21] A recent study in New York state, for example, found that black students were more likely to have teachers who were brand new to the teaching profession, had failed a certification exam, or had a bachelors' degree from one of the "least competitive" colleges.[22] Thus, in order to attract qualified teachers, inner-city schools might need to offer substantially higher salaries.[23]

Again, though, some of the black-white achievement gap remains even if you look at students within the exact same schools, which means blacks and whites who are receiving the same level of school spending. No one has seriously suggested that school spending explains the entire achievement gap.[24]

Stereotype Threat

Claude Steele and Joshua Aronson famously argued that black performance in school or on academic tests may be depressed by "stereotype threat," which is a student's fear of confirming the negative stereotype that blacks are not as smart as whites. In other words, if a black student sits down to take a test and then starts to be nervous about failing to perform well, that nervousness could turn into a self-fulfilling prophecy.[25] While their research is often misinterpreted—even in psychology textbooks[26]—as having found that blacks absent stereotype threat performed at a level similar to whites, Steele and Aronson actually controlled for preexisting SAT scores. Thus, it was only those blacks and whites with similar SAT scores who did equally well on a test when stereotype threat was absent. But that finding cannot show how we could get the average black SAT score to equal the average white SAT score in the first place.

Nobel laureate James Heckman and two of his colleagues claim that there is "no evidence that [stereotype threat] accounts for an important fraction of minority-white test score gaps."[27] That said, there is one recent study that attributes 40 percent of the achievement gap to stereotype threat.[28] In two randomized field experiments, researchers gave black and white students an essay assignment that presented them with a list of values (such as relationships, art, athletics, et cetera) and then asked them to write a paragraph describing which value was most important to them. The whole exercise took around fifteen minutes. A substantial majority of the black students who wrote about their most important value ended the school year with a grade in that particular class that was 0.26 to 0.34 points higher than the black students in the control group, thus closing the racial achievement gap by about 40 percent. A two-year follow-up study showed that African-American students who had written about their affirmative values had an overall GPA that was 0.24 points higher than the control group.[29] This is a stunningly large effect, and to be frank, it almost seems too good to be true.

In any event, the very notion of stereotype threat could turn out to involve the "acting white" criticism itself. After all, the essence of "acting white" is that a black child feels he is being stereotyped as less suited for the world of academics. Thus, when a test is given under stereotype conditions (such as with an instruction that one's intelligence is being tested), black children may be subtly and perhaps subconsciously reminded of the "acting white" threat. This is speculative on my part; I have not yet found any experimental research that even considers this possibility, although one theoretical article does point out that stereotype threat can arise from fear of how one's own group will react.[30] It is a question worthy of further investigation.

Family Environment

It is normally assumed that middle-class families do a better job of preparing their children for school, which implies that poorer families (more likely to be black) are not as likely to feature intensive academic preparation at home. In one intriguing study, researchers found that middle-class families speak millions more words to their young children than do poor families.[31] Granted, this study was based on a projection from observations in a mere forty-two homes, but it was not the first to suggest that lower-class "parents tend to talk less often to their children than do middle-class parents,"[32] or that middle-class parents give their children a more intellectually stimulating environment through active questioning of their children about household objects or books, outside activities, and the like.[33]

This pattern of child-rearing could stretch back to the time of slavery. Think about the typical set of black parents in 1870. They would likely have grown up as slaves, and would have had little formal education. They would never have been exposed to anything remotely resembling a twenty-first-century middle-class upbringing, where parents eagerly teach their two-year-olds the alphabet, colors, shapes, and the names for countless household objects. These black parents in 1870 wouldn't have even thought to bring up their own children that way.

When their own children became parents one day, in the 1890s or 1900s, this new generation of parents would never have seen a household in which parents diligently talk to their infants about all of their surroundings, read to their toddlers, and so on. They would be unfamiliar with the notion of stepping into that parental role themselves. As one parent told researchers in a 1968 study, "I never know [sic] how to read a book to him until I heard you read."[34]

Thus, the same pattern would repeat itself with the next generation down to the present day. Even at this date, it seems likely that many black children do not receive the same kind of intensive at-home education that many middle-class whites receive during their first few years of life.

From personal experience, I suspect that this factor might be very important. When I was in college in Athens, Georgia, I went once a week to a predominantly black elementary school to read to some kindergarteners. Week by week, I would go to the same classroom, and then take one of the children into the hall where I would read with him or her. Over the course of the school year, I would get a fairly good feel for how the entire class was doing on their reading skills.

The typical breakdown in a classroom was about twenty-five blacks and four or five whites; one year, there was an Asian girl. Unfortunately, the differences were absolutely stunning. Hardly any of the black four- or five-year-olds knew the alphabet, though they all seemed eager to learn to read. By contrast, all of the white kids knew the alphabet pretty well. And the Asian girl could read several grades ahead. One occasion stands out in my memory: A college female named Susanna was there at the same time as me, and she spent the hour reading to the Asian girl while I read to a black child on the other side of the classroom. After a while, Susanna turned to me with her jaw gaping open. She said, "I was just reading the girl this book, and we came across the word 'fleur de lis.' *I didn't know what it was, but then she said, 'Fleur de lis. That's French.'"*

That Asian girl might have been some sort of budding genius, but even so, I am positive that she did not learn to read "fleur de lis" in her kindergarten class. From what I saw of the classes, they mostly consisted of story time, play time, nap time, recess, and snack time. The only conclusion was that (a) the Asian girl had parents who drilled her on reading from day one, (b) the white kids had parents who at least taught them the alphabet, and (c) the black kids had parents who didn't do much at all to teach their kids to read. It was deeply saddening, because although the kids were just four or five, and even though they all seemed eager to learn, I could already see that their education would take far different paths over the next decade.

All of that said, I do not think anyone has the slightest idea how to quantify the effect of this factor. For all we know, it could account for the *entire* achievement gap. I doubt that that's the case—otherwise, I would be writing a different book—but I cannot claim to be sure.

The Power of Peers

As James Coleman said, "the one variable at the level of the school that does make a strong unique contribution is the educational backgrounds and aspirations of fellow-students—the student body variable."[35] In fact, Coleman found that other students' attitudes have more effect than family background or anything about the schools themselves.[36] *That* is why it is important to discuss the "acting white" phenomenon.

So far, there has been only one empirical estimate of the "acting white" effect: Roland Fryer's. He estimates that if we got rid of the "acting white" effect, we would eliminate 11.3 percent of the black-white test score gap for black students with a 3.5 GPA or higher.[37] That leaves a lot of the test score gap unexplained, of course, but so does any other explanation for this gap. (No one would suggest that we cannot talk about poverty just because poverty does not *completely* explain the achievement gap.) Fryer notes that because the "acting white" effect is targeted at blacks in highly integrated schools, it could have a larger effect there: "Eliminating racial differences in the relationship between popularity and achievement has no effect on the mean student or students who attend predominantly black schools—but could potentially be a major reason for the underperformance of minorities in suburban schools or the lack of adequate representation of Blacks and Hispanics in elite colleges and universities."[38]

If anything, Fryer underestimates the "acting white" effect. Recall that Fryer defines "acting white" as the drop in popularity experienced by blacks who have a 3.5 GPA. *But those are the very students who have overcome the "acting white" effect.* The real problem is when a black student who could have gotten a 3.4 instead slacks off and gets a 2.6, because he wants to maintain popularity rather than pursue academic achievement. And needless to say, it is impossible to quantify what a given student *could* have done.

Other scholars have agreed that "acting white" has at least some effect. As one set of sociologists found, their interviewees were "aware of academically able Blacks who, in order to avoid being accused of acting white, deliberately chose not to enroll in higher-track classes and not to maximize their academic achievement." These scholars believe that "acting white" causes at least part of the racial gap in academic achievement, because of the "power of acting white to shame [students] as traitors to the race."[39] Similarly, Ronald Ferguson's multistate survey reported that "almost half of black males in integrated schools who perceive that people like themselves might be targets of acting white accusations, and who report receiving either A-range or D-range grades, indicate that they may hold back from doing their best in school because of what others might say or think."[40]

Apart from the literal "acting white" phrase, numerous studies show that the peer culture in a school is very important.[41] James Coleman found that when more students said that getting "good grades" made someone part of the "leading crowd," it was very much more likely that high-IQ students would get good grades.[42] Coleman concluded that "students with ability are led to achieve only when there are social rewards, primarily from their peers, for doing so."[43] Studies have shown that college students do better when they are randomly assigned to have roommates with higher SAT scores.[44] An even better example comes from the Air Force Academy, where students are randomly assigned to squadrons—groups of about 120—who "live in adjacent dorm rooms, dine together, compete in intramural sports together and perform military training together." Indeed, freshman students are not even "allowed to enter the premises of another squadron." Thus, the academy presents a unique opportunity to see what happens when you randomly assign people to a new peer group and then basically shut off contact with any other potential source of peers. One study found quite large results: "a 100-point increase in the peer group average SAT verbal score increases individual GPA by 0.45 grade points and a 1-point increase in peer group GPA increases individual GPA by 0.65 grade points."[45]

Laurence Steinberg and his colleagues surveyed some twenty thousand high school students, and found that peer pressure has a strong effect on black achievement.[46] By tracking students over a three-year period, they were able to compare "the academic careers of students who began high school with equivalent grades, but who had different sorts of friends during the school years."[47] They found that students whose friends were "more academically oriented" did "better over the course of high school than students who began school with similar records but who had less academically oriented friends."[48]

After finding that Asian-American students performed the best in school, Steinberg points out that this is because "they work harder, try harder, and are more invested in achievement—the very same factors that contribute to school success among *all* ethnic groups."[49] Some have speculated that Asian-American parents scold their children and force them to do homework for several hours per night, while black parents are more easygoing. But Steinberg found that "black parents are just as engaged, and just as involved in their children's education, as other parents are."[50]

Indeed, "Asian students from disengaged homes earn grades in school that are higher than Black students from authoritative homes!"[51]

Steinberg then explains why Asian students do better than other ethnic groups in school: The factor that both "undermines the positive effect of effective parenting in Black homes is the same one that counters the adverse effect of ineffective parenting in Asian households—the peer group."[52] For example, Asian students' "friends have higher performance standards (that is, they hold tougher standards for what grades are acceptable), spend more time on homework, are more committed to education, and earn considerably higher grades in school." As a result, "peer pressure among Asian students and their friends to do well in school is so strong that any deficiencies in the home environment . . . are rendered almost unimportant."[53]

By contrast, black students' friends fall to the opposite extreme. Black students are "far more likely than other students to find themselves in peer groups that actually devalue academic accomplishment."[54] Steinberg made clear, however, that any anti-academic attitude among blacks "is not unique," and that it is merely "an extreme case of what exists within most White peer groups as well."[55]

Steinberg and his colleagues also reject the notion that black youth are discouraged about education solely because they expect to be discriminated against in the marketplace. To the contrary, "much more than other groups, Asian-American adolescents believe that it is unlikely that a good job can follow a bad education," while "Hispanic and African-American students are the most optimistic." In other words, "what distinguishes Asian-American students from others is not so much their stronger belief that educational success pays off, but their *stronger fear* that educational failure will have negative consequences." Thus, it may be "unwarranted optimism"—not pessimism—that is "limiting" the performance of blacks in school.[56]

The role of peer effects—and of "acting white" in particular—could also explain two otherwise puzzling research findings: First, recent black immigrants to America perform better in school than do native African-Americans, but their performance *decreases* as time goes on.[57] For example, one recent study of all the fifth and eighth graders in New York City found that in the fifth grade, the "gap between black and white immigrants" is "statistically no different from zero."[58] There is no achievement gap among immigrants, in other words.[59] But by the eighth grade, "immigrant black and Hispanic students . . . perform worse relative to their white foreign-born peers."[60] So for immigrant black children, achievement is fine in the fifth grade but goes downhill by the eighth grade.

Second, the same study found that black students (not just immigrants) actually achieved "greater gains in test scores between fourth and fifth grades" compared with white students, but that this trend exactly reversed for the seventh-to-eighth-grade years. In other words, "racial gaps . . . appear to be growing for these students between seventh and eighth grades."

Most other explanations for the racial achievement gap do not seem to make much sense here. There is no reason to think that socioeconomic status, teacher quality, teacher discrimination, or school spending suddenly get worse between fifth grade and eighth grade. But we *do* know something that gets worse between fifth and eighth grades: racial awareness and peer effects. The middle school years are *precisely* when the "acting white" criticism emerges, as students become attuned to matters of race for the first time. By the same token, stereotype threat would also be expected to get worse in the middle school years—although again, to the extent that "acting white" occurs, some of the very "stereotype" in "stereotype threat" could well be created by other black children. In any event, the effect of peers strikes me as the most elegant explanation for why the racial gap would improve in the fifth grade (or why black immigrants would perform equally to white immigrants in the fifth grade), but then—in the same group of kids—performance would go downhill just a few years later.

Indeed, in the middle school environment, the "acting white" criticism seems to have a very potent effect. One journalist described an inner-city school in Washington, D.C., where the principal tried to have regular assemblies to honor the high-achieving students: "At the start, the assemblies were a success. . . . But after a few such gatherings, the jeering started. It was thunderous. 'Nerd!' 'Geek!' 'Egghead!' And the harshest, 'Whitey!' . . . No longer simply names on the Wall of Honor, the 'whiteys' now had faces. The honor students were hazed for months afterward. With each assembly, fewer show up."[61] A Chicago educator calls "acting white" the "silent killer" of academic motivation, while a Cincinnati teacher notes that one of his good students had "stopped trying his best" because of "negative comments from some of his black friends."[62]

In the face of these kinds of statements, it is implausible to suggest that "acting white" has no effect. How could it not have an effect? What teenager is going to be immune to a criticism that, on its face, is so devastating?

Some people claim that peer studies are plagued by the problem of "selection effects." That is, people select their friends. (To some extent, that is: we all remember that some high-schoolers are rejected by potential friends.) Thus, the objection goes, maybe the kids who tend to hate school already just find each other and start hanging out. Thus, it is not their friends that caused them to hate school; hating school caused them to choose like-minded friends.

What is odd, however, is that the academic literature always assumes that selection effects are a problem. Everyone seems to believe that we are in danger of *overestimating* the effect of peers if children are simply choosing like-minded friends. By the same token, everyone seems to think that random assignment (if it can be had) would reveal the *true* effect of peers.

I disagree. In fact, the opposite is closer to the truth: It is far more likely that the *greatest* peer effect will be found precisely where children have chosen like-minded friends—that is, where there is a definite selection effect. And random assignment, however useful it might be, will not show you the full extent of peer effects.

Imagine that you are randomly assigned (never mind how) to spend several hours a week for ten weeks with a group of Hell's Angels. Are you suddenly going to grow your hair long, buy a black leather jacket and a Harley, and spend every weekend cruising around on the interstate highway system doing ninety without a helmet? Probably not. (On the other hand, if you find that you are mysteriously drawn to the Hell's Angels lifestyle, imagine that you have been randomly assigned to attend the meetings of a Thomas Kinkade Appreciation Group, or some other organization that you would find repellent.)

Why wouldn't your new peers change your values and tastes? *Precisely because you did not choose to be in that peer group in the first place.* It is not as if you have been sitting on the sidelines, yearning for the day when you could win the approval of the Hell's Angels. In fact, you probably regard their status symbols not with envy, but with a sort of bemused contempt.

Imagine, by contrast, that you have been taking an interest in living more healthily, eating organic food, and so forth. So you start going to Whole Foods or to local farmers' markets, and happen to strike up a friendship with a few other people who are very much into that lifestyle as well. Then you find out that your new friends are vegetarians. Over time, they talk to you about their reasons for going vegetarian; they show you pictures of factory farming; you start to become convinced that the meat production system in America is unhealthy, or even that there is a moral argument against it. Eventually, you end up being vegetarian yourself.

What happened here? The usual explanation would be that the peer effect is somehow *diminished* by the fact that you chose your peer group. I disagree: The peer group that you choose is *precisely* the peer group that will have the most power to shape your choices, to prod you in a new direction, to influence you due to your desire to fit in and meet your peers' approval. *Selection effects are what create peer effects.*

Another important point is that the effect of "acting white" could be harder to measure in proportion to how great the effect is. This is because the greatest effects of peer disapproval often happen at the unconscious level.

For example, I would predict that none of the readers of this book have ever worn a swimsuit to a funeral or a business meeting, even on the warmest summer day. This is not because you made a conscious decision *not* to wear a swimsuit. Rather, even without thinking about it, you know that showing up to an important event in a swimsuit would get you plenty of disapproving looks, and could even cost you some friendships or job opportunities. You pattern your behavior around the social expectations of others, without even being aware of what you're doing. (The same observation could be true of stereotype threat.)

So perhaps the more entrenched the "acting white" phenomenon is, the less that students would even think about it—and the less they would be able to articulate it to a researcher or to someone taking a survey. Middle schoolers cannot always articulate their inner feelings, after all. But they may still subconsciously know that going off to an advanced class would be anathema to their friends. Pursuing schoolwork with a passion would never even arise as a real choice.

What this means is that any empirical measure of peer effects—or of "acting white" in particular—is likely to be understated. How do you empirically measure the *full* extent to which children rule out various choices without even thinking consciously about it?

Some might say, of course, that I am putting too much weight on the *absence* of evidence. As the joke goes, a man says, "There's an invisible cat sitting in that chair." Someone else says, "But the chair looks empty." The man replies, "Aha, that's *exactly what you would expect.*"

Here, though, we have several existing reasons to believe in the invisible cat. We know that there is a large achievement gap that does not fully disappear even when you look at the most advantaged and wealthy black students being taught by good teachers in good schools. We know that "acting white" exists to some extent. And we know that peers have a strong effect on how adolescents behave, both in school and elsewhere. Putting all of this together, it is reasonable to surmise that the "acting white" effect is stronger than any survey would be able to detect, because students could be affected by it in ways that they do not fully realize themselves.

3

THE HISTORY OF BLACK EDUCATION IN AMERICA

History seems an imprecise subject at best. Even when historians are studying a narrow question that, at least in theory, could be pinned down to an exact number, there often is not any way to be sure you have an accurate answer.

Take literacy rates. If you want to know the literacy rate *today*, you can look at a government study that gave a literacy test to a representative sample of people, and scored their answers on a scale of 0 to 500.[1] One can quibble with the methodology, but that kind of study gives us a fine-grained view of literacy in modern America.

But what if you want to know the literacy rate *in the 1700s*? No one was giving detailed tests to nationally representative samples at that time. You would have to look for other clues. For example, several studies rely on how often people were able to *sign their names* to documents.[2] Needless to say, this is a very rough measure; it will not tell you how many people could read college-level texts.[3] Worse, the sample of available documents (such as wills, legal contracts, and so on) is often unrepresentative of the general population. Nonetheless, that is often the best that historians can do.[4]

The same is true of everything I say in this chapter. This chapter deals not with a specific numerical fact, but with a much more amorphous question: what did blacks think of education prior to recent generations?

That is a difficult and vague question. As you will see, I answer this question by relying on many sources—mostly secondary sources—that have pointed to many anecdotes about how much black people valued education during slavery and the Jim Crow era.[5]

Nonetheless, are these anecdotes truly *representative* of how the average black person felt? There are many autobiographies left behind by former slaves and teachers, but these were obviously written by a select group of people. After all, it is not as if the typical illiterate farmer or manual laborer in the nineteenth century wrote an autobiography. George Orwell once said that "history is written by the winners." It is just as apt to point out that history is written by the *literate*, which means that the historical record is inevitably biased toward people who were able to write down their experiences.

Bias might have arisen from other causes as well. Many of the testimonies written in the nineteenth century might have been overly optimistic. After all, black leaders and teachers from black schools had an incentive to paint a rosy picture of their stunning successes.[6] And when nineteenth-century observers marveled (as they often did) about how fervently blacks desired education, perhaps this was partly because the observers had such low expectations of former slaves. For example, a nineteenth-century white teacher who, out of conscious or unconscious racism, expected all blacks to be illiterate and dull would have been pleasantly surprised to find even the slightest interest in education. She then might have unknowingly exaggerated that level of interest when writing a diary or reporting on her activities.

Despite all of the above, history is almost never kind enough to leave behind a random and unbiased sampling of *any* broad social trend. We have to work with the historical record that we have.

That record is remarkably unanimous in what it fails to mention: any trace of an "acting white" attitude in schools during the era of slavery and Jim Crow. This does not prove that such an attitude never existed, of course, but the lack of any positive evidence is striking. I suspect that if an "acting white" attitude had been common in nineteenth-century schools, someone would have written about it. Instead, in virtually every piece of literature on black education during slavery or for the hundred or so years after the Civil War, you find tale upon tale of blacks sacrificing their scarce money and time to pursue education, in the most difficult of circumstances or even where prohibited by law.[7]

With all of these disclaimers in mind, on to the evidence.

The Antebellum Period

Before the Civil War, many states attempted to bar slaves from learning to read. For example, an 1847 Missouri law stated, "No person shall keep any school for the instruction of negroes or mulattoes, reading or writing, in this State," with a potential six-month jail term for violations.[8] Similar laws existed across much of the South.[9] Not just the law barred slaves from an education: slave masters often whipped, branded, cut off a finger, or even put to death slaves who had learned to read.[10] William Henry Singleton recalls being beaten "severely" with a harness strap merely because he had been accused of briefly opening a book while carrying it for his master's son.[11] Slaves occasionally remarked that "whites blocked their learning because whites had recognized the superior intelligence of blacks."[12]

Even in the midst of such oppression, both free blacks and even a few slaves could be found pursuing an education. As Eugene Genovese's classic history of slavery points out, "The roots of black enthusiasm for education lay deep in the slave past. As early as the 1750s, Samuel Davies found the slaves eager pupils when he sought to teach them to read as part of his campaign to win converts."[13]

In 1817, for example, a white missionary opened a Sunday school for slaves in St. Louis, Missouri, and soon nearly a hundred "knowledge-starved pupils" had enrolled.[14] Another white minister in Missouri during the same period wrote that he had been devoted "every Sabbath morning, to the labour of learning them [slaves]. . . . They learned the rudiments of reading quicker than even the whites."[15] Indeed, after one school was closed and a teacher arrested, the black leader renewed his efforts by opening a school on a steamboat kept in the Mississippi River—outside Missouri's jurisdiction—and the "students traveled from the bank of the river to the boat in skiffs." This boat came to be called the "School for Freedom."[16] One former slave wrote that a flogging for attempting to read "only made me look upon it as a more valuable attainment. Else, why should my oppressors feel so unwilling that their slaves should possess that which they thought so essential to themselves? Even then, with my back bleeding and smarting from the punishment I had received, I determined to learn to read and write, at all hazards, if my life was only spared."[17]

Many black schools were conducted in hiding.[18] When James Yeatman issued a report in 1864 on sanitary conditions in the Mississippi Valley, he found numerous such schools: "There is at Groshon's plantation a school of about forty to fifty students, young and old, taught by Rosa Anna, a colored girl," while "William McCuthchen, a colored man, commenced a school on the Currie place" with at least sixty students.[19] One writer recounted: "The plantations of a parish or township would be canvassed, and those in whom they could confide, were invited to attend a 'School' in any location where Secresy [sic] could be secured. Sometimes these schools were held in remote swamps and cane-breaks, where, perhaps, the foot of the white man had never trod."[20] A former slave recalled, "On Sundays, I have seen the negroes up in the country going away under large oaks, and in secret places, sitting in the woods with spelling books."[21]

One black woman from Alabama told an interviewer, "None of us was 'lowed to see a book or try to learn. Dey say we git smarter den dey was if we learn anything, but we slips around and gits hold of dat Webster's old blue back speller and we hides it 'til way in de night and den we lights a little pine torch and studies dat spellin' book. We learn it too."[22] A black woman who grew up in Savannah, Georgia, wrote in 1902: "My brother and I being the two eldest, we were sent to a friend of my grandmother, Mrs. Woodhouse, a widow, to learn to read and write. She was a free woman and lived on Bay Lane. . . . We went every day about nine o'clock, with our books wrapped in paper to prevent the police or white persons from seeing them. We went in, one at a time, through the gate. . . . The neighbors would see us going in sometimes, but they supposed we were there learning trades."[23] As an adult, the same woman taught school on St. Simon's Island; she "had about forty children to teach, besides a number of adults who came to me nights, all of them so eager to learn to read, to read above anything else."[24]

Another woman described clandestine schools in Louisiana:

> Two other schools were taught by colored teachers; one of these was a slave woman, who had taught a midnight school for years. It was opened at eleven or twelve o'clock at night, and closed at two o'clock A.M. Every window and door was carefully closed to prevent discovery. In that little school hundreds of slaves learned

to read and write a legible hand. After toiling all day for their masters they crept stealthily into this back alley, each with a bundle of pitch-pine splinters for lights.[25]

The Postbellum Period

Despite their keen interest, not many slaves were successful in becoming educated—the literacy rate was only about 5 percent in 1860.[26] But after the Civil War was over,[27] former slaves pursued education with vigor,[28] and the illiteracy rate dropped to 33.6 percent by 1910 and 14.6 percent by 1930.[29]

Freed slaves were eager to be "able to read the Bible and teach it to the young, understand their legal rights, negotiate labor contracts, and buy or lease land." Thus, for example, one former slave from Vicksburg, Mississippi, said, "I must learn now or not at all . . . so I can read the Bible and teach the young."[30] An autobiography of a black educator observes: "The scholars at the night school were mainly of the older people who had spent their early years in slavery. All they wished to hear was how to read the New Testament."[31] Similarly, an old man going to school in Mobile, Alabama, said, "I will not trouble the teacher much, but I must learn to read the Bible and the Testament."[32]

After the Civil War, many philanthropically minded Northerners—mostly whites but occasionally blacks[33]—went to the South to become teachers in black schools. These Northern "missionary" teachers (one prominent group called itself the American Missionary Association)[34] aroused special resentment among racist whites and Klansmen, who saw them as troublemakers.[35] One Alabama newspaper wrote, in typical nineteenth-century colorful style, "False calves, palpitating bosoms and plimpers are all the rage now in the land of wooden hams among the poor, slab-sided old maids who are coming south to teach the Negroes to lie and steal."[36] Female teachers in Alabama were sometimes told in public to "go to the devil," while their schools were occasionally the victims of racially motivated violence or arson.[37] In Florida, Northern teachers were "recipients of many taunts and sneers," and one teacher was driven away after several shots were fired through her door.[38] In North Carolina, the Ku Klux Klan flogged a white teacher, cut the hair off from one side of his head, and left him in the woods, for the offense of "teaching niggers."[39]

This opposition from racist Southern whites was due, in part, to the fact that many blacks equated education with "political and economic freedom," and the "struggle for schooling by both free and enslaved African-Americans demonstrated . . . the pervasive value placed on learning, even in the face of extraordinary threats and punishments."[40] As a freed black pastor is said to have remarked, "Ignorance is slavery for a man's mind."[41] In Alabama in 1865, a convention of blacks resolved that "the education of our children and youths [is] vital to the preservation of our liberties."[42]

Thus, whites were very nervous about the possibility that educated blacks would start to become politically powerful.[43] In 1903, a Tennessee newspaper editorialized: "At present there is no danger from the Negro. The question that demands answer from us and which clouds the future like a monstrous pall is 'Are we not by educating the Negro sowing the seeds of a dangerous force that will one day arise and make demands with which we cannot comply?'"[44] Similarly, an Ohio newspaper wrote in 1827: "If we enlighten [blacks'] minds by education, what a new world of misery does open to their view. Knowledge would open their eyes to their present degraded state—their incapacity of enjoying the rights of citizenship, or of being received into the social interests of the whites as friends. They would be rendered uneasy with their condition, and, seeing no hopes of improvement, would harbor designs unfriendly to the peace and permanency of our institutions."[45] One observer "said he heard hundreds of times, while on tour in the South, that 'learning will spoil the nigger for work,' and 'Negro education will be the ruin of the South.'"[46] Another common maxim was, "When you educate a Negro, you spoil a field hand."[47]

Despite this strong opposition, many blacks of the postwar and Jim Crow eras were determined to push for education. James Anderson's superlative history of black education notes that "virtually every account by historians or contemporary observers stresses the ex-slaves' demand for universal schooling."[48]

The national superintendent of schools for the Freedman's Bureau—John W. Alvord—wrote in 1866: "Throughout the entire South, an effort is being made by the colored people to educate themselves. . . . [E]very-where some elementary text-book, or the fragment of one, may be seen in the hands of negroes."[49] In Louisiana, Alvord saw a petition "from plantations across the river, at least 30 feet in length, representing 10,000 negroes. It was affecting to examine it and note the names and marks (x) of such a long list of parents, ignorant themselves, but begging that their children might be educated, promising that from beneath their present burdens, and out of their extreme poverty, they would pay for it."[50] Alvord also said, "Here is a people long imbruted by slavery, and the most despised of any on earth, whose chains are no sooner broken that they spring to their feet and start up an exceeding great army, clothing themselves in intelligence. What other people on earth have ever shown, while in their ignorance, such a passion for education?"[51]

Alvord's employees often corresponded with him, sending back reports of how eager blacks were to obtain an education. The superintendent for North Carolina wrote to Alvord, for example, of the "impoverished colored man who built a log schoolhouse with his own hands and hired a teacher out of his own pocket" or "Little Lizzie who ran home from school each day to teach her aged grandmother the alphabet." To be sure, as one scholar points out, Alvord himself had "shamelessly encouraged his underlings to provide him with 'incidents for popular reading,'" thus creating an incentive to exaggerate. Still, "The eagerness for learning which [the letters] reflect was not a figment of the superintendent's imagination. No matter where [the North Carolina superintendent] traveled in the state, he met with the same enthusiastic reception; sometimes he addressed crowds of up to two-thousand freedmen."[52]

Observers throughout the South had experiences similar to Alvord's. As Booker T. Washington wrote, "in every part of the South, during the Reconstruction period, schools, both day and night, were filled to overflowing with people of all ages and conditions."[53] One observer in Virginia wrote, "Spelling is with them an exciting past-time. When at work toting the barrack-boards to the wharf, men, women, and children spelled aloud for their own private ears, though we heard now and the 'B-o-a-r-d, Board,' 'H-o-u-s-e, House.'"[54] A Georgia doctor wrote that "we have hundred—hundreds—of smart little colored children and youths, who are burning with anxiety to learn."[55] A Northerner who moved to Georgia to set up a plantation and a school for blacks noted that "at noon and at night, at nearly every cabin door could be seen a little knot of [blacks], with a little paper or book in their hands, doing their best to master the alphabet and its succeeding mysteries."[56] He added that "so great was the desire for instruction on the part of the blacks, that these teachers were often compelled to resume their task in the evening, after the labors of the day were over."[57] As a Northerner visiting Alabama wrote in 1869, "there is something very touching about seeing the extreme eagerness of the old freedmen to learn."[58] A teacher in Norfolk, Virginia, "tried to limit her school to fifty students, but the students begged so hard that she had to admit more."[59] At a South Carolina school, one of the teachers remarked that the "enthusiasm of the children to learn is intense. Their school-hours seem like one bright holiday, and their progress is remarkable."[60] Another teacher from Virginia wrote, "The children . . . hurry to school as soon as their work is over. The plowmen hurry from the field at night to get their hour of study. Old men and women strain their dim sight with the book two and a half feet distant from the eye, to catch the shape of the letter. I call this heaven-inspired interest."[61]

Many testimonies say that black people were so eager for education that they were upset at the prospect of any vacation—whether summer vacation, Christmas vacation, bad weather, or even weekends. For example, in Alabama, "so great was the blacks' desire for education that the pupils of one school in 1866 selected some of their own classmates to continue the school during the summer when the white missionaries returned to the North for a vacation."[62] Similarly, a Northern teacher working in Nashville wrote: "Parents & children, husbands & wives are earnestly and unitedly engaged in this good work of education . . . . Some are never absent and express a regret when Saturday night come[s] for then there is no night-school for them. There is great pleasure in teaching such pupils."[63] From Georgia, one black teacher said that blacks "begged for learning 'as a thirsty man would beg his neighbor or a friend for a drink of water.'"[64] Another teacher "marveled over her pupils who traveled long distances to school each day in the winter despite pouring rain and freezing temperatures. One day she tried to send her class home early because of the cold weather, but all insisted on staying in the icy building."[65] A teacher in South Carolina "reported that at the start of Christmas holidays, one of her students asked that she not give them a long vacation, and another urged,

'We want a few days, but not long. We like to read.'"[66] Similarly, a teacher in Virginia noted that at the beginning of summer vacation, "several students came to her in tears and said, 'Now, Miss Dodd, you ought not to stop school, for we are just beginning to learn." Another observer in Florida wrote: "The eagerness and thirst for knowledge manifested by the freedmen's children has been to me a matter of continual surprise. They gather around the schoolroom door long before the hour of opening, study diligently through the regular school hours, and beg for admittance to the adult school at night, at which time they may frequently be found in the same class with their parents helping them through the mysteries of the alphabet."[67] Yet another observer wrote in the *National Freedman* in 1865, "You will be agreeably surprised [to see] a class so interested in having a good lesson as to forego the pleasure of the usual recess, and remain engaged with their geography lesson."[68]

Indeed, many people claimed at the time (probably with more than a little overenthusiasm) that blacks were *more* interested in education than were whites.[69] One state superintendent noted in 1869 that "as a class they are eager to learn, while the poor whites are indifferent."[70] A white man in North Carolina claimed, "The colored take more interest in education than the whites."[71] A black preacher in 1865 observed: "The ignorant whites had every chance to learn, but didn't. We had every chance to remain ignorant, and many of us learned in spite of them."[72] Another observer in Florida wrote: "It is astonishing how apt the little Negroes are to learn. I may safely say that the freedpeople, as a general thing, manifest greater interest in education than do the whites."[73] A Georgia missionary teacher said, "In seven years of teaching at the North, I have not seen a parallel to their appetite for learning, and their active progress."[74] Another observer in Virginia claimed that a "pro-slavery" acquaintance had "declare[d] that, if there was any difference, so far as the mind is concerned, between the colored population here and the native Virginians, the advantage is on the side of the colored people."[75] A teacher in Arkansas reported: "I never saw people learn so fast. It generally took me three months to teach white children what these will learn in ten or fifteen days. But I am satisfied the difference is caused by more intense application."[76]

Again, these many accounts may smack of exaggeration or overoptimism, and there is at least occasional evidence that blacks in the wake of the Civil War were sometimes uninterested in school.[77] Still, there is no counterevidence that any black children thought of education as "acting white."

Despite their overwhelming poverty, blacks in the Jim Crow era built numerous schools and collected money to pay schoolteachers' salaries.[78] In impoverished sections of Mississippi, for example, blacks "taxed themselves and formed all-black boards of directors that oversaw the erection of a number of schoolhouses and churches."[79] In Mississippi, over a seven-year period in the early twentieth century, blacks with "patches on their trousers and dresses" contributed $100,000 to the Mississippi Industrial College.[80] One anthropologist, on "studying the black community of Indianola, Mississippi, marveled at the PTAs' 'indefatigable . . . efforts [to] maintain and improve the schools."[81] A teacher in Alabama described "Negro pupils who lived in miserable shacks without adequate food and clothing," and who "had eaten no food for twenty-four hours but they would come to school."[82]

As James Anderson points out, "these school construction campaigns were not isolated incidents but examples of widespread grass-roots reforms that epitomized the educational beliefs and behavior of black southerners."[83] In some instances, blacks had already paid taxes for the construction of white schools, and yet gave some of their few remaining dollars to build black schools.[84] As one observer in Missouri wrote, "the negro property holders not only cheerfully paid the school tax for the education of white children, but also generously contributed from their limited incomes to sustain the private schools for colored children."[85]

As the twentieth century progressed, Northern philanthropists also helped to build black schools across the South. Most notable was Julius Rosenwald, the founder of Sears, who contributed millions of dollars that helped build thousands of black schools that were attended by a quarter of all Southern black schoolchildren as of 1932.[86] Despite Rosenwald's massive generosity, the money he gave averaged only about 15 percent of a school building's costs; the rest was made up by contributions from black citizens and public funds (often collected from black taxpayers).[87]

M. H. Griffin of the Rosenwald Fund wrote of his effort to construct a black school in Autauga County, Alabama: "Children without shoes on their feet gave from fifty cents to one dollar and old men and old women,

Rally in Welsh, Louisiana, in effort to build a school, 1917. (Papers of Jackson Davis, MSS 3072, negative number 1385, Special Collections, University of Virginia Library, available at http://mcgregor.lib.virginia.edu/davis/advanced.html)

Julius Rosenwald (left) at the opening of the four thousandth Rosenwald school in 1928. (Papers of Jackson Davis, MSS 3072, negative number 6613, Special Collections, University of Virginia Library, available at http://mcgregor.lib.virginia.edu/davis/advanced.html)

whose costumes represented several years of wear, gave from one to five dollars. . . . Colored men offered to pawn their cows and calves for the money. . . . They raised in this way one thousand dollars, and we started out for a contractor."[88] Griffin observed a similar scene in Greene County, Alabama. At a fund-raising rally, the black master-of-ceremonies said, "'We have never had a school in this vicinity, most of our children have grown into manhood and womanhood without the semblance of an opportunity to get an insight into life, etc.' As he spoke, tears began to trickle down his face. . . . One old man, who had seen slavery days, with all of his life's earnings in an old greasy sack, slowly drew it from his pocket, and emptied it on the table."[89] As Griffin recalled, the old man said, "'I want to see the children of my grandchildren have a chance, and so I am giving my all.'"[90]

As I said at the beginning of this chapter, the historical record may be inaccurate or biased in many different ways. Still, no historical sources suggest that "acting white" was a problem during the years of slavery and segregation.[91]

4

WHAT WERE BLACK SCHOOLS LIKE?

"We had teachers who were interested in us getting the best and doing our best, and that's what we were required to learn. I would not trade my education that I received . . . for the education kids are receiving today."

—A Missouri woman who attended segregated schools in the 1940s, and whose daughter attended an integrated school in the 1960s

"It was like a family. You knew all the children. You knew their parents, and they all had gone to the same school. We didn't have the same resources that the white students had, but we had teachers who made sure you did the very best you could with what you had."

—A elderly black woman from North Carolina

Before I explain what was lost when schools were desegregated, we have to discuss one more question: What were black schools really like in the decade before that happened?[1]

The Deprivation of Segregated Schools

Segregation was a monstrous moral evil, one that shortchanged the black population in too many ways to detail here. We are all familiar with the tales of how black schools through most of the Jim Crow era were starved for resources.[2] Black schools often consisted of dilapidated clapboard shacks, with perhaps a pot-bellied stove for heat in the winter.

An elderly teacher from Atlanta recalls, "That school was in such bad shape you could study botany through the floorboards, astronomy through the roof and the weather through the walls."[3] Similarly, a Freedman's Bureau agent in 1870 wrote that black students in Missouri attended classes "in churches and cabins with walls admirably adapted for ventilation and for admission of copious shower baths of rain."[4]

School supplies typically consisted of old books that the white schools had discarded. As one North Carolina teacher recalled, "I was so sick of having the books in our classroom that had been used 5, 6, 7, 8 times, and they were discarded, old books discarded from the white schools."[5] Another teacher from Virginia recalls another teacher complaining that the books from the white schools were so old and "dirty I don't even want to touch them myself."[6] From Atlanta, a teacher recalls: "I'll never forget opening my English text book and seeing 'Avondale White School' written in it. We always got the hand-me-downs. It was insulting."[7]

For many decades, black teachers were paid much less than white teachers, and per-pupil spending was much lower as well. In 1913 in Georgia, the white teachers' average salary per month was $44.29, more than double the black average salary of $20.23.[8] In Arkansas, the legislature in 1909–10 gave white teachers $12.95 per month compared with $4.59 per month for black teachers.[9]

Many towns didn't have a black high school—or perhaps any black school at all—and the black children either went without schooling or had to travel miles to a neighboring town. Black children in Warren County, Virginia, had to be sent for the weekdays to Manassas, Virginia, to attend school. One resident recalls: "That was really where segregation hurt me the most, because it was so sad to see 12 and 13 year old students having to leave their home to go to another city and stay from their families for the whole week. The public school system paid for their board, rather than to build a school for them."[10] In Fayetteville, Arkansas, the black Lincoln School ended at the ninth grade; black students who wanted to continue through high school had to move to a boarding house in Fort Smith, fifty miles away.[11]

Interior of a black school in Prince Edward County, Virginia. (Papers of Jackson Davis, MSS 3072, negative number 0787, Special Collections, University of Virginia Library, available at http://mcgregor.lib.virginia.edu/davis/advanced.html)

Class photo at a one-room black school in Virginia. (Papers of Jackson Davis, MSS 3072, negative number 0874, Special Collections, University of Virginia Library, available at http://mcgregor.lib.virginia.edu/davis/advanced.html)

The Revisionists

In the past ten or twenty years, several scholars (most of them black)—Vanessa Siddle Walker, Jerome Morris, Vivian Gunn Morris, David Cecelski, Barbara Shircliffe, and more—have taken a somewhat revisionist position. These scholars have written numerous books and articles that take issue with the usual depiction of segregated schools as dens of unmitigated oppression and misery. While they are careful to note that they do not romanticize segregation itself, they point out that there were many black segregated schools that offered a good education, that made black children feel at home, and that encouraged black children to pursue education with a passion. As Walker says: "It is true that these schools were often treated unjustly and victimized by poor resources. But in spite of the legalized oppression, many teachers and principals created environments of teaching and learning that motivated students to excel."[12]

Indeed, Walker said that she began studying segregated education in depth when she noticed an "unnerving contrast between the bright photos of engaged young people in yearbooks of the [black] school and the often listless black students she encountered in current-day schools." There are several important ingredients in a good education—"dedicated teachers," "strong principals," "order," "high expectations," and "community and parental support"—and what is "astonishing," according to Walker, is "how many black children attended schools during segregation that delivered on these objectives, and how few do so now."[13]

Because I present the other side of the story—the one that is often ignored—some people might interpret my book as having argued that segregated schools were equal, or that they were good schools in an absolute sense, or that segregation was justifiable in any way. Such an interpretation would be wildly incorrect. We all know that segregation was morally wrong, that segregated schools were deprived and underfunded, and that many black children never had the chance to attend school at all. Moreover, studies in the segregation era found that black pupils in black schools were several years behind the white grade level.[14] Nothing that I say in this book should be read as disagreeing with or undermining those facts.

Nonetheless, the story of black people under segregation is not unremittingly depressing. Even in the midst of the greatest oppression, black people were often able to fashion community schools that had at least some praiseworthy qualities. As a result, students in segregated schools thought of education as a quintessentially "black" experience, not as "acting white." We should be able to admire the hard-won achievements of black people in the face of such staggering adversity, without being thought to have made light of the adversity itself.

The Schools as Community Centers

The black school was the most important institution in the black community, next to the church.[15] The black school "served as a rallying point and meeting place for political and social community affairs," as it was often "the only place where two hundred or three hundred people could gather for a dance or meeting."[16] As one researcher said of a black school in Nashville, the fact that "teachers and parents shared churches, grocery stores, and social groups, promoted stronger bonds between the school and the community."[17]

One Texas resident recalls: "We were really proud. Jackson was the first real high school we had. . . . A school was more than just a place to learn. It meant you had teachers living in your community. Teachers were important people."[18] Blacks in Centerville, North Carolina, recall "their segregated school as being a tremendously important focal point for their cultural and community identity."[19] A former student from Alabama wistfully recalled: "There was a real sense of community. I mean the school being the centerpiece of the . . . small black community. And there were churches, four consecutive blocks there were churches. . . . So, everything kind of focused and circulated around that little area where we lived. And you felt connected to the people who were there, with the older people, younger people, generations of people that lived there."[20]

Many older blacks similarly recall the close cooperation between schools and parents.[21] As one North Carolina resident said: "You knew you better behave in school. If you didn't do your work, you knew what was waiting for you when you came home. You knew that the teacher would tell your parents in no time."[22] A resident of Jacksonville, Florida, recalls the Dunbar High School there in similar terms: "The teachers we had in those days, they knew you personally. . . . It was like having your dad at school all day."[23] From Fort Myers, Florida, an article on a black school lost to desegregation notes: "Teachers knew parents. Parents knew each other. Students spent their after-school hours walking home in pairs and groups, afraid to get into too much trouble because someone's mom or dad or uncle or grandmother would make sure they got their licks if they caused problems."[24] A black teacher from Kansas City recalls: "The black community was close-knit. All of the teachers knew the parents and the students. In those days when you got a job teaching, you taught forever. That's what I've done. Just like my teachers knew my parents for a long time, I know the parents of my students."[25]

In black schools, the black students were naturally the center of attention in community activities and celebrations, such as May Day events (which were quite common).[26]

Many blacks also recall their high school as a "home space" or "safe space" that "provided a shelter from the pains of the outside White world," and that they felt a "sense of protection or a feeling of being looked after by the adults in their community."[27] Here is a typical account about a black school in Florida:

> In Old Dillard School more than 60 years ago, Annie Gamble found refuge. Within the walls of that two-story, four-room schoolhouse, Gamble found a place safe from the white children who would spit on her and call her "nigger" when she and her mother went shopping in downtown Fort Lauderdale.
>
> She found a place, one of a very few places, that she and the other black children growing up in Broward County in those days could call their own.
>
> "That was all we had, church and school," said Gamble, now 72. "There was nothing else for us."[28]

Caring Teachers Who Pushed for Success

Two universal themes in the literature on black education are, one, the teachers deeply *cared* about their children's academic success, and two, the teachers *pushed* the children to do their very best.[29] As always, however, let me begin by mentioning several sources of bias. First, the level of "caring" is impossible to measure empirically, especially when we are talking about decades long past. All I have are anecdotes. Second, people

Graduating class of a normal (or teacher training) school in Elizabeth City, North Carolina, 1921. (Papers of Jackson Davis, MSS 3072, negative number 1925, Special Collections, University of Virginia Library, available at http://mcgregor.lib.virginia .edu/davis/advanced.html)

The May Queen, Booker T. Washington High School, Suffolk, Virginia, May 10, 1940. (Photo courtesy of the Library of Virginia, available at http://www.vcdh.virginia .edu/HIST604/hamblingallery/source/photo03.html)

might be inclined to remember the past through rose-colored glasses. Thus, when elderly black people praise the teachers of their youth, they might be affected by nostalgia (just as it might be the case that today's children will one day say the same about their teachers). Third, black people might be more reluctant to criticize their old teachers in print; that is, the historical record could be skewed toward positive memories. I freely admit that these sources of bias are potentially significant.

It also bears repeating: no one should read this section as suggesting that we should go *back* to segregated schools. That is not my argument in any way. All that I am doing here is praising the achievements of black people under dire oppression. Nor am I arguing that black teachers were superior in all respects—in fact, black teachers were often less qualified (in the traditional academic sense) than white teachers—let alone am I arguing that any school with black teachers is bound to succeed. My only argument here is that black teachers in segregated schools, whatever their other disadvantages, were often able to create an environment in which academic success was admired.

There is far from enough space to discuss the many dozens of articles and books in which black people all across the country testify that black teachers loved and cared for their students.[30] Here are a few examples: One man who grew up in Washington, D.C., recalls that his segregated education "was a good one, primarily because of the interest of the teachers, teachers who are willing to go above and beyond the job. . . . They went out of their way with you as a person, to give you advice, to help you, to talk about your family problems or personal problems."[31] From Atlanta, one teacher "speaks reverently" of the education he received in black schools: "Black schools may have lacked resources, but they provided a caring environment designed to uplift a people. 'We weren't allowed to feel inferior.'"[32] A woman from West Virginia says: "Our segregated schools were wonderful. Whatever we were given book-wise we used, and we had the most wonderful teachers. They made you realize that no matter what, you had to excel. The teachers taught us not only from our books, but they taught us about living. They wanted you to be the best you could be."[33]

In Hyde County, North Carolina, "The teachers were like second parents, at turns demanding and nurturing, making house calls and doubling as Sunday School teachers."[34] A student from Alabama recalls: "The teachers cared about you. . . . Trenholm was a family. You knew it when you were there. And it was not just during the school day, but all the time. You felt like people cared about you."[35] Another student from the same Alabama school recalls that she "already knew almost all of the teachers when she enrolled in first grade. They were her neighbors. She went to church with them and she saw them at the grocery stores and at social and recreational events in her community."[36]

In her superlative book about the Tampa black schools and their destruction, Barbara Shircliffe quotes a former student who said: "At Middleton as a student, we were indeed a family. We were embraced by teachers, protected, taught everything that they thought we would need to get out there and improve the world, as such. Whatever you did in school, everybody knew it, your mom also knew it. . . . We were a *proud, proud, proud* group; a *proud* group of kids."[37]

In addition, black teachers often pushed and inspired their students to succeed academically.[38] As one former student from a North Carolina black school recalled: "They encouraged the fainthearted, and boosted the ego of the underachiever. . . . They aroused hunger before serving the main course."[39] A 1961 graduate of a segregated school in Fort Myers, Florida, recalls: "They pushed you because they loved you. They wanted you to do better than they did."[40]

Charles Harris, who was one of the first blacks to integrate a Virginia school, said: "There were some advantages to segregated schools at the time. Our black matriarch teachers really instilled in you that you could be as good as anybody. You were on a mission to be the best you could be."[41] William Pollard, a dean at Syracuse, "believes, in fact, that his education in the segregated schools of North Carolina was better than the education his sons are receiving today. 'My teachers would not accept mediocre work, because they knew that I could not function in a racist world being a mediocre person.'"[42] From Florida, a former student at the Lincoln School in Tallahassee recalls that the teachers "would take you wherever you were and push you as far as you could go and then some."[43] A former student from the black school in Little Rock points out: "In the days before integration, [Dunbar teachers] told us we were somebody. They told us we had something to contribute and expected us to become productive citizens. . . . In spite of the inequities, we had teachers who loved us, who cared for us, who expected—and demanded—that we do our best."[44]

A woman from Florida writes: "I am a product of a segregated school system. Funny, I now wear that distinction as if it were a badge of courage, a symbol of accomplishment. . . . Instructors pushed and challenged students, sometimes with the tough love that can come only through familiarity. A large percentage of the teachers knew the parents and had attended the same schools."[45] One former student from a black school in Williamsburg, Virginia, said: "The plus for us was the dedication of the teachers as we further advanced up the grade level. There was no such thing as 'you couldn't learn.' Teachers served as surrogate parents. Teachers encouraged us to do the best we could."[46] Another former student from Maryland said that "in the African American schools, teachers were relentless. They did not let up on you because they knew what you had to do to make it in the world."[47]

The sentiments described above might seem foreign to white readers, particularly the suggestion that black students had pride in their segregated schools. Didn't the Supreme Court hold, for example, in *Brown v. Board of Education* that students in segregated schools had suffered from a lack of self-esteem? True, the Supreme Court thought, partly based on Kenneth Clark's research, that black children in segregated schools had low self-esteem because they were likely to choose to play with a white doll.[48] But Clark's own research actually showed that *Northern* children in nonsegregated schools preferred white dolls more often than Southern children did.[49] The notion that segregation caused low self-esteem was quickly disproved by many studies,[50] and by 1980, one researcher noted that "the weight of empirical evidence suggests that segregated blacks evidence self-esteem significantly higher than that of their desegregated peers." The same researcher found, in a study of 194 Southern schools, that black self-esteem was "lower in racially balanced schools than in predominantly black schools."[51]

The Supreme Court's speculation on the self-esteem issue is also inconsistent with much anecdotal evidence. As one student from a North Carolina school said, "Yesterday, [in] the all Black school, we had pride, we had dignity, we had self-gratification."[52] When I mentioned the *Brown* finding to one woman who had integrated an Oklahoma school as a youngster, she thought the very notion was utterly ridiculous: "You go around a bunch of old black ladies," she said scoffingly, "and you'll *find* some self-esteem."[53]

In admiration for their service, black teachers were treated with great respect by the black community. As Vanessa Siddle Walker notes, "During the era of Negro segregation, teachers were valued by the community as representatives of their people who had made it."[54] One teacher from Virginia recalled: "I remember several Christmases, even though the families didn't have money to go out and buy the teacher a gift, the children would come to school with gifts, something that their families had raised. If you'd go to the home, the parents would often invite you back to dinner."[55] Another black teacher remembered: "For most black people, the teacher was *the* person in the community. . . . That was because primarily [teaching] was the profession that most blacks went in if they wanted to get ahead and so forth."[56] As a student said, "There was prestige. My parents thought preachers were good, but teachers were great!"[57]

The fact that teachers were so widely respected helped black parents to trust and reinforce the school's values.[58] This too is a near universal theme in many articles and interviews. For example, at a black school described by Jerome Morris of the University of Georgia, one of the teachers was a godmother to certain students; other teachers lived in the black community and knew the "parents and grandparents on a personal basis," thus making them "comfortable calling or visiting the families" if a student acted up at school.[59]

Moreover, black teachers and principals served as respected role models for the young black schoolchildren in their care. As Horace Tate said, "In the old days, the black principal was to the black community what the mayor was to the whole town."[60] In Rock Hill, South Carolina, Robert Barber said that his teachers "went the extra mile to instill the importance of a good education." For him, "it was the black male teachers who stood out." "It was something to aspire to. It was my first time seeing a black male with a tie. I had somebody there who understood where I came from."[61] Black principals were commonly treated as an "unchallenged spokesman for the black community," both in school and in political activities.[62]

In all of the articles and books about black schools before desegregation, I could find only one person who was upset at how his teachers treated him: "'I had all black teachers, and not one of them ever said, George Allen, you ought to go to college,' he recalled bitterly. 'Two of them discouraged me from taking an examination that would have given me a full scholarship. They had targeted this hoity-toity, light-skinned young lady whose parents were the funeral directors, and they promised it to her and she got it.'"[63]

The Curriculum

Blacks in the Jim Crow period had a long-running debate over what should be taught in black schools. On one hand, many people argued that the most practical curriculum would be industrial or vocational in nature, including subjects such as cooking, sewing, agriculture, machine shop, shoemaking, hatmaking, and the like. But there were also many black people who wanted a more classical education, with a focus on academic classes such as literature, geometry, and Latin.[64]

Prominent black educators like Booker T. Washington were convinced that an industrial education would be more practical for the majority of blacks.[65] Washington mocked the notion that "knowledge, however little, of the Greek and Latin languages would make one a very superior human being, something bordering almost on the supernatural,"[66] and remarked that "one of the saddest things I saw . . . was a young man, who had attended some high school, sitting down in a one-room cabin, with grease on his clothing, filth all around him, and weeds in the yard and garden, engaged in studying French grammar."[67]

Many white authorities, as well, were more comfortable with the industrial model of education, because they thought it was more fitting for the supposedly limited capabilities of black people. A Tennessee report on education stated that "the hope of the colored race is in industrial education . . . they will find their greatest contentment and prosperity in the field, on the farm, in the work shop, in the factory and mine; and their training should be of this character."[68]

At the same time, many black people were determined to seek a classical liberal education for their children.[69] One black teacher recalled in her 1913 autobiography that "freedmen now began to pour into Ohio from the South, and some of them settled in the township of Oberlin. During my last year at the college, I formed an evening class for them, where they might be taught to read and write. It was deeply touching to me to see old men painfully following the simple words of spelling; so intensely eager to learn."[70] She then described her school in Philadelphia:

> In the year 1837, the Friends of Philadelphia had established a school for the education of colored youth in higher learning. To make a test whether or not the Negro was capable of acquiring any considerable degree of education. For it was one of the strongest arguments in the defense of slavery, that the Negro was an inferior creation; formed by the Almighty for just the work he was doing. It is said that John C. Calhoun made the remark, that if there could be found a Negro that could conjugate a Greek verb, he would give up all his preconceived ideas of the inferiority of the Negro. Well, let's try him, and see, said the fair-minded Quaker people. And for years this institution, known as the Insti-

Black students mending shoes in a school in Hope, Arkansas, 1916. (Papers of Jackson Davis, MSS 3072, negative number 1100, Special Collections, University of Virginia Library, available at http://mcgregor.lib.virginia.edu/davis/advanced.html)

tute for Colored Youth, was visited by interested persons from different parts of the United States and Europe. Here I was given the delightful task of teaching my own people, and how delighted I was to see them mastering Caesar, Virgil, Cicero, Horace and Xenophon's Anabasis. We also taught New Testament Greek. It was customary to have public examinations once a year, and when the teachers were through examining their classes, any interested person in the audience was requested to take it up, and ask questions. At one of such examinations, when I asked a titled Englishman to take the class and examine it, he said: "They are more capable of examining me, their proficiency is simply wonderful."[71]

One black educator's autobiography recounts his frustration at trying to set up a practical industrial curriculum at a new school in Alabama, only to run into objections from the parents: "They were much opposed to industrial education. When the school was started, many of the parents came to school and forbade our 'working' their children, stating as their objection that their children had been working all their lives and that they did not mean to send them to school to learn to work."[72] A visitor to a Tennessee school in 1914 reported that black teachers were "attempting to teach four years of Latin, and neglecting a great deal of the [industrial] school work."[73] Similar curricula were to be found all across the South, everywhere from big-city Houston to small towns in Alabama.[74] A report on black Baptist colleges in 1903 concluded that their "major problem was too much emphasis on classical and higher literary training," including Latin and Greek.[75] An elderly former teacher points out, "Most people are shocked when they learn that I was a Latin teacher, perhaps because they don't expect a black woman to be a Latin teacher."[76]

Indeed, the classical curriculum sometimes took place in secret. One observer heard a teacher claim that a black college in South Carolina "was able to teach Latin only because they called it 'agricultural Latin.'"[77] At the Risley High School in Georgia, the white school board thought that "young blacks were being trained for lives of manual labor," but (according to a former student) the opposite was true: "They [the school board] were never brought into the main building where the laboratories were and where Mrs. Mollette was teaching Shakespeare, Thoreau, Emerson,

Langston Hughes and Countee Cullen. They never saw any of that."[78] Sometimes the classical curriculum took place alongside industrial classes; at the Orange County Training School in North Carolina, students "practice cooking and carpentry each morning; in the afternoons, they read poetry in their English Club, debated in their Young People's Literary Society, and rehearsed their productions of Shakespeare's plays."[79]

Blacks' demand for classical education aroused resentment and ridicule among some philanthropists who saw themselves as well-meaning: Jackson Davis of the General Education Board of New York City once wrote, "Many of the principals are not able to resist the popular demand of colored people for pretentious and high sounding courses."[80] Similarly, a Northern philanthropist wrote in 1916 that he was amazed to find "the large place given to foreign languages and especially to the ancient languages" in black schools.[81] The president of the University of Tennessee said in 1901, "Nothing is more ridiculous than the programme of the good religious people from the North who insist upon teaching Latin, Greek, and philosophy to the negro boys who come to their schools."[82] Another Northern philanthropist contended: "Probably not 5 percent of this southern expenditure for Negro education goes to industrial education to help the Negro fit his environment. The remaining 95 percent is wasted in so-called academic education."[83] Indeed, a representative from the Rosenwald Fund "concluded that blacks were making choices not on the basis of need but out of hunger for prestige and *a tendency to imitate whites*."[84]

In addition to the drive for classical education, black schools were able to spend time addressing black cultural achievements, such as celebrating Negro History Month, singing the Negro National Anthem, and reading the works of black authors and poets.[85] A Mississippi black man writes: "Even though we were being educated by colored teachers who in many instances came from backgrounds as deprived as our own, we were always motivated to be the best colored people. Our teachers made sure we knew the life histories of Dr. George Washington Carver, Mary McLeod Bethune, Marian Anderson and Jackie Robinson."[86] Black history was a regular part of the curriculum in black schools. "That helped to develop pride," said a former teacher from the famed Dunbar School in Washington, D.C. "Because the world seems to be run by the other race, it's important to see where our successes are. There can never be too much of that."[87]

Funding

Funding for black schools vastly improved as the twentieth century progressed. In part, this was because many Southern school boards were extremely nervous about integration, and so—especially after *Brown*—they rushed to improve black schools or even build new ones, in the hopes of keeping local blacks happy where they were.[88] The school board in Southampton, Virginia, built five new elementary schools for blacks, and their modernity contrasted with the "older schools White children attended."[89] In 1949, Houston built a new $2.5 million black high school, at the time the most expensive high school in the city; it was intended to "shore up the argument that segregated facilities could be equal."[90] In Hughes, Arkansas, the town built two new black schools in the 1950s; the mayor was quoted as saying, "We wouldn't be building these two nigger schools if we were going to integrate."[91] In Tampa, Florida, officials built a new black school in 1956; one graduate of that school says that the school board saw this as a "way of avoiding integration."[92]

More broadly, while per-pupil spending in black schools was only about 43 percent of white spending in 1940, it had risen to 70 percent just twelve years later.[93] Teacher salaries started to become more equal as well: In 1952, there were actually four Southern states where black teachers had *higher* salaries than white teachers. This was because educated blacks had so few career choices at the time, and so many of them went into teaching that the pool of black teachers was more qualified.[94] Indeed, when the Coleman Report was issued in the 1960s (probably the largest education study of all time), researchers found that "lower-class and black children attend schools with characteristics that are measurably *equivalent* to those in schools attended by middle-class and white children."[95] Economists have found that the wage gap between black and white men dropped between 1960 and 1980, and that 20 percent of this drop could be explained by the fact that black schools had improved between 1915 and 1966.[96]

In any event, black schools could be *good* schools, at least by the mid-twentieth century. Graduates of Houston's Wheatley High School, formerly a segregated school, recall a time when it was "arguably the finest black public high school in the South, when it brimmed not just with great athletes, but with extracurricular activities, when its students excelled in speech and debate and drama and music, when students showed up at seven in the morning for an extra college-level algebra class taught by an inspiring teacher."[97] To be sure, the black children who attended such schools were likely a somewhat stratified elite, just as were the whites who attended quality high schools at the time.

Some might point out, of course, that today's inner-city black schools —such as in Washington, D.C.—often perform very poorly. But I am *not* arguing that any school that is predominantly black (or predominantly white, for that matter) will therefore be a good school. There are many other factors that affect whether or not a school achieves good results— the quality and experience level of the teachers, the abilities of the principal, the curriculum, parental involvement, family socioeconomic status, neighborhoods, and so forth. An impoverished and gang-ridden inner-city school in the twenty-first century is not going to be able to imitate the vibrant black community of the 1950s or 1960s, simply by virtue of having a student body that is mostly one race.

Let me reiterate that the historical record may be biased. As I noted above, people who recall black schools fondly might be overly nostalgic. Still, whether or not black schools were as wonderful as might be remembered, no one recalls those schools as a place in which education was viewed as the province of white people.

Moreover, as I have also noted, there were many towns where black schools (especially black high schools) were not available at all. This was a serious problem, and one that I do not discount. To repeat, I do not intend to venerate the old system of segregated schools; rather, I am making the more limited point that where black schools did exist in the 1950s and 1960s, they were often better schools than many white people might stereotypically think. Even if good black schools were not available everywhere, there were still many cases where dedicated teachers and principals provided black children with strong role models of black academic success, pushed them to succeed, and provided them with a nurturing and safe environment.

But, as we shall see in the next few chapters, that world of black educational success was about to be undermined.

5

THE CLOSING OF BLACK SCHOOLS

"I don't know why they closed our school, it was good. It is just another way white folks have of messin' over us, I guess."

—Black student from Memphis, circa 1972

"We were just a little pocket of black folks with our own school, and then they took it away."

—Black former PTA president from Georgia

"It was bad. It was terrible. More than anything, it was unbelievable."

—A 1966 graduate of a black high school in Tampa that was closed

"*Brown* was turned against us. We lost our schools."

—Elias Black, Jr.

"The Supreme Court decision of 1954 didn't give us school integration in Tuscumbia, it gave us school elimination. It eliminated the black schools and forced the black children to go to the white school."

—William Mansel Long of Tuscumbia, Alabama

"As far as we can determine, the black high school was the only long-term publicly supported institution that was pervasive across the black community, and that was controlled, operated, staffed, populated, and maintained by blacks that has ever existed (or most probably will ever exist again) in the United States."

—Frederick Rodgers

During school desegregation, black schools all across America were closed or drastically redesigned (for example, a black high school might have been converted into an integrated elementary school). As a result, the safe and sheltering environment of black schools—once the center of the black community—disappeared. In their place was the integrated school, which was more unfriendly to black students, and less likely to feature black role models of academic success. As a result, black students became alienated from the world of school. They began to think of the school as a "white" institution.

When Did Desegregation Occur?

The Supreme Court's 1954 decision in *Brown v. Board of Education* was a moral victory, but Southern states took to heart the Supreme Court's holding that desegregation should happen with "all deliberate speed."[1] The result was that outside of a few border cities, very little desegregation occurred during the first decade after *Brown*. As Gerald Rosenberg puts it, "The statistics from the Southern states are truly amazing. For ten years, 1954–64, virtually *nothing happened*."[2] Instead, desegregation began only after Congress enacted the Civil Rights Act of 1964, which required that states desegregate their schools if they wished to keep federal funding, and which allowed the attorney general of the United States to file desegregation lawsuits.[3] The Department of Health, Education, and Welfare began enforcing that law in the 1965–66 school year, and by the next year, "156 Southern school districts had lost their federal funds."[4] Desegregation also got a kickstart in 1968, when the Supreme Court rejected "freedom of choice" plans that had merely allowed black students an option to attend white schools (an option that about 15 percent of the black students had chosen), and held instead that segregation must be addressed "root and branch."[5]

How much desegregation actually occurred depends on how you define "desegregation." Between 1968 and 1988, the "percentage of Blacks who had no White schoolmates fell from 61.3 percent to 5.6 percent in the South, from 22.9 to 15.3 percent in the Midwest and from 6.4 to 3.9 percent in the West."[6] From another view, blacks in the South "attended schools in which the average White enrollment rate was 17.9 percent in

1968, 40.8 percent in 1980, and 40.1 percent in 1988, despite a 6.5 percent decrease in the proportion of students who were White from 1968 to 1988."[7] Gerald Rosenberg points out that the number of blacks who had any white classmates skyrocketed from a mere 6.1 percent in 1965–66 to 91.3 percent in 1972–73.[8]

To be sure, that same time period saw the rise of an important phenomenon: white flight. Oddly enough, the very existence of white flight was controversial when sociologist James Coleman first pointed it out in the early 1970s: the president of the American Sociological Association actually proposed to censure Coleman. At the time, sociologists were afraid that if the existence of white flight became known, some people might start to think that desegregation was not really worth the effort. A more blatant case of prejudice stifling academic inquiry would be difficult to find.[9]

Sociologists were not able to withstand the facts for long, however, and Coleman was eventually vindicated. The amount of white flight was substantial: one scholar looked at the forty largest American cities whose students were at least 5 percent black in 1968, and found that white enrollment dropped in *every single district* between 1968 and 1988. In fact, "the proportion of White students dropped by more than 35 percentage points in Birmingham, Boston, Dallas, Houston, Long Beach, Los Angeles, Milwaukee, and Seattle and by at least 25 percentage points in 10 other cities."[10] In a few locations—such as Atlanta and Washington, D.C.—black students actually had fewer white classmates in 1988 than in 1968, because white students had almost completely vanished from the public school systems in those cities.[11]

White flight could be seen as posing a problem for my theory: After all, how can I blame desegregation for turning the school into a white environment, if white students left so quickly that desegregation never really took place in many cities?

There are three responses. First, white flight did not occur instantaneously; rather, it happened over a period of several years, or even decades. Second, it is not necessary for white students to be a majority of the student body for an "acting white" effect to take place. All that is really necessary is that you have one or a few "advanced" classes that are mostly white. When that happens, the arena of scholastic achievement starts to

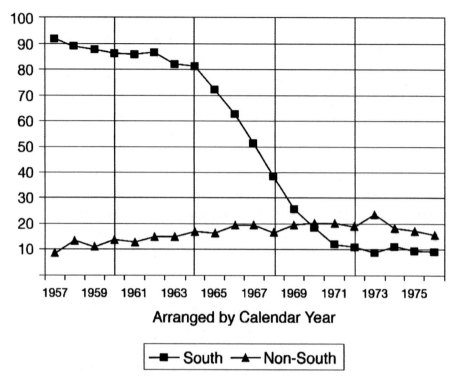

Percentage of black students attending all-black high schools, 1957–76. (From Orley Ashenfelter, William J. Collins, and Albert Yoon, "Evaluating the Role of Brown vs. Board of Education in School Equalization, Desegregation, and the Income of African Americans," *American Law and Economics Review* 8, no. 2 (2006): 213–248, reprinted by permission of Oxford University Press)

look more and more like it is reserved for whites. (We will examine this point in more detail in the chapter on academic tracking.)

Third, not just student bodies were desegregated. Perhaps more importantly, the teachers and principals were desegregated as well (some teachers, and especially black principals, were demoted or fired, as we will see in the next chapter). As a result, the teaching force became mostly white, nearly everywhere you look. Indeed, white teachers currently make up an overwhelming majority even in schools that are 70–80 percent black and Latino. The only place where white teachers do not dominate is where the school's student body is 90–100 percent minority—and even in those schools, a full 40 percent of the teachers are white.[12] The average black student in America between 1988 and 2004 faced a teaching workforce that was around 70 percent white.[13]

Take one specific example from an article about Columbus, Ohio: "Black teachers [now] make up only about 24 percent of the teaching force, while black students comprise about 60 percent of the student population. . . . A veteran black teacher remarked that Columbus had all-black schools before desegregation, and it had virtually all-black schools after desegregation. The crucial difference was before desegregation, *black teachers* taught black students and had more power to influence their lives."[14] As I argue in the next chapter, the increase in the number of white teachers with black students may have made it harder for some black students to identify with their teachers (who, to be sure, may have been wonderful teachers in many other respects).

Black School Closings Across America

If you want to desegregate the schools, where do you bring the black and white students together? White-controlled school boards almost always answered that question in one way: the white school. After all, they did not want to send white schoolchildren into black schools, to be taught by black teachers and disciplined by black principals.[15]

That racial impulse was not the only factor, to be sure. Courts contributed to the black school closings discussed throughout this chapter, by condemning the mere fact that some schools continued to be racially imbalanced. This was taken as a sign that a school board had "the affirmative duty to take whatever steps might be necessary" to eliminate racially-identifiable schools.[16] Otherwise, the mere fact that a traditional black school had many black students would not, in itself, have required local authorities to transfer those black students elsewhere.

Moreover, in the drive for desegregation, black civil rights leaders had consistently maintained that segregated schools were inferior. I want to be very clear here: Those civil rights leaders were correct, in that segregated schools often *were* inferior on the whole. I am not contending that segregated schools were superior or that civil rights leaders were misguided in their overall aim of desegregating the schools. At the same time, the view that traditional black schools were inferior naturally led to one conclusion when it came time to desegregate: the inferior school would have to close, or at least be heavily restructured. And as discussed throughout this chapter, the closing of black schools had unintended consequences.

Whatever the cause, a large number of black schools were closed. In North Carolina, for example, out of 226 formerly all-black high schools that had existed as of 1964, only 13 survived as high schools by 1972. The rest were either closed or changed to elementary schools.[17] Thus, over a very brief time in the mid-to-late 1960s, black high schools were almost completely eliminated in that state.

The same thing happened across the South. In Topeka, Kansas—where the *Brown v. Board of Education* case originated—all four black schools were closed.[18] Most of the black schools in Arkansas were closed.[19] As of 2002, only three of the ninety-four historic black schools remained in Oklahoma; as a black principal from Oklahoma says, "One hundred years of history went into the trash."[20] All of the black schools in Delaware were closed by the mid-1960s.[21] Howard University professor Alvis Adair collected specific examples of black high school closings in Mississippi, Connecticut, Virginia, Illinois, Wisconsin, Missouri, Tennessee, Rhode Island, Louisiana, and more.[22] Similarly, I have found numerous examples of school closings all across the country.[23]

The closing of black schools has even continued into the twenty-first century. In Lafayette, Louisiana, a school desegregation order in 2000 required the "school system to close down two predominantly black inner city elementary schools immediately and bus the students affected by the closures to five predominantly white schools on the other side of town." A pair of scholars who studied desegregation in Louisiana pointed out that there was "considerable black disenchantment" with this desegregation plan, and that a "typical comment came from a black resident who lives across the street from one of the closed schools. He told us that he had attended that school as a child in the 1950s and 1960s, and he resented the neighborhood children now being bused to schools that would not, in his opinion, emphasize black culture and history."[24]

Even black private schools had to close as well, not by force but due to increased competition. Before desegregation, black people had established close to a hundred boarding schools across the country. After desegregation and the wider availability of public schools, most black boarding schools started losing students, and all but four had to close.[25] Again, while it is a resoundingly good thing that more public schools were available to black students, some of the institutions that black people had created for themselves were destroyed as a byproduct.

One reason for closing a black school was that it was more decrepit and out of date than the white schools. In some cases, however, the black schools that were closed were actually newer than the white schools. As we have seen, white school boards across the South had spent the 1950s building new black schools in an attempt to forestall desegregation. Even so, those brand new schools were often closed when desegregation occurred. In one North Carolina town, "the [black] school, a solid brick structure built in 1959, was actually in very good condition. Yet, with the arrival of desegregation—and White resistance to it—the town's 'negro' school was closed, and Centerville's African American schoolchildren were sent to neighboring communities for grades 1 through 12."[26] Similarly, in DeKalb County, Georgia, after a 1969 court desegregation ruling, the county's "remaining five black schools—some only a few years old—were ordered closed. When students returned in the fall, they found themselves sent to nearby white schools, a move that cost most of them their standing in athletics and extracurricular activities. . . . The closing of the schools is an especially bitter memory for [former teacher Narvie] Harris. 'With every court decision, the responsibility for desegregating fell upon blacks,' she explains. They're the ones who had to leave behind their friends to travel across the county to attend white schools."[27] In Richmond, Virginia, a teacher recalls that the closed black school "was built of better material than the integrated school I went to."[28] And Lee James of Gulfport, Mississippi, told me: "Our school was newer than Gulfport High. In 1969, they desegregated. White school had been built in 1938, and our school had been built in 1953. The black school became the Job Corps."[29]

Let's take a specific example: Butler High School in Gainesville, Georgia, a town about an hour northeast of Atlanta. This black school's history was extensively described in Winfred Pitts's book *A Victory of Sorts: Desegregation in a Southern Community,* on which the following section depends.[30]

In the early 1960s, Gainesville's schools were too crowded. Instead of adding on to the white high school (the most efficient solution), the school board chose to build a brand new black high school—Butler—in 1962. Even though Butler was newer than the white schools, under a desegregation plan it was closed after merely seven years.[31]

Despite Butler's short lifespan, former students had fond memories of their community school. One member of the class of 1968 said: "You had a closer bond going to a black school. You were encouraged to do more. What happened at school carried over into home. . . . We had role models. The teachers and parents were our role models."[32] A former teacher said, "There was an awful lot of pride at Butler."[33] One former student says: "Our teachers and counselors were the best. They instilled in us that we could compete with anyone out there in the world." Another student adds, "Those were the happy days."[34] Other former teachers recall, "Butler was like the center of life" for the black community, and "most of your activities centered around the school."[35]

Not everyone in Gainesville lamented desegregation, of course. Some people told Winfred Pitts that integration had brought greater economic opportunities.[36] Still, the black community was hard-hit when Butler was closed. One student remembers: "I was very hurt. I thought they [the school board] didn't care. They took away our history."[37] Another student adds: "Our children had to give up all their clubs. Those kids went over [to Gainesville High School] with nothing to do. They had a hard time exhibiting their talents at Gainesville High. We were so involving in fitting in their culture and forgetting our own."[38] Another student says: "[Butler] seniors were quite upset about it. I didn't like it, but I remember feeling helpless because I didn't know what to do."[39] A former counselor from Butler expressed grave disappointment: "What it [the school closing] was saying was that our pride and our joy has been taken away from us, and it's simply because of the fact that there are some people who look at Butler as being just a black school."[40]

Some black teachers in Gainesville disappeared. One former teacher recalls: "The attrition rate [of black teachers] was tremendous. Many of our teachers just packed up and left."[41] This comment was backed up by overall statistics: In 1966, Gainesville had 115 white teachers and 70 black teachers. Three years later, there were 122 white teachers but only 22 black teachers remaining.[42]

The loss of black teachers changed how black students felt about school.

One former student recalls: "Going to Butler, there was never any feeling of inferiority as far as race was concerned. You were never made to feel like you couldn't accomplish. . . . Your teachers always made you feel like you could jump to the moon if you wanted to. . . . That base of support was gone. They didn't just lose teachers, they lost mentors, a base of support and community. The nurturing element—there was no nurturing element."[43] Similarly, another former teacher remembered that, at Butler, "everybody knew you were supposed to do your work," but "when I worked Gainesville High it was different. Black students were not expected to perform. . . . It is bad to know you are not expected to do as well as Whites."[44]

Along with the loss of black teachers, many black businesses in Gainesville started to disappear, as black people began to shop in white establishments (a trend that was not reciprocated by the white population). Soon, "just about all of the successful businessmen African American children saw were white."[45] The former principal of Butler notes: "They lost seeing teachers at church, cafes, other places in the community. [Formerly,] they may see the teacher in the community out for a walk . . . [or at] the same beauticians and the same barbershops. All that connection is gone."[46]

In the integrated high school, many of the black students were placed in lower tracks. One student recalls, "There were some of my friends who had been in above-average classes who were encouraged not to take these classes. I had some close friends who told me they had been down-phased —that the teachers were actually marking [courses] out and saying, 'You don't need to be in this class.'"[47]

As well, the traditions of Butler disappeared: "Their mascot, the Tiger, and the school colors of purple and black were gone—replaced by the Red Elephant and red and black. Their yearbook and student newspaper were gone. Their varsity teams and pep rallies being led by Butler cheerleaders were gone. With the exception of five teachers, the faculty of caring black teachers who knew the students and their families had been disbanded, replaced by a sea of white teachers who knew almost nothing about them or their families."[48]

The experience of the black school closing in Gainesville shows in a nutshell why desegregation often led to black disillusionment with the world of school. As a former student pointed out, "You have a certain amount of pride and school spirit when you feel ownership in something, but they didn't feel any ownership in anything."[49]

What happened in Gainesville was not unique. Many black communities across the country faced the same hardships once their schools closed.

Loss of Community

The black school had been one of the central institutions in the black community. It was a place where the community bonded together in pursuit of educating its children.

After desegregation, that community center often disappeared.[50] As one black teacher said, "There is one big difference between what I have to do and what the teachers taught me in Kansas City. They didn't have to expend as much effort getting to know the parents. Because the black community was much more cohesive and close-knit, teachers were much more likely to see parents in their day-to-day activities."[51] In interviews with black parents, Frederick Rodgers found many who felt that even though the "school facilities were better now," there were still "several disadvantages they saw as resulting from integration."[52] For one, the segregated school "had been located closer to the students' homes," and "gave the students a sense of solidarity." Parents remarked, "Activities there were not just school activities but they were for the whole community, and we looked forward to them," or "we miss the Glee Club, the Better Speech Club, all the plays we had."[53] Moreover, the integrated high school "deprived the black students of their sense of identification with the school and gave them a feeling of alienation, leading to decreased participation in activities." "Many of the students recognized that their own lack of involvement in activities was accompanied by the withdrawal of their parents and the black community as a whole."[54] At a forum in Chapel Hill, North Carolina, "many members of the black community said that although integration was an important goal . . . , they anticipated a merger of black and white schools, not the destruction of black schools, with black students forced into white schools that had no place for them. The academically strong black schools were the linchpin of a proud black community, and integrated schools never offered anything equivalent, many said."[55]

The black community was also undermined by the fact that black children displaced by school closings were not sent to the same white school. Instead, they were often scattered to different white schools across town, thus dividing neighborhoods and communities.[56] As Carlesa Finney, a Maryland school board member, told me: "One thing we lost was a sense of community. . . . With integration, many of our African American communities were split. In Arundel County, we had students going to seven different schools to achieve integration mandates. Often they couldn't go across the street to get homework from a friend, because they went to a different school."[57] An article about an Atlanta high school notes: "Hamilton wasn't just closed. It was drawn and quartered. The students were split among four schools . . . in an effort to spread the benefits and burdens of desegregation."[58] In Peoria, Illinois, despite "strong opposition" from the black community, the desegregation plan "led to the phasing out of at least one predominantly Black school, conversion of another Black school and large scale busing of Black students; thus scattering Black students among predominantly White schools."[59] In a North Carolina town, "African Americans . . . once a solidly cohesive group, subsequently found their young people scattered, rationed out to schools in wealthier surrounding towns in the district to help those schools achieve racial quotas."[60]

When the best black students were partitioned off into different white schools, they were no longer as capable of forming a positive peer group for the lower-achieving black students. In Houston, for example, while the formerly black Wheatley High School remained open, desegregation "drew the most ambitious students off to other schools."[61] In Birmingham, "Parker was once a school where the children of doctors and ditch diggers learned side by side, but integration allowed the best and the brightest students to attend the better-equipped schools elsewhere in the city, and eventually in the suburbs."[62] And in Washington, a former teacher recalls: "I was at Dunbar when integration came and—whomp— it knocked us out. We had been getting the cream of the crop, but with integration, students had to go to schools in their zones. I lost some of my finest teachers, because there just was not the same demand for subjects such as Latin or advanced calculus."[63]

This subdividing of the black community caused strong emotional reactions. Consider this interview from a doctoral student's dissertation:

At the end of her 11th-grade year, her all-Black school was closed. She began sharing how the classmates that she had been with since first grade were broken up by the desegregation plan in their town. She began to cry. She attempted to stop, but did not succeed. She placed her hands over her chest and began to rock back and forth. As she gulped for breath, she tried to talk. No words came out. The tape was stopped for 15 minutes. She put her hand over her face and just leaned down and wept. As the tears began to slow, I talked softly to her and shared tissues I had found. "I didn't know how much that hurt me, hurt us. We were so close and they just sent them back," she said almost at a whisper but very bitterly.[64]

To be sure, we cannot blame desegregation alone for the loss of the close and cohesive black community that many older blacks recall. Much of that closeness was sadly destined to disappear anyway, due to broader societal trends that took place during the twentieth century—including the growth of big cities (and the demise of small towns where everyone knew each other), the construction of interstate highways through traditional black neighborhoods, the rise of urban renewal programs (colloquially known as "Negro removal" programs), or the rise of television and the automobile. Indeed, many of the nostalgic testimonials to the old black schools may be deeply affected by these other factors. Still, the closing of black schools could have contributed to loss of community spirit, and accordingly undermined the ability of some black students to feel strongly attached to their schools.

Loss of Black Culture and Opportunities for School Involvement

For obvious reasons, black schools had provided black children with numerous opportunities to be involved in school activities—including cheerleading, cultural events like May Day celebrations, and school societies and clubs of all sorts. Whether or not these activities were strictly academic, they allowed schoolchildren to feel an emotional attachment to their school.

This changed with desegregation. No longer could black students count on being involved with all school activities and clubs, let alone chosen as leaders.[65] Instead, as Frederick Rodgers notes, the closing of black schools meant that "many black students lost opportunities for leadership roles that they had had under the segregated system," and that "black parents and the black community as a whole could no longer identify with the integrated school, and they turned away from it."[66] In the course of several interviews with black schoolteachers, Rodgers noted that "fewer black students now participate in activities, partly because they do not identify with the school, and partly, some of these teachers feel, because they are not encouraged to participate as they were in the past."[67] Moreover, the lack of student involvement meant that "parents no longer have an opportunity to assist their children or to express themselves through school-related activities, as they once did."[68] "They had been proud of their schools and their accomplishments then, but now they had lost interest in many of the activities, since they no longer identified with the school."[69]

In Nashville, "the esprit de corps in the black segregated schools was quite noticeable. . . . In the desegregated schools black students, especially black girls, huddled together. Very few of the black girls participated in extra-curricular activities."[70] Vivian Gunn Morris and David Morris observed that blacks in an Alabama school "were very unlikely to hold as many top offices in school clubs" in the white school.[71] The strong "family atmosphere" in the black school where "everyone cared for" one another was lost when blacks were forced into the desegregated school.[72]

Moreover, when black schools were closed or converted to integrated schools, the new schools often destroyed or replaced the school symbols that had united the black school and the community.[73] A 1970 report noted that out of "321 black schools integrated under the new integration plans, 188 had their names changed. School trophies, colors, mascots, and symbols frequently disappeared. In some areas black schools were integrated only after insulting efforts to 'deniggerize' the school were carried out (replacement of all toilet seats, fumigation of the school, etc.)."[74] As one former student from North Carolina puts it: "Essentially everything about Lincoln High School was erased. And now that I think about it's almost comparable to the whole slave trade actually during the middle passage particularly in North America. The purpose was to erase people's connections to Africa."[75]

A student from the former Booker T. Washington school in Reidsville, North Carolina (which was converted into an integrated school), says: "We lost the name of the school, the name of the newspaper, . . . the name of the football team, we lost school colors, we lost everything that was associated with Black History. Everything was lost because of integration."[76] Similarly, in Greenville, Mississippi, a "historically Black high school was not only converted to a junior high school, but all symbols of its Black heritage were also removed and eliminated. These symbols included class pictures hung on the walls, plaques, citations and trophies. All that represented Black school pride and accomplishments was wiped out."[77] In Bogalusa, Louisiana, "the school board preserved only memories of White glory in the integrated high school's trophy room, while the prizes of five Black state football championships were consigned to the Black YMCA. Even the former Black high school's identity was erased as Central Memorial High School, named in honor of World War II Black war dead, became Bogalusa East."[78] A former student from a West Virginia school notes, "When the high school closed, all those trophies, those pictures, they were burned in the incinerator."[79] At another former black school, "the white choral director changed the alma mater because 'it didn't make sense.' The foyer's portrait of George Washington Carver came down. The traditional 'sway' in the seniors' steps at graduation gave way to a march to accommodate white student preferences."[80]

The result of these cultural changes, according to one black teacher, was more disillusionment: "I just feel like we had a certain racial pride for excelling that we lost in integration. I felt we could nevermore have the power of determining anything because we were so outnumbered. The black students felt that the whites were coming and taking over their school."[81] As a black teacher in Hattiesburg, Mississippi, said: "Black students were proud of their school, which had its own band and majorettes, its own football team which the entire Black community and some of the white community supported with a certain kind of pride. . . . But, with forced integration, Black students had to give up and leave buried with the segregated Black school the Black way of doing things. So, from this point of view, forced integration is not still a good idea."[82]

Strong Emotions

The closing of black schools drew forth strong emotions, especially among blacks who had made great sacrifices to build those schools.

Take Second Ward High School in Charlotte, North Carolina's, for example. As the first black high school in Charlotte, Second Ward was an admired and well-loved institution. Former students say, "we had nourishing and nurturing in the classroom without the strife of racial overtones," and "times have changed, but if it had to go back the way it was, black on black, it would be better than what it is now." Says one graduate: "I don't advocate segregated schools today. But there are attributes of that time that need to be in place today. Our teachers, they'd look at you, almost as if they were wanting to will a good education into your head."[83]

But Second Ward was destroyed after desegregation.[84] Students were devastated by the closing of the school. Said one person: "An institution was being closed. And not necessarily for progress, but because of integration. . . . Well, it was heartbreaking. It really was. It really was." Another person said, "We thought that it was the utmost in betrayal."[85] A teacher said, "We had to go to quotas electing student council, quotas for electing cheerleaders, and social events because, especially those social things —the prom. The prom had meant so much to students, and . . . when we made the transition from Second Ward to West Charlotte, you had dual bodies, and just trauma. I still kept contact with those kids from Second Ward, and they would call and sometimes cry."[86]

In Tuscumbia, Alabama, the former principal of the black high school said that when the buildings were torn down, "I saw a lot of people standing on the street crying. . . . And it was like somebody had died, to pass by there and see that building gone like that."[87] Other former students had similar reactions: "Oh, it was devastating. It was like a piece of me had just died." Another said: "The school was the center, was a nucleus of my life. And to have that ripped out is like saying which one of your children are you going to give up."[88] A former teacher said, "It just kills me dead. . . . We had these people raising money selling ice cream and hot dogs [to build the black school]."[89] When the school was closed, black students "lost their school colors, their symbols, and their mascot. All of these symbols were important socially and emotionally to the students and

Students watch the demolition of the Second Ward School in 1969; Second Ward had been the first black high school in Charlotte-Mecklenburg, North Carolina. (Photo courtesy of the Public Library of Charlotte and Mecklenburg County)

to the African American community."[90] In one published interview, Vivian Gunn Morris describes being "floored" by the "depth of feeling" over the school closing, and says that "people were tearing and crying."[91]

As one researcher put it, the closing of a Nashville black high school "shut down a 70-year-old institution of the black community. This closing evoked a variety of emotions—anger, sadness, hopefulness, and pain. In short, it was not simply the end of an era, it was the loss of tradition, ownership, and the collapse of a school community."[92]

When the Lincoln High School in Leon County, Florida, was closed, it was "devastating," like "the time we heard that John F. Kennedy had been assassinated," says one graduate. Another former teacher and student says: "That was like the final hammer. Blacks were seeking for equality of facilities, equipment and on and on. I know they never asked for their schools to be closed."[93]

One recent article noted that both black high schools in Tampa, Florida, were "closed in the 1971 desegregation of Hillsborough County schools."[94] According to Fred Hearns, who graduated in 1966: "It was bad. It was terrible. More than anything, it was unbelievable. What we thought is that they would improve our school and bus in some white kids."[95] Instead, the article notes, "black children were scattered across 11 different high schools."[96] Another article about the Tampa experience quotes a local resident saying it was "as if death had come to a community."[97]

One researcher observed in his study of the school desegregation process in Chesapeake, Virginia: "Student comments about the closing of [the black school] consistently reflected their anger about the unfairness of it. 'Why was it always black schools that were closed?'" or "'funny how all plans involved closing black schools.'"[98] One white woman who was a student at the time remarked "that she felt that the blacks had been 'uprooted from school and left on the doorstep, like orphans.'"[99] In fact, when the researcher tried to contact former students by looking through the yearbook, he soon discovered that "many black students did not have their picture taken . . . , such was their bitterness over the loss of their school."[100]

When the Rougemont school in North Carolina was closed in the 1970s, one of the teachers recalled that she "cried for almost a week. It was just like you were losing a friend." A community resident said: "It hurt the community; everybody. We had one of the best schools in [the city]. We had good teachers. Why did they want to change it?" Another resident noted: "Many students from the area stopped education after integration came. There wasn't a strong push. Things seemed to have broken down."[101]

The Stephens-Lee school in Asheville, North Carolina, was another one of the casualties of integration. Says a former student: "The school board voted to close our beloved 'castle on the hill,' and later the building was torn down. Only the gymnasium was left. Yet, the spirit is so entrenched in us that class reunions are the social event of the summer, and a national alumni organization is running strong." She adds, "Greensboro is full of Stephens-Lee High School alumni. Just ask any one of them about 'that old Stephens-Lee spirit,' and watch their eyes light up."[102] Arthur Edington was a graduate of Stephens-Lee High School in the 1940s; he later became the principal of another black school that itself was closed in the 1960s. He says: "I am proud that I was able to give leadership to Hill Street School, but I was sad to see the black schools shut down. Those schools served as centers of the community. It caused a lot of stress. It affected me so much I had to go on tranquilizers when we closed [the black school]."[103]

One account from Tallahassee notes: "Integration forced the close of the original Lincoln High School, which meant black students would move on to schools where they'd finally get new textbooks and better facilities. But it was hard for many students to imagine a place that could provide a better education and more caring environment than Lincoln. 'We were segregated,' said alumnus Nick Nims as his voice cracked with emotion. 'But we were a good school.'" Another former student remembers being "shocked, confused, angry" when he found out about the school closing.[104]

In Austin, Texas, the closing of the black school "was devastating to the Black community," because that school had represented "something more than just a high school"—it was a "symbol of achievement and a symbol of accomplishment for the community."[105] A black administrator later said: "Yes, it was kind of a sad moment because of all the admiration and all of the love that many members of the community had had for Anderson High School, which had been a great high school and had been, for them, the institution of greatness that they had experienced. They felt that they were good, and they had a lot of pride in Anderson High School, a tremendous amount of pride."[106] A former student said, "When it was closed down it was a shock to us, and we were very angry, we were very resentful, we were very rebellious, we were very upset that it seems like the doors were just shut down and we were just shipped off to the other schools."[107]

A recent book, Barbara Shircliffe's *The Best of That World,* which details desegregation in Tampa, Florida, is full of such poignant moments.[108] The theme of her book is that "nostalgia for the all-Black school reflects the ironic legacy that school desegregation has had for African Americans."[109] One elderly woman said: "We didn't know we were poor or . . . that we weren't getting the very best education at that time. We always knew that the White kids had better books and better schooling materials. But our teachers were teaching us with what they had. . . . We got the best of that world. And if I had a chance to go back now, and which path that I could choose, and if I could have gone to an integrated school . . . I would still have chosen to go to a segregated school."[110] Shircliffe quotes a doctoral dissertation that had interviewed Tampa parents: "There was no denial (among parents) of the often unequal conditions that existed in these schools. . . . African Americans simply referred to those days as a time when they *knew* that their children were valued and supported by their teachers and their schools."[111]

When the local black schools were closed, however, blacks no longer felt at home in the world of school: "Vivian Williams, the first African-American teacher to integrate Hillsborough High, recalls tensions between Black and White teachers and White students there. Part of the problem, according to Williams, was that White teachers and White students felt that it was 'our' school and African-American teachers and students should adopt 'our' culture."[112] One former student recalls that she and several classmates refused to buy class portraits and senior rings at their new integrated school, because they "still considered themselves 'Blake graduates.'"[113]

Former students from the black schools in Tampa are still angry. Shircliffe quotes Carlton Williams, a former student at the Blake school in Tampa: "[The closing of Middleton and Blake] really did damage the community because these schools were each a focus of community reference for east Tampa and west Tampa, and to close them down like that

. . . was a deep insult to my community, a very, very deep insult. Why do you think the committees are trying to have Blake rebuilt—because it has taken us 30 years almost just to come to terms with how fiercely angry we were about that, but what could we do?"[114]

As Shircliffe notes, for many, "the closing of the high schools represented the 'death of a community' and a 'deep insult' to African Americans in the county." Moreover, many teachers and former students blame the school closings for "contemporary problems plaguing Black communities: low levels of educational attainment, high rates of joblessness, family dislocation, and crime."[115]

While one former student did caution against overly romanticizing the old schools, perhaps the most negative statement came from Alvin Hamilton, who said: "Integration cost Black people a whole generation of kids and that's the kids that you see now. . . . Because you don't just take a kid out of a neighborhood, throw him in the classroom with a bunch of strangers that are probably two or three reading levels ahead of him, and say, 'Okay, here's your brand new book, you're sitting in this nice air conditioned class, now you should be able to keep up.' That is why the concept of getting back to the neighborhood schools is great because it worked and because integration is not working."[116]

Kathy Clay-Little, who was one of the first to integrate an Oklahoma school, told me: "I remember when we started to talk integration. I remember black people being very upset that they were going to have to give up their school. I remember this old preacher talking about it in his sermon, and he just started blubbering. He said, 'When they take away our schools, all we will have left are our churches.'" Clay-Little added, "I think in the implementation of *Brown*, black people were horribly ripped off. . . . When we came out of that black school, we could read, write, and cipher. Today our black kids are coming out of school and they can do none of that."[117]

There are many middle-aged or elderly black people today who sponsor reunions for their old segregated schools,[118] or try to rebuild those schools as historical sites,[119] or set up memorial Web sites.[120] The love they felt for their schools, and their abiding sense of loss, is poignant.

Consider a typical story about the Booker T. Washington black school in Greensboro, South Carolina.[121] The journalist notes: "Booker T.

wasn't just another school. Inside its doors, you could find comfort, pride, identity. You could escape the harsh realities of racism. . . . For decades, the red brick Booker T. Washington High School was a tie that bound Reidsville's black community. During the days of Jim Crow segregation, the all-black school was equal parts classroom and community center." Students recall that teachers pushed them to succeed: "What was injected in me was that even though our situation was hard, you could still become a doctor; you could still become a lawyer," says a former student.

In 1969 the school had to shut down. Desegregation had arrived, and the "Booker T. Bulldogs were no more." The building eventually was turned into an alternative school known as the SCORE Center. The principal of SCORE "would see the past reflected in the faces of the people who dropped by just to look and reminisce. 'I don't know what it is about that bulldog, but it brings tears to their eyes.'"

But now, the alumni "are on a mission to restore their past," by collecting old memorabilia, forming a heritage association, and staging reunions. On Memorial Day weekend in 2004, a crowd gathered to have a "homecoming" where a giant placard of a bulldog was installed at the old school. "'He went in there like he was waiting to come home,' Simpson said, dancing and high-fiving some of the other spectators. Off to the side, Mary Bratcher, class of '63, watched, tears pooling in her eyes. 'This was our little corner of the world,' said Bratcher, 59. 'It's history, just a pride you can't imagine. I tell you, I'm just ecstatic.'"[122] In late 2005, the alumni opened a museum dedicated to their old school.[123]

In Fort Myers, Florida, a 1954 graduate of the old Dunbar school said: "I would call those the glory days. We loved them and wanted our children to be a part of them." In 1969, Dunbar was closed as part of a desegregation plan. A former student points out, "Integration was one of the worst things to happen to black kids. We lost our community." "Integration didn't solve Dunbar's problems, alumni said. Rather it broke the heart of the community and scattered the students to high schools across the county." But in 2001, as part of an alumni attempt to revive the school, "Dunbar held its first homecoming football game in 33 years."[124]

In Wilmington, North Carolina, the Williston High School was closed in a desegregation plan in 1968. "When Linda Pearce of the Class of 1963 hears the Williston school song, it still makes her cry," because the "loss to the black community was immeasurable" when that school was closed; it was like a "death in the family." Another former student says: "When integration came, it was devastating because we were so used to having our own school. It was heartbreaking."[125] One alumnus writes: "Being snatched from the comfort of our own environment was unreal. It was like a nightmare . . . unwarranted and unjust. We lost the bond between school, parents and teachers."[126] A 1994 news report noted that thirty members of the alumni association held monthly meetings, an annual reunion, and an annual dance, as well as reviving the school's glee club.[127] They also published a memorial yearbook titled "Lest We Forget," on the twenty-fifth anniversary of the school's closing.[128]

In Charlotte, North Carolina, black alumni of the Reid School, which was closed in 1966, wrote a commemorative book, started a scholarship fund, and built a monument to their old school. One graduate said: "When they came to tear it down, I stood there and cried. Then I picked up some of the bricks. I still have them in my yard. I made them into a border for my flower bed." Another graduate spoke wistfully of going to "see where you had your high school days, and you see nothing there but a park." Another graduate said: "As I reflect back on my days at Reid High School, Lord, my heart is full of pride because of the start that Reid gave so many black youth. We had to make do with substandard materials and left over books, but we had one thing that as an educator I realize now that no one can take from us. And that is we had dedicated, sincere educators in the classroom. They served as our mothers, our fathers, and often times, our conscience."[129]

Black Protests Against Desegregation

The closing of black schools was so unpopular that, in more than a dozen little-known incidents in civil rights history, blacks actually led boycotts and marches *against* desegregation plans. Most dramatically, the black community in Hyde County, North Carolina, in dismay over a desegregation plan that closed the local black school, boycotted the public schools for nearly a year.[130] These residents staged numerous marches and protests during that year. "We were going against the powers-that-be to maintain ownership of the only thing we had: the schools," said a black resident who boycotted his junior year of high school.[131] David Cecelski, who wrote a book on the Hyde County boycott, notes that "when he talks to black audiences of a certain age, 'I'm still always taken off guard by the depth of bitterness' about the loss of their schools."[132]

On a somewhat smaller scale, blacks boycotted classes for about a month in Portsmouth, North Carolina, to protest a desegregation plan that would have converted the traditional black high school to a vocational school. According to a newspaper account, boycotters staged a protest "chanting 'You're not going to take our school.' They sang the school's alma mater, with its lines, 'Forever and a day we're yours; yes, yours a thousand-fold.'"[133]

In Chesapeake, Virginia, several hundred students "stage[d] a march on city hall during school hours to protest the closing [of the traditional black school called Crestwood]. A substantial number of students actually left school and walked the several miles from Crestwood to city hall where they made their discontent known. . . . The students sang and linked arms as they marched in what one student remembers as rainy weather."[134] The Crestwood school was kept open for one more year, but then closed. "No one can say what happened to the bulk of the trophies, class pictures, uniforms and other paraphernalia. Like the school, they just vanished."[135]

In Ohio, a school board proposed in 1973 to convert a black high school to a junior high school and special education center. According to one account, "The black community rose in protest. 'We refused to allow them to put Spencer High School on the blacklist,' declared one Spencer alumnus. 'Why they wanted to do that, I can't understand. I believe that the main thing is to remove . . . any references that could be something that stood out well from the black community.' A black teacher remembered, 'Everybody got up in arms. They were about to have the whole town burned down.'"[136]

In Charlotte, North Carolina, a desegregation plan in 1969 involved "closing seven all-black schools and assigning those three thousand students to outlying white schools, a scheme that had been used in Buffalo and Syracuse," thus provoking "strident protests from the African American community."[137] One local black minister organized a "Black Solidarity Committee" that "led rallies, marches, and a petition drive" threatening an economic boycott.[138]

There were also protests across several counties in Florida. As Barbara

Shircliffe notes: "In Florida and other southern states, African Americans began actively protesting the closing and downgrading of historically Black schools. . . . In 1969, school protests and boycotts occurred in Lee, Gulf, Sarasota, Orange, Daytona Beach, and West Palm Beach counties."[139] In 1970 in Tampa, Florida, several hundred black students participated in a walkout; later, black students from four black schools held a rally to oppose desegregation plans that would close their schools.[140]

Finally, protests occurred over the closing of Hamilton High School in the Atlanta area. The school had opened on the day after the *Brown v. Board of Education* decision in 1954. Said one former PTA president, "We were just a little pocket of black folks with our own school, and then they took it away."

> [Parents] spoke against the closing at school board meetings. They staged protests. In April 1969, hundreds of students walked out of their classes at Hamilton and joined their parents in a 2 1/2-mile march to the DeKalb courthouse. "Why close all black schools and no whites?" pleaded one of their signs.
>
> But the all-white school board had made up its mind, and the courts so ordered. Narvie Harris, still supervising schools for blacks, was heartsick and torn. She supported desegregation, but she was "dumbfounded, angry and hurt" about the one-sided way it was playing out. "People fought so hard to get those schools," she says, "and then they were taken away. Just closed."
>
> During the final week of classes that May, students assembled in the gym to bid farewell to Hamilton. They signed yearbooks and hugged teachers and sang songs. Juanita Harden Nelson, who would have to get her diploma elsewhere, performed a solo from the Sidney Poitier movie "To Sir, With Love." . . . As she picks up the melody all these years later, her eyes dance at the memory. "There was lots of crying," she says.[141]

I spoke with Daniel Buggs, who led the protests over Hamilton as a sixteen-year-old junior back in 1969. He said, with a touch of bitterness, "What led me [was] that had been the hub of our community—our schools and our churches. It was an every day thing, generating unity and brotherhood and sisterhood. It was family. . . . I was willing to fight for that. It was all I knew from elementary to my junior year. That school that led us and nurtured us. You gonna just close that off and tell us—no explanation—'OK, there's not enough Caucasian kids going to your school, so we're going to close you down and bus you.'"[142]

The Change in Attitudes

In all of the ways detailed above, the closing of black schools meant that black schoolchildren no longer saw school as a familiar and well-loved institution of their own community. Instead, school belonged to, and was run by, whites.

Thus, one study found that black parents were more alienated from the desegregated school that their children attended than were white parents.[143] Another broader study of a nationally representative sample of eighty-seven high schools—on a longitudinal basis—found that "the integrated setting itself appears to detract from the positive benefits of academic excellence," because "increased isolation in a mostly white environment can produce behavioral problems that make high school graduation and college attendance less likely."[144]

Anecdotal evidence shows that as black students were moved into white schools, some began to feel alienated and detached. One black girl who desegregated a school in Georgia said: "It wasn't really our school. Like we had lost our own school, you know, and all we had now was the whites' school."[145] Blacks often "felt as if they were in an alien environment."[146] Alvis Adair used the same phrasing: "Black students are thrust into these alien settings as undesirable 'outsiders' or 'intruders.'"[147] Blacks in North Carolina found that the "most difficult part" of the black school's closing was the "sheer strangeness" of the new white school.[148] A black teacher says: "I went to an all-black school for ten years, and then we were desegregated. It was very painful. I come from a small town, a very close-knit black community that focused on home and church. I had to go into another world I knew nothing about."[149]

As one black teacher from Virginia said: "I think when they integrated the schools, instead of the black kids seeing themselves as people who could go in there and make progress, they got linked and then linked themselves to all the bad things that the kids were doing. I can only relate to when I was in a segregated school. You'd go to high school commencement and I could see these kids walking up there with these four-year scholarships to places like Fisk and Howard or A&T or wherever. Now when I go to a high school graduation, the only kids I see getting the scholarships are white kids."[150]

Dudley Flood, who is on the Board of Governors for the University of North Carolina, spent many years coordinating integration plans in the state. Recently, he has said that with the closing of black schools: "It wasn't unusual to have whites welcome blacks into their schools. But it was clear the black children were the visitors. This was not their school. Their school was gone."[151] Scholar bell hooks writes about "attending all-black schools where black boys excelled . . . and the way that changed when schools were integrated. White teachers were not eager to teach black boys and white parents were not eager to have black boys sitting next to their songs and daughters. Suddenly, smart black boys were invisible."[152] In a North Carolina town, a principal spoke of the alienation experienced by the black community after desegregation: "The [black] students . . . don't feel as if this is their school. And the parents say: 'No one has ever invited me to come to this school.'"[153]

Indeed, white students themselves often took the attitude that the school was their own white institution. In Chesapeake, Virginia, for example, white former students reported having thought, "This is our school and they're just going to have to adjust," or "this is our territory" or "here they come to take over our stuff."[154] Black students obviously figured out that they were not welcome: "Even the teachers 'made us feel like they didn't want us to be there.'"[155]

The world of school had become white.

6

THE LOSS OF BLACK TEACHERS
AND PRINCIPALS

Dr. Evelyn Granville received a Ph.D. in mathematics from Yale in 1949. She finds it upsetting that black students today are criticized for "trying to be white" if they work hard in school, Granville says. "I was trying to be like my teachers"—that is, her black teachers in the segregated schools she had attended in Washington, D.C.[1]

But with the closing of black schools, most black students had to answer to white teachers and principals. As a result, black children were even more alienated from the school environment. No longer were they taught by black adults who had served as role models of academic success. Instead, they began to see the academic environment as one in which success required the approval of whites.

Firings and Demotions

One of the lawsuits that led to the *Brown v. Board of Education* decision was filed in Topeka, Kansas. But few today recall that teachers in Topeka were threatened with *firing* if the lawsuit in *Brown v. Board of Education* was successful. National Public Radio has observed that "over the next few years [after *Brown*], more than 80 percent of Topeka's black teachers weren't allowed to teach in desegregated schools."[2]

This is just an anecdote from one town, to be sure. On a nationwide scale, it is difficult to determine how many black teachers may have lost their jobs or been demoted due to desegregation, even while overall numbers of black teachers increased (as discussed below).[3] Anecdotes of firings or demotions are plentiful. Robert Hooker's 1971 report for the Race Relations Information Center noted that "demotion of black principals and teachers is more prevalent than outright dismissal." Examples include relieving "former department heads of their titles," sending high school teachers to elementary classrooms, assigning teachers to subjects outside their expertise, and making black teachers into "co-teachers" or "teachers' aides" or even "hall monitors." Nonetheless, Hooker documented numerous cases of dismissals—up to two thousand in Alabama, more than two hundred in Arkansas, several hundred in Florida, and so forth.[4]

In a North Carolina town, black teachers "were relieved of their positions entirely or demoted," thus breaking "what had been for many of the town's African American residents—despite myriad hardships, battles, and sacrifices—a chain of successful educational experiences."[5] Also from North Carolina, two former teachers recall, "Because they needed to consolidate, they took the white music teacher from the other school and made her the music teacher for the integrated school. And our black music teacher who had a number-one glee club and outstanding students in voice and the bands and the little flute bands and whatever and put her in a fifth-grade classroom. I thought that was outrageous." In that county, "more than half of the black elementary schoolteachers left. Only a handful of principals remained."[6] Looking back on the consolidation of black and white schools in West Virginia, one black resident recalled: "We felt short-changed and angry. . . . At [the newly integrated Welch Junior High] there were no black teachers, no role models. We lost all that. We had black history at [Dunbar] school, [and] when we went over there, there was none."[7]

A National Education Association task force in 1965 similarly found that "in a system with no classes for Negroes, there were simply no positions for Negro teachers," as it is "widely assumed by many school board members that Negroes, both students and teachers, are intellectually inferior."[8] Michele Foster, a professor of education at Claremont-McKenna College, describes numerous specific examples of black teachers who were fired or displaced in Missouri, Oklahoma, Texas, and elsewhere.[9] Etta Joan Marks, a teacher in Texas, recalled: "Most of those who worked with me in the segregated school didn't have jobs [following integration]. . . . Only four of the twelve black teachers were retained in the system."[10] In El Paso, Texas, one black teacher recalls that "experienced teachers were driving buses because that was the only job they were offered."[11]

Black principals were the most disadvantaged. As a black man from Maryland observed, "If you're going to combine these two school systems —you've got a Black superintendent and a White superintendent—who is going to be out of a job?"[12] This observation is borne out by the facts collected by the United States Senate in 1971, showing that the number of black principals in nine Southern states declined from 1,424 in the mid-1960s to a mere 225 in around 1970. In about three or four years, the number of black principals had been reduced in these states by more than 84 percent.[13] Alvis Adair notes that the jobs of some 600 black principals disappeared between 1964 and 1970 in Texas,[14] while Frederick Rodgers pointed out that between 1963 and 1973, the number of black principals in North Carolina dropped from 226 to a mere 15.[15]

When not fired altogether, many black principals found themselves re-assigned to a "subordinate administrative position," or transferred to a teaching position, or demoted to an assistant-type position.[16] As Linda Tillman explained, "Since racial patterns in most communities, especially those in the South, did not countenance blacks supervising whites in any capacity, much less teaching, principals of formerly black schools usually were reassigned as assistants to white principals or as central office super-visors."[17] A twenty-three-year principal of a black high school in North Carolina "became Director of Migrant Education and Coordinator of So-cial Services with the County Board of Education."[18] A black former prin-cipal noted: "We were integrated in the fall of 1970. . . . I felt that I would remain in my position as principal of the middle school. I later found out through some contacts that this was not true. They had already hired a young white without telling me a 'damn thing.' I saw then that the su-perintendent was determined to make me an assistant under a little white upstart. The students got wind of what was going to happen and started to raise hell, boycotting classes, striking the buses."[19]

In Kentucky, one esteemed black principal was pushed out the door be-cause they "didn't want to see a black person be in charge of white teach-ers" in the integrated school, "in spite of the fact that he had more formal education than any of the teachers in the whole system." He was brought up on bogus charges of malfeasance, including accusations that he gave away too many free lunches to poor students. As a local NAACP official noted, "Despite all of [the principal's] education, and all of his training and his skills; they brought such minor charges. And he just broke down and cried. It has always stuck in my mind how you could just take a strong black man and tear him to pieces like that."[20]

As Michael Fultz notes in his excellent review of the literature, however, the numerous anecdotes of black teachers having been fired must be reconciled with "a seemingly antithetical" fact: "according to United States Census statistics . . . , the absolute number of Black teachers in the South grew substantially throughout these years, increasing in the southern areas covered by *Brown I* from approximately 76,390 in 1950 to 146,872 in 1970." Fultz suggests that even though the absolute number of black teachers rose over that twenty-year period, it's "more meaningful" that the number of black teachers in the South fell from "19.8 percent of the total in 1950 to 17.4 percent in 1970."[21] According to Fultz, the percentage of teachers who were black should have remained more constant.

All of that said, there is no inherent reason that the percentage of blacks entering the teaching pool should have remained constant throughout the 1960s and 1970s. After employment discrimination was made illegal by the Civil Rights Act of 1964, many blacks—who formerly would have had to teach school out of sheer necessity—would have found themselves with a far wider range of career possibilities.

Indeed, while some black teachers and principals may have lost their jobs or been demoted under desegregation plans, it is entirely possible that some of them were simply less qualified or prepared than the white teachers and principals. As Adam Fairclough notes, many black teachers under segregation—however well-meaning—were not as qualified as the white teaching force.[22] Moreover, if a local school board *had* installed less-qualified black teachers and principals in a white school, that could have exacerbated white flight.

Nonetheless, even if we assume that every single job loss or demotion was rational and justified, and that the overall numbers of black teachers hired outweighed those who lost their jobs, the fact remains that desegregation affected the way that black children perceived the world of school.

They no longer saw as high a concentration of strong black role models, and the caring and nurturing environment of the traditional black schools dissipated.[23]

One study presents intriguing evidence from the National Educational Longitudinal Survey, which (among other things) looked at how eighth graders responded to numerous questions about their educational expectations, their attitudes toward teachers, their attitudes toward math and sciences, and so on. The scholar found that "blacks' odds of having a high belief [that is, positive attitudes and expectations] are between 1.2 and 1.6 times greater in predominantly-minority schools than in separate-white schools," and that "blacks and Latinos report less optimism and less pro-school attitudes in predominantly white schools than in predominantly nonwhite schools, especially nonwhite schools that employ many nonwhite teachers." To be sure, the scholar included a disclaimer pointing out that integrated schools also have several benefits (including smaller class sizes, middle-class peers and neighborhoods, among other things); she nonetheless noted that "being situated in a white environment does have an effect," and that "predominantly black" schools have at least one "advantage" in that "they promote optimism and pro-school attitudes."[24]

Outside of rigorous survey evidence, it makes sense that the diminished role of black teachers and principals would have had a dramatic effect on black children's attitudes, their views about school, and the energy that they put into academic success.[25] As Dudley Flood said in 1971: "In black culture, the black principal was about as high on the totem pole as it was possible to be. They could affect more things in Negro people's lives than any other person. [The loss of black principals] really takes a toll—an immeasurable toll—on the morale of the black community."[26] Dale Cushinberry, principal of Topeka High School, told the *New York Times* in 2004: "You have to ask yourself, what did it matter? If you listed the pluses and minuses, there'd be a lot of things on the negative side. The assumption was that black kids could sit next to white kids and become smarter. But what I knew about black schools is that those teachers were you, those principals were you. They saw my parents at church, at the grocery, at the beauty parlor. I couldn't get away with miscreance or subpar performance."[27]

One black administrator at a Chicago high school "spoke with longing and wonder about the segregated schools he had attended in Meridian, Mississippi. 'I think it was bad, I really do,' he said of integration. 'It may have been necessary, but I think for the average African-American it was probably one of the worst things that ever happened in this country. That's looking back on it.' Then he caught himself. 'I shouldn't say the worst thing that ever happened. I think that it had to happen, I really do. . . . But boy, there were some great teachers [in the black schools]. There were some teachers who could just take anything and make it come alive for me. . . . Integration took all that away because, number one, who were the teachers who were let go? Black teachers, African-American teachers. Principals were let go. So what you found yourself in was a school that was supposedly integrated, that had none of the things that you were really interested in.'"[28]

In a study that interviewed 75 percent of the black principals in one Southern state as of the mid-1970s, one principal commented that "the desegregation of the public schools has done more damage to the black educational administrator than any other single factor in history." Another principal similarly remarked, "In my opinion, the desegregation of the public schools has been probably the greatest catastrophe for the model image of blacks in our time. . . . In many cases, the few black administrators who are left are not looked upon as anyone with authority."[29]

One woman from Florida said, "Missed [integration], thank the Lord, by two years. I'm not saying I'm not for integration. But the community and the caring our children got in an all-black school is something that I think they're missing now."[30] In North Carolina, blacks sent to integrated schools "especially missed the black teachers and principals who had been their most important role models and counselors," and who had created a "daily shelter for black children to learn in—one with high expectations, strong role models, and constant reinforcement of their dignity and self-respect."[31]

Lloyd Daniel, who went on to become a Missouri state legislator, said that when he was bused to a desegregated school, his experience went downhill: "[Teachers] were always black in the segregated school and better teachers who understood us better, cared more about us, and we made much more progress. The absence of black teachers retarded all of our development."[32] Similarly, a black resident of North Carolina told author David Shipler: "This might not set so well with some people, but I don't think integration was necessarily the best thing for everybody. In this part of the country, anyway, the kids are still sitting in the back row. And when there were black teachers teaching black kids, they knew your mother, they knew your father, and you had to be accountable to that teacher. She was more than a teacher. The principal was like our grandfather, an authoritative figure. When you walked down that hall, you better not do anything. . . . You knew that you had to carry yourself in a certain way. . . . We didn't have the best materials, but we had the best nurturing. The teachers knew what we had to face and knew that we had to try extra hard, and they tried harder to make us to strive."[33]

One resident from Hyde County, North Carolina, commented that her children "who graduated and went to school with predominantly black students in their formative years were more focused, more dedicated to, and interested in school and school life. And it seemed to me it was more valuable to them. . . . It was more like what I was accustomed to, the way that I grew up: the teachers caring, they could identify, they were held responsible, and they were disciplined." As for a son who went to an integrated school: "The teachers said that he was very bright. He just didn't seem to be motivated and nurtured in the school. It wasn't the same nurturing of the children that the older children got from their teachers in the black schools."[34]

George Wright, a University of Texas at Arlington dean who grew up in segregated Lexington, Kentucky, writes of the "highly dedicated teachers that I encountered," who "had very exacting standards and refused to allow any misbehavior by their students," who "had a sense of pride in race and believed that any inappropriate act by students reflected poorly on the entire race."[35] But when the last black school in Lexington was closed in 1964, Wright was moved to a white high school. He "experienced segregation within a predominantly white environment": "Where previously I had found numerous forms of enjoyment behind the wall of segregation to such a degree that I was unaware that I was segregated, . . . I realized [in the white school] that I was an outsider."[36] As a student Wright dreamed of becoming a high school history teacher, but when he told one of the school's history teachers this, the teacher replied "that I lacked the smarts to do that"—it was the "worst thing that happened to me in high school," he recalled.[37] Summing up, Wright says that "the indifferent attitude that I received from white teachers in high school was encountered by other blacks and it destroyed their dreams and led to their dropping out of school."[38]

A Florida woman recalls: "When you had all black schools, you had all black teachers and the teachers wanted the kids to learn . . . . There was no way a kid would finish high school and not know how to read. No way a child was going to be disrespectful in the neighborhood without somebody's mama saying something. The problem with segregated schools was not the teachers, but the lack of supplies and proper facilities. We weren't begging to go to school in a mixed atmosphere. . . . I think integration hurt more than it helped. Our kids went to the other schools and saw the way other kids were acting and so they started acting that way, too."[39]

A retired teacher in Little Rock observed that her oldest children were "taught by all black teachers" who "seemed concerned about the children," and "there was a lot of competition among the children then, and they just wanted to learn." But her younger children attended integrated schools, where "the white teachers did not relate to the black children . . . some of the children resented the white teachers, and they did not do as well as my first set of children did."[40]

These changes in attitudes could contribute to lower academic performance. Although the research is not unanimous—and I have the formidable Roland Fryer and Steven Levitt against me on this point[41]— several studies find that black children do better academically when they have black teachers. One researcher found that both black and white students who have a same-race "role model" have better attitudes about academic achievement and even have "relatively better academic performance more than a year after the initial assessment."[42] In a study of Texas students, Eric Hanushek and his colleagues found that "black teachers tend to be more effective with minority students. Estimates range in size from 0.05 to 0.10 standard deviations."[43] Similarly, after studying a well-known Tennessee experiment that involved random assignment, Thomas Dee found that each year with a same-race teacher "increased math and reading scores by roughly 2 to 4 percentile points."[44] Dee also points out that the estimated 3.1 percentile point increase in math scores amounts to "35 percent of the corresponding black-white test score gap."[45] One scholar also found that "increasing the percentage of math teachers who are black has a nontrivial, positive impact on the likelihood that a black geometry student will enroll in a subsequent rigorous math course."[46]

To be sure, the positive effect of black teachers on black students is just a small factor. I am *not* suggesting that black children must be taught by black teachers to succeed; nor am I suggesting that where black children do have black teachers, their education will automatically be excellent. As is always the case, education is influenced by many, many factors. If there is a positive effect of same-race teachers, it would no doubt be outweighed by many other factors, such as the teacher's ability and qualifications, the curriculum, the peers in a given school, the socioeconomic status of the neighborhood.

Other Impacts

Outside of the loss of black academic role models (especially black principals), there were many other effects when black students were sent into schools where the majority of teachers and principals were white.

White Teachers Who Did Not Push Blacks to Succeed

Although the following point is difficult to prove empirically, many people believe that white teachers in newly integrated schools didn't care enough to push black children to succeed academically. Whether this was because of outright racism, lower expectations, disillusionment, liberal paternalism, or whatever other cause you can imagine, the result was the same: teachers that often did not inspire the best performance from their students.

For example, a 1944 graduate of the Dunbar School in Washington, D.C., remarks: "We had black teachers who pushed in the same ways that our parents did. White teachers don't have the same high expectations."[47] Another older woman from Virginia noted: "I think we were taught in our day to strive and work harder, even though we were under disadvantages. Teachers were good then, they were so good. . . . I don't believe that white teachers push the blacks like a black teacher would push a black child. I don't know whether there's fear there, or just what it is. That's my concern. A black teacher will push you."[48] A teacher in Ohio "lamented the loss of that 'loving, nurturing touch' black teachers provided. In place of their veteran teachers, former black schools got inexperienced white teachers, many perceived as unresponsive to black children."[4]

You find the same sentiment among blacks who were the first to integrate their local schools. Ingrid Burton Nathan, a teacher at Lake Mary High School in Seminole, Florida, was the first black student to attend Sanford Junior High School in 1965. She recently told a newspaper that "today's schools don't provide black children with the support that existed during segregation, when black teachers were part of the community and kept in contact with parents. Today, black students often do not relate to white teachers."[50] Similarly, one former student who integrated a North Carolina school says: "When I first integrated? For the most part I felt that the white teachers were rather insensitive. . . . Now I know some of my friends can tell you some pretty blatant kinds of things that happened but from my own perspective I feel that for the most part the more subtle racism [was] that they simply ignored [us] and did very little to cultivate any type of relationship with us."[51]

I spoke with Artemise Clemons, who integrated a New Orleans high school in 1968. She told me that in her previous black school, "Teachers really cared about me academically. They always made sure I did the best that I could do. I felt loved, not only from teachers but my principal as well. In entering the school, I didn't have to enter a hostile environment. We were all black. . . . If I could do it all over again, I would stay in the black environment. . . . If I could go back, I wouldn't do it. Everything was different [in the integrated school]—the culture—it was white, it was layed out white. . . . My principal—Mr. Price—if a child didn't show up in school, he got in his car and went around the neighborhood. If I missed school at the white school, I was just out. I wish for those days [segregation], it was just a better day."[52]

In some cases, of course, white teachers at the time of desegregation were guilty of racism. A black teacher from Texas said: "The teachers made it clear that blacks were not welcome. In the classroom, the white teachers would put the black kids on one side of the room and the white kids on the other side."[53] Another teacher agreed that the attitude of white teachers was, "These black kids can't make it."[54] Yet another stated that "a lot of these [white] teachers haven't cared about black kids."[55]

In other cases, some white teachers coddled black students out of pity, timidity, or patronizing attitudes.[56] Well-intentioned or not, the result was the same: students who were not pushed to succeed and try their best. As University of San Diego law professor Roy Brooks notes, "African American teachers have fewer feelings of 'liberal guilt' than many white teachers and consequently will tolerate less trash talk and 'acting a fool' in class than their white counterparts."[57] In the earliest study to find the "acting white" criticism, one student noted that "some teachers are harder on Negroes, and some are easier on Negroes, just because they're Negroes. There're some people who're so conscious about the Negro getting a fair shake that they're overly easy."[58] In a 1975 study, researchers found that white teachers were less likely to push black students to succeed, and pointed out that "oppression can arise out of warmth, friendliness, and concern."[59]

As one black teacher said, "The worst cases I had came from children who had been pampered by white teachers."[60] Another veteran black teacher opined: "All students will con teachers if they let themselves be conned. But it's often easier for black students to con white teachers because the students know that the teachers will pity them, feel sorry for them, and make excuses. . . . White teachers tend to give up too easily on the kids. They take the kids' resistance as not wanting to learn. But as soon as the teachers stop pushing, the students say that teachers didn't care because if they had they would have kept on pushing them."[61] Another veteran black teacher said, "I've seen white teachers let black kids misbehave and then when I ask them why they say, 'I thought that was a part of his culture.'"[62] A black teacher from St. Louis noted that "too many teachers" had "low-level expectation[s]" of black students, and that while desegregation had many advantages, one disadvantage is that "most of the people in the county schools don't respect our abilities."[63] Black students in Alabama claimed that when they performed well at an integrated school, white teachers referred to them as "unusual Negroes," indicating that the teachers had "low expectations."[64] In Houston, one school's "new white teachers lacked experience teaching inner city black children, and, of course, they didn't live in the community with the children they taught. 'A lot came in and tried to be kids' friends,' says [a former student], 'instead of their teachers.'"[65]

One black teacher said: "People who don't share this past wonder how anything positive could have gone on in segregated communities. . . . I am not romanticizing segregation, and I certainly don't want to go back to those days. But there are lessons that can be learned from my experiences and the experiences of thousands of other black people like me who lived under segregation. Our teachers could see our potential even when we couldn't, and they were able to draw out our potential. . . . [T]housands of black children could still benefit from studying under the kind of teachers that taught me."[66] Another former student said of his segregated school: "The best experience I have ever had [is] going to a segregated school. . . . In segregation, we learned, the teachers taught us and we learned. They cared about each child. But, in desegregation, it's sad to say that's not true."[67]

Different Teaching Styles After Integration

In the world of black schools, black teachers had commonly urged their students to be "twice as good" as whites in order to have any chance of succeeding in the world. But in an integrated setting, black teachers now felt restrained—for obvious reasons—from giving their students that same exhortation.[68] Everett Dawson, who taught high school in North Carolina from 1943 to 1984, says:

> I became disillusioned with what I saw in desegregated schools. The biggest difference is that we were able to do more with the black students in all-black schools. In other words, if I wanted to I could come in this morning . . . and ask, "Why are you here? Are you here just to make out another day? . . . Do you know where your competition is? Your competition is not your little cousin sitting over there. Your competition is that little white kid sitting over in the other school. He's the one you have got to compete with for a job. And the only way that you're going to get that job is that you are going to have to be better than he is." . . .
>
> Once you integrated, and had mixed groups, I didn't feel comfortable getting into the things the whites did to us as black people.[69]

Dawson continues: "Again, what black kids miss as a result of desegregation is the serious kind of conversations that we were able to have in all-black schools. Black kids are not hungry now. . . . They don't hunger and thirst for education. And the reason they don't hunger is because nobody tells them that they need to hunger and thirst for education. Once they went into the integrated situation there was no one pushing them."[70] A black teacher in San Diego notes, "There are some things I might be able to tell them [black students] that a white teacher might have difficulty conveying, because the students assume that the white teachers are getting after them for the wrong reasons."[71]

Another black teacher from Virginia argued: "Our teacher could stand in front of our class and say . . . that every job we went for we'd be competing against a White person and so we had to look as nice as they do or better. . . . You can't stand up in front of a class and say that today."[72] Similarly, Charles Sherrod of Albany, Georgia, pointed out: "You can't say to a black youth in the presence of a white staff person, 'Son, you got to be better than them. You got to think faster, run faster.' That kind of prompting helped us through. There's no more of that."[73] From North Carolina, a former teacher recalls: "I think that was one motivation of each teacher: knowing that they had to prepare the children to be better than . . . the white students in order to have any opportunities. Therefore, they had to put an emphasis on the reading and the writing and communications and doing it right."[74]

Differences in Teacher Quality

Another problem with the way desegregation was implemented was that some of the best black teachers were reassigned to white schools, while some of the worst white teachers were sent to those black schools that remained open in some capacity.[75] One Houston black school "lost as much as half of its experienced teachers to other schools."[76] A black principal remarked: "They took my best teachers, in my opinion, some of the best teachers you'll find anywhere. In return they sent me the white principal's 'Ivory Soaps.' . . . A lot of them had teachers they were trying to get rid of for years, and this was a good opportunity . . . [Q: What do you mean by 'Ivory Soaps'?] Oh, those are the individuals who float around from place to place in a school program and don't and perhaps can't do a decent job anywhere."[77] Or as a teacher from Birmingham recalls, "I distinctly remember them taking some of our very good black teachers and sending them to white schools, and they sent us—I'm not saying that the teachers weren't good, but they sent us all of the white teachers that were kind of new, rookies."[78] A black school principal in Arkansas recalls that the superintendent "took his best teachers and replaced them with white teachers of a lower caliber, which severely hurt the quality education program he was trying to establish."[79] From Alabama, a former teacher recalls that the school board reassigned black teachers with master's degrees, while sending the "inexperienced" white teachers "right out of college" to one former black school: "They pulled the best that we had and took it over there."[80]

Even apart from teacher quality, there's evidence that white teachers who ended up in black schools tended to have higher numbers of transfer requests, because they didn't want to work there. As one article put it, "One can only speculate about the quality of the instructional programs in black schools which are characterized by teachers assigned to these schools against their will, teachers who request transfer as soon as they are eligible, teachers who are unable to transfer because they are not accepted by the requested school, and teachers who perceive their work site as unacceptable."[81]

The Role of School Discipline

Numerous scholars have pointed out that black children are disciplined, suspended, or expelled from the public schools at disproportionate rates.[82] To be sure, some of this discipline could be because black students really do misbehave more often on average,[83] which might be due to impoverished upbringings, peer groups in the neighborhoods, a greater rate of fatherlessness in the black community, or other factors. Indeed, one study that took place during segregation noted that black students in segregated schools were more "delinquency prone."[84]

At the same time, white teachers and principals in integrated schools were sometimes thought to be unfair in choosing whom to discipline and how. At the time, black students often complained that they were punished for types of behavior that white students got away with—cutting in line, leaving a tray on the cafeteria table, disagreeing with the teacher, and so on.[85] As one black teacher from Virginia said of her white principal shortly after desegregation, "I knew lots of other cases where he'd hit black kids with a paddle, but I've never heard where he had hit a white kid with a paddle; they have discipline problems too."[86] In a study of a desegregated school, one scholar claimed, "Black students were regularly suspended for offenses for which whites were merely reprimanded."[87]

Thus, if higher disciplinary rates in any way resulted from discrimination, it should be no surprise that black children might start to resent the whole world of school, and to think of it as an imposition of "white" values.

In any event, discrimination isn't even necessary for resentment to arise. Even if black children really do misbehave in higher numbers in school, they will resent being punished. After all, children do not typically enjoy punishment, no matter how justified it might be. Then, just by the fact that punishment is being meted out by a white teacher or principal, the typical black student might feel resentment toward the white world of school.

Of crucial importance, too, is the way that black parents view school discipline. It's a commonplace observation that in the days of black schools, black teachers were able to discipline black students with the full support of the parents and the community. In most cases, the black parents knew the teacher or principal from church or community activities, and often had been a student of a particular teacher or principal themselves. Because of the close-knit nature of the community, there was a degree of trust between the parents and the school authorities. As one study found, black students in segregated schools were much more likely than white students (in white schools) to be satisfied with the level of discipline in their schools.[88]

This trust, however, began to break down once black children were in an environment controlled by mostly white teachers and principals.[89] Even if discrimination were completely absent in each and every case of school discipline (which seems a rather optimistic assumption), black parents and children might very naturally *suspect* that discrimination had played a role. If you're a black parent, and you hear from a black principal that a black teacher has had problems with your son talking back, you have no reason to think that racism is involved. But if you hear from a white principal that a white teacher saw your son get in a fight, you may have more trouble trusting that the principal and teacher are being totally fair.

As one teacher from Virginia put it, "The relationships between black teachers and parents and the support we used to enjoy aren't like they used to be. And as a result children—black children—are suffering."[90] A teacher in Chicago said: "I can remember I made a stray mark on a test once. To the kids this meant racial prejudice. One stray mark on a piece of paper and three hundred years of discrimination comes up in your face. You'll break your neck for those kids, but they'll never really trust you. No matter what you do, to them you are still white."[91] In one Ohio community after desegregation, "Black teachers and students said discipline was harsher for blacks. A black student explained, 'There were a lot of black students paddled and a lot of white parents called on the telephone.' "[92] A 1970s study of two newly desegregated schools noted that black parents were "suspicious of any kind of control by whites," and were "ready to complain if black children were suspended or expelled in too large numbers."[93] A woman in Oak Park, Illinois, speculates on why her three daughters chose to go to black colleges: "They probably suffered a lot in this experiment [of desegregation], because they had to deal with teachers who had never had black students and who had all the stereotypes about they can't learn, they're lazy, their parents are uneducated, you know. . . . [At a black college, you could] be in a class and know if you didn't get the grade, it was because you did not do the work. It didn't have anything to do with the color of your skin."[94]

A former student from Maryland described the contrast: under the "close-knit structure that was in the segregated system," "I couldn't walk down the hall and kick a door without somebody . . . grabbing me by the collar and taking me to the principal's office. And then the next thing I know when I get home in the afternoon, my parents sitting there saying, 'Well this happen.' I say, 'Well—' 'Don't even try. I know Mr. So-and-So isn't going to tell me a lie.' Bam. That's it." But in the integrated school, "if they say the child did something and the parent knows full well the child wouldn't do such a thing, . . . those types of situations occurred. And it led to a lack of continuity in the classroom."[95]

In short, whether or not the suspicion of racial discrimination was correct in all instances, the very *possibility* for such suspicion made it harder for black children to feel that they really belonged in their school.

With desegregation—as important a goal as that was—the black community ended up losing control over its most important public institution.

For many blacks, school had been the one place where they saw other blacks succeeding, where they were taught by black teachers who strongly believed in their potential, and where they did not have to deal with racism in any direct way. But with desegregation, those black schoolchildren were suddenly thrust into schools where their presence was resented, where they faced teachers who often either slighted or patronized them, and where they were part of an identifiable minority that (due to past discrimination) was often less prepared than white students.

7

THE RISE OF TRACKING

"Desegregation destroyed us."

—Rev. Vernon Dobson, a 1941 graduate of a black high school
 in Baltimore

"Integration? What was it good for? They were just setting up
our babies to fail."

—Gwendolyn Hopson

Desegregation and the Rise of Tracking

The term "tracking" refers to the way schools group students into classes according to ability.[1] Although tracking had been used in public schools for many years, it became a racially tinged process after desegregation.[2] Ironically, the use of tracking was contemplated by Thurgood Marshall. In his argument before the Supreme Court in *Brown v. Board of Education,* he was asked whether black children could achieve at the same level as white children. Marshall answered in his typical colloquial style: "Simple, put the dumb Colored children in with the dumb White children, and put the smart Colored children with the smart White kids."[3] Needless to say, even though many segregated black schools were doing the best that they could, they were not fully able to overcome centuries of slavery, oppression, and economic hardship. As a result, when black children were thrust en masse into white schools in the late 1960s, not all of them were performing well enough academically.[4]

The use of tracking had the effect of keeping most black children in a slower class, apart from many white students in a more advanced class. Indeed, I have come across some indignation over a perception that "special education"—which is intended for disabled children—allegedly became a dumping ground for black children. A woman from Austin, Texas, said: "Back then it wasn't a thing called special education when I went to school. All children learned their multiplication, all children learned the different English curriculum, nouns, pronoun. I mean, they didn't separate who was unable to learn and who could learn."[5] Wanda Jackson, an educator in Houston, told me: "Once integration came, the value system in education—as far as blacks—was that the standards were lowered. By lowering, I mean, all of a sudden you have special education created. When we were segregated, every child could read. Teachers did not tolerate foolishness, clowning around."[6] Lee James, the pastor of a Baptist church in Gulfport, Mississippi, told me: "We didn't have special ed, because the children weren't allowed to be that dumb. Teachers just didn't tolerate any mischief."[7] And as one former teacher points out, "When the children were integrated into white schools, they lost something. Integration has helped in some ways, but it has hurt our black children in some ways. Now, instead of seeing black children winning prizes for their achievements, you see them all in special education classes. This has caused them to lose their pride, their self-esteem."[8]

Beyond special education, one set of scholars notes that "the use of academic grouping and discipline to resegregate classrooms has generally been associated with desegregation."[9] For example, "When South Carolina was forced to desegregate its schools, racial separation shifted to the classrooms. The use of testing to group, or 'track,' children began as a deliberate way to divide blacks and whites. The powerful School Committee encouraged the practice in its 1964 report to the Legislature."[10]

In an Ohio community, "high schools tracked students in English and math by the second year of desegregation. Tracking grades 7–12 became official district policy in 1974–75, with students grouped in three levels by reading achievement test scores. The highest track was overwhelmingly white, the lowest predominantly black."[11] In Maryland, one long-time black teacher noted that "desegregation, or integration, of the schools was not easy. Many of our children were placed in special education classes without proper testing. They 'seemed slow.'"[12] In Selma, Alabama, one former educator noted that tracking began after "desegregation occurred in 1970."[13] In St. Louis, a principal "noticed shortly after the desegregation program that there was a rapid increase in the number of white suburban students trying to get into honors English in ninth grade," and he suspected that this was because of white parents "who did not want their children in classes with African-American students."[14]

In one early study of a desegregated school, "there was little desegregation in classrooms," because of tracking. As one black student said, "It's possible to go all through the years of high school and not have a single white person in your class."[15] Another study notes that when the black schools were closed in two Southern counties, the teachers in white schools tended to regard them as of low worth: "Black students had been regarded by staff as having low ability," and when desegregation occurred, blacks "were placed in separate classrooms and labeled educable mentally retarded, learning disabled, or behavior disordered."[16] A teacher recalls:

> When the school systems integrated, they . . . [had] white children in one class and black children in another because . . . white were smarter. . . . Your predominantly low groups have been black children. They were when I came here. There hadn't been a white face in what we call a low group. And your gifted children were all white.[17]

On studying around sixty-five hundred children during desegregation in the school system in Riverside, California, social scientists concluded that "when entering the receiving classroom, the minority child was likely to be nearly two years behind academically"; for such a student, the "only academic salvation lay in social acceptance by the Anglo majority," because it would be "extremely difficult for him to improve his performance . . . within his small, isolated, low-achieving ethnic clique." This "salvation" was rare, however, because during the six-year period of the study, "little or no real integration" had occurred, and if anything, "ethnic cleavage became somewhat more pronounced over time."[18]

Today, black high school students are not often found in the higher-ranked classes, which are typically designated Advanced Placement (AP) or

International Baccalaureate (IB) courses. One study that looked at nationally representative data found that 15 percent of black eighth graders were in high-ability English classes, compared with 32 percent of whites.[19] Another pair of scholars found that "Asians have over an 80 percent chance of being in college prep math, whites have a 43 percent chance of taking college prep math, and blacks and Latinos have less than a 15 percent chance of taking college prep math."[20]

In analyzing a large random sample of high schoolers in Charlotte, North Carolina, Roslyn Mickelson found that "tracking resegregates students such that the lowest tracks (special education) are largely Black and the highest tracks (AP/IB) are overwhelmingly White."[21] This disproportionate representation was present even after Mickelson controlled for prior achievement. For example, among the students whose sixth-grade test scores were in the 90th to 99th percentiles—the top 10 percent of all students—"52 percent of Whites but only 20 percent of Blacks were in AP/IB English."[22] According to Mickelson, tracking in the Charlotte system "began at about the same time desegregation efforts commenced." Specifically, "when Whites from a prosperous neighborhood desegregated the flagship high school in Charlotte's Black community (West Charlotte High), the 'open program' or higher track was instituted to create an environment that would encourage Whites to participate in desegregated education."[23] Indeed, when a black principal in 1997 tried to enroll more black students in the higher track, a "major struggle ensued" with several "veteran White teachers" and "middle-class White parents who feared greater enrollment of Blacks in the top academic classes would result in the dumbing down of the curriculum."[24]

How Tracking Contributed to "Acting White"

Here is what many black children faced once they had been reassigned to desegregated schools: They were sitting in a classroom with mostly other black students in what they believed to be the "dumb" class, watching as the white students headed to the "smart" class down the hall. (Even in the absence of tracking, a black child might have found himself sitting next to a white child who came from a more privileged background and was better prepared for the school environment.) In such circumstances, it is not surprising that some black students would have started to lose confidence in their academic abilities.

For example, in North Carolina's desegregated schools, "Black students were having social, personal, and academic difficulties in adjustment. . . . In many instances remedial classes had been set up which were all black, or predominantly black, which made the black students feel inferior."[25] In a 1970s study of two desegregated schools, Mary Metz found that although the school population was 32 percent black, "there were only two black children in eighth grade Honors classes at the two schools together."[26] In the lower tracks, "most of the children felt divorced from the school's values and accustomed to conflict with the teachers."[27]

A report on early desegregation in Louisiana noted, "Ability grouping 'has knocked the ambition out of the children. . . . When I try to tell some of my own children to work, they won't, because they know they're in the lowest sections and the school expects them to be bad.' Black students themselves say they find being assigned to low sections so degrading that they would prefer outright segregation."[28] Economists who examined the famous "High School and Beyond" database found that "blacks in almost totally white schools are, indeed, significantly more likely to dread English and math than their counterparts in all-black schools."[29]

A long-time teacher said that integration has "separated our black kids. It has divided them." When a few kids from the "projects" are bused to a white school, they "group together. They want to be seen; they become behavior problems. Then, they're put in special education classes. . . . They congregate. They don't do their work, [thus] they're labeled as slow. Then they're tracked. What happens as a result of that? Low self-esteem. 'I'm slow anyway, so why try?'"[30]

Not only did tracking cause black children to become dispirited with schoolwork, it encouraged the "acting white" charge. After all, what happens if you are sitting in a roomful of black students, and one of them leaves to go join the white class down the hall? People start to mutter, "What's the matter with her? Does she think she's white?" Just as with the elimination of black schools, the classification of white students as "smart" hammered home the message: "Academic pursuit is for whites, not for you."

Indeed, many scholars and observers have noted that "acting white" is closely tied to academic tracking.[31] This was true as far back as the earliest study to find the "acting white" criticism. In that study, students at a desegregated school remarked that "all the Negroes" are in the "dumb math class," while there "aren't many Negroes" in the accelerated classes.[32] Less colloquially, the scholars themselves noted that "only one or two black students are present in each of the college preparatory classes; most other black students seem to be in courses such as shop or others which involve manual work."[33] This directly led to the "acting white" criticism: As one student put it, "I participate in speech; I'm the only Negro in the whole group. . . . I'm always contrasted in pictures of the group. However, the Negroes accuse me of thinking I'm white. In the bathroom one day, they'd written across the wall in big letters, 'Al Carter is an Uncle Tom.' I think it's this kind of pressure from the other Negro kids which causes me the greatest concern."[34]

Similarly, one researcher found, when studying an integrated school in the Northeast from 1975 to 1978, that "both white and black students . . . have come to see academic effort and achievement as characteristically white," that "whiteness has become associated with success in . . . the most fundamental role of children in the school situation—that of student," and that both "teachers and parents told researchers that black children who consistently perform very well are sometimes pressured by their black peers not to work so hard."[35] This was because black students saw that "succeeding academically often means leaving their friends behind and joining predominantly white groups within their classes."[36] Indeed, even within classes, "teachers, both black and white, often set up and enforce racially segregated seating patterns as a by-product of their desire for academically homogeneous sub-groups in their classes."[37] In the scholar's words, the "very obvious white domination of academic life . . . fosters in many black students a sense of alienation from the school."[38]

John Ogbu found that tracking contributed to "acting white" in Shaker Heights, Ohio; he quotes one black student as saying, "You don't want to go into a class where you're one of four or five people of your race. I think that's a very intimidating situation."[39] As Ronald Ferguson of Harvard pointed out in his own study of Shaker Heights, "Concerns about the potential of social isolation is one reason that black students, especially males, might choose to avoid honors and AP courses. . . . For example, at a recent conference of high-achieving minority teenagers . . . , one black male said, 'If you're a girl, some guy's always going to talk to you,' but if you are a guy, you might end up all by yourself. Hence, when they do enroll in honors and AP classes, black males often take special measures to maintain their standing 'within the fold' among other black males."[40]

Sociologist Karolyn Tyson, who otherwise is a skeptic on the "acting white" issue, blames the "acting white" effect on the fact that schools often place blacks and whites in different academic tracks.[41] That is, if "higher-level classrooms and programs are disproportionately populated by Whites, and scholastic achievements and honors also appear to be reserved for whites, academic achievement is simply added to the list of behaviors around which students (Blacks and others) draw racial boundaries."[42] Two sociologists recently noted that when "few black students take challenging classes, those who do so could be seen as deviating from normative black behavior or as acting white."[43]

A recent story from Michigan notes that "it was almost 20 years ago, in 1987, that Tiombe Earhart . . . first was told she was 'acting white.' She and her family had just moved to Kalamazoo from Detroit. There, she had attended the predominantly black Renaissance High School and had taken college-prep courses. When Tiombe Earhart started a similar track at [the integrated Kalamazoo high school], she found herself one of a few blacks at the school. Attending the math and science center, coupled with having clear diction, made her a target for critics."[44] In another story, *New York Times* reporters found: "As students notice that honors classes are mostly white and lower-level ones mostly black, they develop a corrosive sense that behaving like honors students is 'acting white,' while 'acting black' demands they emulate lower-level students. Little wonder that sixth grade, when ability grouping starts here [New Jersey], is also when many interracial friendships begin to come apart."[45] A girl from Virginia notes: "I've had people criticize me because I'm in an honors English class. I'm the only black girl in my class and there's one other black boy. . . . Some of my friends don't seem to understand I'm trying to better myself and whenever I explain it to them, they keep insisting I'm trying to be white. I'm not."[46]

Some people would claim that black students are placed in lower-level classes only because of discrimination. Ironically, that sort of discrimination is more likely to occur in integrated schools than elsewhere: In an all-black school, it is difficult to imagine how there could be racial discrimination in classroom assignments. Thus, even though blacks and whites with the same achievement levels are equally likely to end up in a college-bound track,[47] this is more often the case in black schools than in racially diverse schools. According to sociologists Samuel R. Lucas and Mark Berends: "The more racial diversity there is, the more likely white students are to be in the college prep track and the less likely black students are to be in the college prep track. . . . [But] blacks in all-black schools are more likely to be in the college preparatory program than are comparable whites in all-white schools."[48] In other words, "Where blacks encounter students of other races, promising blacks enter lower track levels; where comparable blacks study alone, they enter the school's college preparatory curriculum."[49] Another study found that the more black teachers there are, the less likely it is that black students will end up in the lowest tracks.[50]

Moreover, when all-black schools did use tracking, there was no reason for the parents to suspect that their children had been misclassified due to racial discrimination. But when white teachers in integrated schools told black parents that their children were slower—*even where the classification was correct*—black parents found themselves not knowing whether to trust the school. As one article puts it: "A black father who had several children in the elementary school when desegregation began said that blacks were worried about discrimination by white administrators and teachers: 'They've got a percentage set . . . for how many blacks are allowed to make the grade. . . . I know one little boy who got 100 on the spelling papers he brought home to show his mamma—and he was real smart. . . . But they didn't let him pass his grade because they already had their percentage of black children."[51] In the context of desegregation, tracking became yet another wedge driven between the black community and the schools.

Getting rid of tracking—or "detracking"—might have some benefits, but likely would not address the "acting white" phenomenon. One detracking program in San Diego took a select group of minority children (those who had high-enough grades and achievement scores) and put them in college-prep classes. Among other things, this particular program essentially created a new peer group—students outside the program tended to be "jealous," while students in the detracking group felt "an increased commitment and loyalty" to each other precisely because they were a bit "defensive" about having been chosen.[52]

This is just what we would expect from social psychology: Create a new group that feels a bit competitive with outsiders, and they will start to be loyal among themselves. Putting students in a college-prep class as a group also overcomes the collective action problem, where no student wants to be the first minority to join such a class by himself.[53]

Moreover, the detracking program in San Diego took only a select sample of black children. If detracking were applied across the board, differences in academic ability would still exist. Within each classroom, it would still be clear that certain students were smarter and better prepared than others. As well, teachers are only human; they cannot help but recognize and smile upon achievement when they see it.

Thus, slower students in a given classroom would quickly realize that other students were smarter, more accomplished, more likely to know the answer when called upon, and more likely to be praised by the teacher. As one scholar argued: "If students enter the desegregated situation with a lower level of skills they are fated to be perceived as having little academic ability in almost every class they attend—there is no escape from this fate. This will occur even if there is no tracking or ability grouping."[54]

Moreover, I do not think that detracking, in and of itself, would ever be implemented on a broad scale. It would be politically difficult to get rid of all academic distinctions, such that no English class is any harder or any easier than another. Like it or not, many parents of academically advanced children want the option of sending them to a "gifted and talented" class.[55]

In sum, the practice of separating the "smart" children from the rest had devastating consequences in desegregated schools. It usually removed black students from white students in class, and contributed to the widespread feeling that the handful of black students who join advanced classes are thereby deserting their friends and acting superior—that is, "acting white."

8

WHEN DID "ACTING WHITE" ARISE?

"Lindsey Clark is African-American. But because she's smart, her black classmates tease her sometimes and tell her she's 'acting white.' 'I didn't want to do well on a test once,' said Clark, 13, a seventh-grade honor student at the Smart School charter school in Lauderhill. 'Kids tell me, you're always acting like a white girl. If you see what color I am in my face, I'm not white,' she said."

—*South Florida Sun-Sentinel,* 2004

The past few chapters have explained why desegregation set the stage for the "acting white" criticism to emerge in the school setting. This chapter shows that "acting white" did indeed start with desegregation. "Pioneers"—or the first black children to integrate local schools—often faced criticism from their black peers for "acting white."

I admit right off the bat that the evidence in this chapter is anecdotal. It would be wonderful if someone had thought to do a survey every year over the past century, asking a random sample of black people nationwide about the "acting white" criticism in education. Unfortunately, no such survey exists. That said, while anecdotes are not necessarily "data," that does not mean that anecdotes can be dismissed. In the absence of systematic data, the only reason to reject anecdotes is the fear that they have been cherry-picked and do not fairly represent the broader truth. But the anecdotes that I have found are *unanimous* that "acting white" (in school settings) arose at the time of desegregation, not before.

You may wonder how I collected the many anecdotes in this chapter.

Sheer hard work is the answer. I have examined literally thousands of sources over the past several years, including academic journals, academic books, newspaper articles, Web sites, recordings and transcripts from historical archives kept by state governments or universities, biographies and autobiographies, popular histories of race in America, as well as personal interviews. All the while, I kept an eye out for anyone who mentioned "acting white" in connection with desegregation; anyone who *denied* that "acting white" was connected with desegregation; and anyone who ever mentioned whether "acting white" occurred in schools *prior* to desegregation. Obviously, I have not read everything ever written. But it does seem telling that after reading thousands of sources, I am not even tempted to cherry-pick, because *100 percent* of the anecdotes are consistent with my theory.

One final source of potential bias: few people ever have their words inscribed in history books or news articles. Countless utterances disappear into thin air the moment they are spoken. Thus, it is possible that the term "acting white" could have cropped up at an earlier time, but that there is simply no written record of it.

This chapter has three sections. The first section describes the often hostile reception many black students found when they entered the desegregated environment. The second section discusses the many black people who recall being accused of acting white along with desegregation. The third section bolsters the case by showing that the "acting white" criticism was virtually unheard of in earlier generations.

Hostile Reception in Integrated Schools

In many communities, integration did not happen in one fell swoop. Instead, integration plans often occurred piecemeal—perhaps with the upper grades being integrated years before the lower grades, or with one school in a given town being integrated before the rest. As a result, there were often black students who were the very first to integrate their local schools, either as part of a small group or even alone.

These "pioneers" incurred the brunt of white resentment toward integration.[1] They were ridiculed, ostracized, ignored, left out, subjected to protests (from Little Rock to Boston to Detroit), and occasionally they experienced violence. Melba Pattillo Beals, for example, was one of the nine teenagers who were the first blacks to attend Central High School in Little Rock, Arkansas—the site of Governor Orval Faubus's infamous pledge to keep segregation forever. At first, the threats of violence were so extreme that she had to attend school under the watchful accompaniment of soldiers from the 101st Airborne Division. Even when the initial threats of violence subsided, she faced extraordinary obstacles throughout the entire school year: she was regularly hit, kicked, tripped, called a "nigger," and even worse. On one occasion, students broke eggs over her head, and another time a student threw a lighted stick of dynamite at her. Perhaps the worst incident was when another student rushed up and threw acid in her eyes. Her eyesight was saved only because the 101st Airborne soldier assigned to protect her quickly rushed her to a sink and ran water over her eyes for several minutes.[2]

Derrick Bell, a long-time civil rights lawyer and the first black professor at Harvard Law School, was present for the initial desegregation of the schools in Harmony, Mississippi, in the fall of 1964. As he tells the story, only one black family in Harmony was willing to participate at first—the parents of a first-grader named Debra. She was alone in integrating the local school; no other black student joined her. She initially had to be accompanied by federal marshals who were there to protect her from racially motivated violence. Her father was "fired from his job that very day, and whites attempted to burn down his house."[3]

Or consider the experience of Mae Bertha Carter, as told to National Public Radio's *Morning Edition* on October 2, 1995. She had worked picking cotton for thirty cents an hour in Drew, Mississippi, close to where the White Citizens Council was started. As she told her interviewer, "I always would say to myself, 'Well, bein' black, that's a disadvantage—just bein' black—but, being uneducated, that's another disadvantage.' So, I couldn't change the black, but we certainly could change and get a good education for our kids." Carter and her husband decided to try to put their children in the local white school in 1965 under the "freedom of choice" system that Mississippi had established (intending, of course, that black people would make the correct "choice" to stay away from the white schools).

The Carters, however, were determined to make the choice to send their children to white schools. The rest of the black community thought that the Carters "had lost their minds." As for the local school officials, says Mrs. Carter, they "were shocked that morning that we walked in the superintendent's office. . . . Well, what they did, then they started puttin' pressure on us—all kinds of pressure." That pressure took the form of vandals who "plowed under the Carters' cotton crop before they could harvest it," and local hoodlums who fired guns into the family's house. And of course, the Carter children faced hostility at the white school. In Mae Carter's recollection, her children faced "spitballs, nigger calling, even the teacher set up in the class teaching a history class, and when they get down to some—He would say 'nigger, and nigger, and nigger,' teachin' a history class, and that hurt those children."

Jo Ann Bland, who integrated an Alabama high school in 1970, said: "It was *awful*. It was already traumatic enough just to be going to high school for the first time. To go to a place where you're not wanted by the students and teachers because they felt we were forced upon them made everybody unhappy. There were just eight of us, and sixteen hundred and ninety-two of them, dedicated to making our lives miserable. I cried every day."[4] A black student in Georgia said that his integrated high school felt "like trespassing, man. That's how it is when you step on the man's property."[5]

These experiences were by no means unique. For example, a 1968 survey of several hundred black high school students found that "almost one-half of the group encountered considerable resentment and hostility when they entered desegregated schools," and only 15 percent "felt included and welcome."[6] One of the first black students bused to a Florida high school said, "At 14, it was like someone took a knife and cut off everyone you've known."[7]

When she talked to eleven black adults who had been the first to desegregate New Orleans schools in the 1960s, Leslie Baham Inniss found lingering bitterness over the entire experience.[8] Two potential interviewees had been "apparently destroyed" by the experience—one man had "suffered a nervous breakdown in his junior year at a desegregated school," while a woman's family claimed that she was "strung out on drugs" because she "has never gotten over the [school] experience."[9] Out of the people who were available for interviews, one former student told Dr. Inniss, "We had to learn their way of doing things—acting, talking, dressing—their way of being, but nobody was interested in our way. We wanted so badly to be accepted, we tried to do and be all they wanted and we were still rejected. Even today, I have a really big problem with rejection of any kind."[10] Another said: "To this day . . . I never eat breakfast. . . . I know it's because for those four years my stomach was so much in knots I couldn't eat before I went to school and then I couldn't eat lunch. I wouldn't sit in the lunchroom because of the things they would do. . . . [D]eep down you know that it's stuff that still affects you."[11]

One student recalled that at her graduation, the school played the song "It's So Hard to Say Goodbye to Yesterday," and "all the white girls would start crying because they were leaving and we were crying because we couldn't wait to leave."[12] The comments of other black students are even more forceful: one "extremely angry and bitter male" states that "forced integration was the worst thing that happened to our race,"[13] while one woman reported that she "would never even consider sending my children to an integrated school."[14] Another woman claims that "the desegregation process destroyed my whole foundation of self-worth."[15] A man recalls feeling "like I'm in no-man's land."[16]

Integration pioneers also lamented the lost opportunities to participate in school activities. One teacher at a newly integrated school said, "I always worried about the talents that the black students were not allowed to use . . . in their role as pioneers." She recalled that one black girl "said all her life she always wanted to be a cheerleader," but "cried inconsolably because she knew she would never be a cheerleader at this school because no one would elect her."[17] Another woman made similar comments: "In our segregated neighborhoods and schools we didn't feel deprived, we didn't even know that we lacked self-esteem, we were happy and secure in our all-black neighborhoods and our all-black schools. We felt that we belonged, hell, we did belong. There was no fear of trying to join the band or the drill team, or of trying out for cheerleader."[18]

Wanda Lloyd, who grew up in Savannah, asked her parents if she could participate in school desegregation in the mid-1960s. Her parents' response: "Absolutely not." Lloyd may have been disappointed, but today she writes: "What a blessing for me. My high school years—separate but so-called equal—were full of the support and nurturing of black teachers in an environment that set many of my schoolmates and me on a solid course for success. Our teachers knew our parents from relationships in our all-black neighborhoods, in our churches and in the community. My transferred friends, who had been near the top of their classes in segregated schools, saw their grades suffer and had almost no support from teachers in their new school. They were subjected to hostile treatment of the worst kind, with white students tripping them on stairways, tossing spitballs at them in class (with no recourse for discipline by their white teachers) and name-calling using the 'N' word."[19]

Sarah Johnson's children were among the first to integrate the white school in Greenville, Mississippi. Johnson recalls that her oldest daughter "was among probably 30 blacks in that school. She had the experience of being called n————. . . . As I look at schools now, and as I look at what my kids got and what I got, I think it would have been better for them to have gone to a segregated school. In a segregated situation, I got more attention. The teachers were more concerned with us."[20] Another pioneer from Arlington, Virginia, later said: "A lot of the black high schools in the nation were closed because of integration. A lot of our past is lost. I went to the black high school from the seventh through the eleventh grade, but I was not invited to class reunions. You pay a price. Your personal life gets lost. It was a sacrifice. It might have helped African Americans, but the damage done to us individually is still there."[21]

These sorts of experiences, in some people's minds, seemed to confirm the troubling truth of what W. E. B. Du Bois said in a famous article from 1935: "A separate Negro school, where children are treated like human beings, trained by teachers of their own race, who know what it means to be black in the year of salvation 1935, is infinitely better than making our boys and girls doormats to be spit and trampled upon."[22] Derrick Bell later reconsidered the value of his 1960s civil rights work: "What did it mean? Why was I trying to get these children admitted to schools where they were not wanted?"[23] Whereas at the time he lavished attention on a few success stories, he now says that he "paid far less attention to all those students less able to overcome the hostility and the sense of alienation they faced in mainly white schools. . . . Truly, these were the real victims of the great school desegregation campaign."[24] Similarly, Bell wrote in a 1980 essay that he would prefer for his children to attend an all-black school: "There is a subtle but real harassment faced by students in mainly white schools that is manifested by a low academic expectation from at least some teachers, and a general sense of minority subordination to white interest."[25]

My point here is not to argue that desegregation was a mistake. Nor, for that matter, am I arguing that black people in general are in favor of segregation. I am merely trying to point out that despite all the good that desegregation may have done, there were nonetheless some black children who could understandably have become alienated from the now-hostile environment they faced in school.

The Rise of "Acting White" In Schools

Before the 1960s, there were plenty of blacks who may have disliked school—just as there are many whites today who have such attitudes. A teacher in Chicago in the 1920s, for example, claimed that her black students had a "general antagonistic attitude toward everything pertaining to the school."[26]

Still, the "acting white" criticism in school is intimately associated with desegregation. Pioneering blacks were often ridiculed for "acting white" in their newly integrated surroundings. The perception was that they had forsaken the black community to seek academic success in a white environment.

The very first scholarly study that found the "acting white" criticism had examined a desegregated school. One student pointed out, "Maybe it's easier in an all-Negro school; may there aren't as many pressures. Certainly you don't have to be worried about being called an Uncle Tom for associating with whites. Everybody in an all-Negro school is probably in one accord—all striving to learn."[27] Janet Ward Schofield spent the 1970s studying a desegregated school where more than 75 percent of the students in the advanced classes were white, while a similar number in the "mentally retarded" class were black. After noting that "traditional stereotypes about the intellectual superiority of whites could hardly help but be reinforced,"[28] she noted that black students "tended to see academic effort and achievement as characteristically white," and that they often believed that "students worked for good grades primarily in order to look better than their peers."[29]

Another early study of a desegregated school found that "many blacks wished access to the college preparatory curriculum, and those who desired such access 'understood' that their success required 'acting white.'" Students "who were relegated to the basic, or standard, curriculum . . . chided their more successful peers for 'acting white.'"[30] Yet another in-depth study of a school before and after desegregation noted that "middle-class blacks were ostracized as 'Oreos'" if they declined to go along with "militants" and "cut off" their "white friends," that one black "honor student" was called a "Tom" for having too many white friends, and that "during the early years of desegregation, when militant blacks drew a hard separatist line, they mocked studious blacks who did their homework like 'whitey.'"[31]

Recall the Carters from Drew, Mississippi: Their daughter Beverly was in the third grade when they successfully installed their children in the local white school. Beverly experienced hostility from both whites *and* blacks:

> How I hated recesses. None of the other children would play with me . . . I wanted to say to Mama, 'I want to go where people will play with me, or, you know, like me.' But I never did. White kids would come by and call me names, from 'nigger' to 'walking Tootsie Roll.' God, I wanted to cry, to disappear, to go home. I never cried, at least not until I was older . . . when I was in the fifth grade I did. We had just moved into the city limits of Drew and now I had a chance to meet some black children my own age. Somehow they could not understand why I was going to an all-white school. *They said that I thought I was white . . . that hurt more than any of the bad names the white kids had called me—and I cried.*[32]

Shirley Bulah, a fair-skinned black girl adopted by a black couple in Hockessin, Delaware, had participated in a school desegregation lawsuit.[33] But "far from being heroes in Hockessin, the Bulahs became the focus of the color consciousness that sometimes besets black communities. Mrs. Bulah later recalled that 'some of the colored people were whispering that just because Shirley is fair-complexioned *we thought she was white, and that we were suing because we didn't want her to associate with colored children.*"[34]

Dwight Thomas of Atlanta was fifteen years old when he became the first black student to attend Avondale High School. He told the *Atlanta Constitution*, "When I walked into the lunchroom, it was one of the weirdest, coldest feelings; it was like it would be if E.T. had landed." Students would tell cruel jokes: "I smell a Gar," said one student. Another answered, "What kind of Gar? A Cee-Gar?" The response: "No, you know what kind of Gar I'm talking about." But the hostility did not come just from whites: Thomas also says that he was *"criticized by many blacks for 'assimilating' into the white world."*[35]

Elaine Thorpe Cox was the only black student to attend her school in Florida in 1962.[36] As she told the *Tallahassee Democrat*, she "remember[s] the children being polite, but I didn't feel much warmth. . . . It was polite isolation." At the same time, however, Cox faced rejection from other blacks: "Some of my black friends were upset with me. *They thought I was trying to be too good for them.* I did feel like I was in the middle of two worlds."

Lorenzo Bowman had attended an all-black school through the third grade, but was then "one of the first Black students" to be "forced to attend a school closer to my home that was all White." He remembers a feeling of "isolation and loneliness" that became "even more intense" in junior high school. Then, in high school, "I realized that not only was I different in the eyes of my fellow students who were members of the dominant race, but I was also different in the eyes of my fellow African-American students. As a result of 'tracking' in high school, I was assigned to the College Prep Curriculum; while I did want to go to college some day, I did not know that I would always be one of two or three students of color in each class and would be labeled as someone 'who was trying to be White' by my fellow Black students."[37]

Ron Kirk, who later became the first black mayor of Dallas, was one of the first black kids to integrate a junior high school in Austin, Texas. As he puts it, "The curious thing was this: After a day of all of us struggling to make this whole desegregation thing work, we would walk home and run into neighborhood friends, and they would ridicule us and want to fight us because we were going to school with white kids. So in the course of a single day we might get beat up because we were black, then get beat up again because we weren't black enough!"[38]

Many blacks have also told me that they experienced the "acting white" criticism as students in newly desegregated schools in the 1960s. For example, Ingrid Burton Nathan of Florida was depicted in a local news story as being worried about " black students who seem more concerned with their social life than their schoolwork. Nathan, the first black student to integrate all-white Sanford Junior High School in 1965, said today's schools don't provide black children with the support that existed during segregation, when black teachers were part of the community and kept in contact with parents."[39] When I asked her where she thought "acting white" came from, Nathan responded: "*In my opinion it didn't start until desegregation. There were no whites to 'act like' before desegregation.* In my school, Crooms Academy, we were all black, and there were hundreds of bright students. The brightest kids were 'black.' We were competitive also. The cream rose to the top, as usual. There were lazy kids and hard-working kids. But the teachers connected more with them. They lived where the kids lived. There was the village. Now the village is gone."[40]

Elvert Barnes grew up in southern Maryland and attended an integrated school starting in the mid-1960s. He told me: "I did find with integration . . . I made good grades. I kept hearing the phrase 'you're acting white, you're acting white.' Didn't happen before integration, it happened afterwards."[41]

Author Kitty Oliver notes that "there was a time when black students wouldn't dare tease a student, but rather would applaud them for their achievements." But then, "desegregation created a clearer division of white and black. Once black and white students started attending school together, the association shifted and black students began to tease one another by pushing their smart peers into the 'white' category."[42]

Leo Hamilton, one of the first to desegregate a school in Baton Rouge, says: "We were at a school where people didn't want us there. But, you had a problem in the neighborhood because you didn't go to school with these [black] people anymore, and there was a group of people . . . who resented the fact that . . . you were at school with those white folk. You know. 'What, you want to be white? You can't come to school with us?' So, you had to deal with these idiots at school. Then, you have to come home to deal with all these other idiots who were against you because you weren't in school with them, and you were all of a sudden trying to be white."[43] Yvonne Butler McPherson "remembers people saying, 'Oh, they want to be white now,' when she and other African-Americans integrated L. W. Higgins High School" in New Orleans.[44]

A former student from Maryland recalls: "But after they integrated schools, all hell broke loose. We were really in the middle. We had been accepted by most of the white students here, and when they brought all the other blacks that weren't accepted, we were kind of in the middle. They called us 'Toms' because we got along with some of the white kids and they didn't."[45] Tracie Powell of Atlanta recalls that when she participated in an integration program in DeKalb County, "My black friends from the neighborhood thought I was stuck up because I went to a white school; we argued about whether white was synonymous with 'better.'"[46]

Jesse Williams, who was the first black woman to integrate the faculty at Shaw High School in Shaw, Mississippi, in 1968, recalls that as a result she received "great pressure" from "both races": "The blacks mistrusted me for leaving. The whites mistrusted me because I was black."[47] A former student from North Carolina recalls, "In my high school, at times I was the only African-American in the class, especially in my college curriculum. It was only one or two of us. I received negative responses from both whites and African-Americans. African-Americans felt like I thought I was better than everyone else and I was a bookworm, and whites felt I wasn't smart enough to be in there. We had it from both sides."[48] Daniel Buggs, who integrated and played football for an Atlanta-area high school in 1969–70, told me: "From the black neighborhood, I was called Uncle Tom, from the white neighborhood, I was called a nigger. I was catching it on both ends."[49]

Ironically, some of integration's pioneers themselves said that they wanted to be white. Richard Howell was the first black student to attend Northeast Junior High School in Minneapolis. Years later, a newspaper account of his experience reported: "He says he wouldn't do it again. 'I was never comfortable,' Howell said. 'I was always looking over my shoulder.'" Although other white children ridiculed him at first, he soon "had learned to get along so well that he was voted student council president. But he also knew little about being black. . . . 'To tell the truth,' he said, 'I wanted to be white.'"[50]

Similarly, when psychiatrist Robert Coles studied children who had been through desegregation, he found a boy who "felt a traitor trusting and accepting the friendliness of white people. Several times he could frankly tell me how hard it was for him to respond to some of the genuine respect and affection shown him by white students at school. I suspect he also felt accused by his own people for the increasingly conscious desires he felt to leave their company, to spend his time with white people, even to be white."[51] Another boy in a desegregated school told Coles: "I'll graduate, and some people at the ceremony might even forget I'm a Negro. I'll probably never feel whiter than I will that day."[52]

If all of this seems like a deluge of anecdotes, it is. But given that I have no more systematic evidence here, it seems important to convey the number and one-sidedness of the anecdotes.

"Acting White" Was Unknown in Earlier Generations

So "acting white" often occurred along with desegregation. But did it ever occur earlier? As far as I can tell, it did not. Again, the only evidence is anecdotal, but older black scholars and commentators have said in unanimity that the "acting white" criticism was unknown in their generation. If these anecdotes were unrepresentative, I should have come across at least one person who recalled the "acting white" criticism being common in a segregated school.

Artemise Clemons integrated a New Orleans school as an eleventh grader in 1968. When I asked her whether she had known of the "acting white" criticism in the black schools, she laughed and said, "They wouldn't have said that in that time—you identified with your environment, and your environment was black."[53] Bill Raglin is a school board member in West Virginia who attended segregated schools as a child. When I asked him if he heard "acting white" when he was growing up, he said: "Not 'acting white'! I was in a black school. When you had a black school, you would be criticized for being a nerd or a bookworm or because you didn't play football. They couldn't criticize you for acting white, because there wasn't any white kids there!"[54] Elmon Crier, an educator in Cincinnati, told me that while he deals with "acting white" every day in his current integrated school, he never heard of this criticism as a schoolboy in segregated Miami: "We couldn't 'act white' because there was no white kids with us," he said.[55] Dudley Flood of North Carolina told me, "We were not thought of as 'acting white' because we never saw white people as role models."[56]

Many commentators have noted that "acting white" was unknown in previous generations. Harvard psychiatry professor Alvin Poussaint said: "A lot of black youth now are anti-education and anti-intellectualism, who feel that getting an education is being white, is acting white. We never had that in previous generations, this is something new."[57] Henry Louis Gates, the head of Harvard's Afro-American Studies Department, pointed out that in one poll, black children today identified "making straight A's, speaking standard English and going to the Smithsonian" as "acting white." But "if anybody had said anything like that when we were growing up in the '50s, first, your mother would smack you upside the head and, second, they'd check you into a mental institution."[58] In another article, Gates contrasted "a generation of immigrants from India and west Africa 'who have made it in the system by practicing what our people did in the 1950s' with today's inner-city youth 'who identify "acting white" with standard English, straight-As and the Smithsonian.'"[59]

Beverly Daniel Tatum has observed that "an oppositional identity that disdains academic achievement has not always been a characteristic of Black adolescent peer groups. It seems to be a post-desegregation phenomenon."[60] Similarly, bell hooks points out briefly that "during the years of legalized racial segregation, no one in black communities saw education as a 'white' thing."[61] A 1988 article in the *Washington Post* notes: "Gloria Davidson, head librarian [at a D.C.-area high school], attended a segregated Mississippi high school in the '40s. 'When schools were all black there was pressure in the home and the black community to make something of yourself and education was seen as the way. By the time I got to high school, the low achievers had dropped out and got jobs or moved north. We were told that we had to be "twice as good" to make it but we never thought learning was a special province of whites.'"[62]

John McWhorter has pointed out on numerous occasions that "black people didn't suffer from this until about 35 years ago. There was no such thing as the 'acting white' syndrome in 1910. It's a new thing."[63] In a book review, he noted that "black students began casting scholastic success as 'acting white' only after Jim Crow had ended, in the mid-1960s."[64]

In 2002, McWhorter wrote: "About two hundred African American people have written to me to say that it happened to them. And very consistently, with one possible exception, it was after about 1965. If you were a
smart black kid doing well in school in the 1930s and 1940s, you might
have been teased for being a walking encyclopedia—that's a cross-racial
phenomenon—but you weren't told that you were acting white. One man
told me that when he was coming of age in the early 1960s, he never heard
that, but then his cousins, who were a few years younger, were hit very
hard by it in the late 1960s."[65]

Columnist Leonard Pitts wrote: "You find yourself marveling at how
dramatically African-American mores have shifted . . . . Where earlier generations thought of education as a weapon of advancement and shield of
self-esteem, many in this generation think of it as cultural betrayal. In their
eyes, to do well in school or speak standard English is to 'act white.'"[66]
Social commentator Stanley Crouch observes that in his day, "We read
Julius Caesar aloud in class, saw films about Marian Anderson and Jackie
Robinson, read Dickens and so on. . . . We were not allowed to give any
excuses for poor performance either. If we had come up with some so-
called 'cultural difference' excuse, we would have been laughed at, if not
whacked on the booty for disrespecting the intelligence of the teacher.
Our teachers were tough and supportive. They knew well that the best
way to respect so-called minority students was to demand the most of
them."[67] More colloquially, Crouch has said: "When I was growing up,
Negroes might have been confused about a number of things because they
were Americans and Americans always have a repository of confusion, but
nobody ever told me, whatever his or her station was, that being a dummy
made one a real black person. I never heard anybody say that, not even the
thugs."[68] Film director Spike Lee, actor James Earl Jones, and power bro-
ker Vernon Jordan have all said the same.[69]

In D.C., a black police lieutenant tells of the difference between yesterday's attitudes and today's:

> Driving through the streets, [the lieutenant] ticks off the names of
> the families, recalls where the kids wound up, mostly in solid jobs.
> "There was a tremendous amount of pressure on us growing up
> in black schools to succeed," he says. "To make it you have got to

run twice as fast as the white man. You have to be an hour early. This was instilled. You messed up in school, the teacher hit you upside the head, sent you home, and your parents did the same. Nobody wanted to be known as the F student, as the high school dropout." These days black students who do well sometimes are derided for acting white. "My role models were not athletes of the day, like Jim Brown," he says. "They were Mr. Delaney, the mail carrier who taught us how to use our hands. Henry Parker Sr., who owned a grocery store."[70]

Journalist Leah Latimer notes that in her black school growing up, "My classmates and I never acknowledged racial stereotypes because we never fully realized that we were different. Different from what? Virtually everyone was Black, and our interests and characters were as varied as those of any other part of the population. In the security of the all-Black environment, not having to worry about 'being a credit to our race,' we were free to be successes or failures, winners or losers, bookworms or all-night partyers. We got all the honors and all the demerits."

But after integration, Latimer says, race became "a burden, a limit," in which black students' overwhelming focus had become emphasizing their "Black" identity. After integration, too many black students "don't do things like joining the French club or playing the violin" because "they are too busy being only one thing—Black."[71]

A black pastor from Florida says: "We were told we had to work twice as hard as our white counterparts. Growing up in segregation, we were challenged to outdo whites. . . . [Today,] good students are told by their peers that they are trying to be white. That upsets me. We didn't have to worry about that growing up because all of us were black and we were expected to work hard in school."[72] Another Florida educator says, "In my generation, if we made honor roll, . . . we were lauded as heroes. [Now] it's a badge of honor" for some to make Fs.[73]

Beyond the "acting white" criticism, many people have noticed that black attitudes toward education seemed to shift at the time of desegregation. One longtime black principal noted: "Integration in my opinion hurt black communities, principals, teachers, and students. We simply lost something. I think it was racial pride in our schools, drive and motivation to take control of the schools. To me, the 'I can't' attitude rather than the 'I can' attitude surfaced in our teachers, parents, and children after school desegregation."[74] An article from Indianapolis notes, "'Once integration started . . . , there was a huge shift in the success rate of African-American students and in their attitudes,' said [a middle school history teacher]. 'Many of these children went to suburban schools that didn't want them. And when you integrate kids in an environment that doesn't accept them, you have a minimum level of success.'"[75] In Southampton County, Virginia, one elderly woman says: "School was considered to be a pleasure. They (the students) thought of it as an honor. There was a great deal of respect for the teachers. This changed with integration."[76]

In studying a North Carolina county, one scholar found many parents who "observed a decline in student motivation, self-esteem, and academic performance" when integration occurred and the black schools were closed.[77] One mother said that although her son "would have been considered later a very gifted child, he had difficulty. And I may have, you know, ruined his chances to be that nice, bright student that he would have been because he sort of went into his shell for a while. . . . Being at the white school, I think that triggered it more than anything else."[78]

In all of my research of newspaper articles, Web sites, books, scholarly articles, and dissertations, I could find only one counterexample—one that, incidentally, has never been discussed in any previous literature on "acting white." It occurs in the book *Children of Bondage*, published in 1940 by the eminent black sociologist Allison Davis. Among many detailed profiles of black adolescents from the South, Davis interviews "a Negro boy, fourteen years of age, and dark-brown in color," living in Natchez, Mississippi. In the following passage—which Davis transcribed in a form meant to represent a heavy Southern accent—the boy gives voice to his resentment of certain blacks.

> I can't do nothin to the white folks that talks bout kickin me but talk big, talk back to em, but I shore can handle colored folks who try to *ack lak white folks jes cause they is bright* an got a little more money than some other colored folks. I shore do drop the wood on em an I don't feel bad over it. (Deep thought). I really don't reckon I could ever learn to lak a bright colored person, I don't

care what he'd do for me. I'd always feel funny roun him an the least li'l thing he do or say to me would make me feel lak jes gettin somethin and try'n to kill him. I reckon white folks feels the same bout colored people.

What shore nuff gits me though is some niggers *jes cause they is a little bright tries to ack lak white.* That is when I gits my feelin out on em. I tries to kill em when I gits on em an see jes what good their color does em then. They thinks they is cute jes cause they is bright an got a little more'an the other colored people.[79]

Thus, there is at least one recorded instance of the "acting white" phrase (or "ack lak white") prior to the 1960s, used to label someone who was too "bright." That said, this example is quite ambiguous: as an anonymous peer reviewer pointed out to me, the speaker in the above passage may well have been using the term "bright" to refer to skin color, not intelligence.

Leaving aside this single and ambiguous counterexample, the overwhelming consensus among everyone who has ever publicly commented on this issue is that "acting white" was new to the 1960s generation. Of course, as many sociologists have pointed out, America has long had a strain of anti-intellectualism—both among blacks and whites. But something happened in the 1960s that made some black children start to believe that education was *for white people, not for them.*

Some might ask whether, by my theory, "acting white" should have shown up earlier in integrated schools in the North. As I do not wish to gloss over difficulties for my theory, I admit that I do not have a convincing answer to this question. The best I can do is a series of suggestions. First, while segregation was most common in the South, it often occurred elsewhere as well, as recounted in historian Davison Douglas's useful book on Northern segregation.[80] Thus, a 1963 article titled "A Review of Public School Desegregation in the North and West" reviewed desegregation challenges in "sixty-nine cities and communities in fifteen states from Connecticut to California."[81] A Chicago NAACP official in 1945 said that Chicago schools were "as much segregated as the schools in Savannah, Georgia, or Vicksburg, Mississippi."[82]

That answer gets us only so far, though, given that segregation was not *universal* in the North. Integrated schools did exist in some places. Thus, my second suggestion is that the "acting white" charge might indeed have emerged in the occasional Northern school in the Jim Crow era, but it was not widespread or prevalent enough for anyone to notice or leave behind a written record of the fact. Nor was it widespread enough to have any significant impact on black educational achievement across the country.

Why Other Theories of "Acting White" Are Not Plausible

If "acting white" arose only in the 1960s in desegregated schools, then other explanations for "acting white" lose plausibility. They do not match the timing.

Popular culture. One common theory is that "acting white" arises because black popular culture idolizes hip-hop musicians and athletes. In a *Newsweek* online discussion, Ellis Cose agreed with a questioner who said, "We have made a world where black men shooting black men in movies and music is 'cool,' while black men reading a book or praising education is as scarce as a non-violent rap album."[83] Or as John Obgu said in an interview, "What amazed me is that these kids who come from homes of doctors and lawyers are not thinking like their parents; they don't know how their parents made it. They are looking at rappers in ghettos as their role models, they are looking at entertainers."[84]

Now I agree that popular culture—whether as to whites or blacks—isn't geared toward encouraging school achievement. Still, I find it hard to imagine how black popular culture would have caused "acting white." Hip-hop and rap music did not become common until around 1980, with artists like Grandmaster Flash and the Sugarhill Gang. Those artists couldn't have caused something that began fifteen or twenty years earlier.

Even if the timing matched up, this explanation is unsatisfying. White students also idolize athletes and musicians far more than Nobel Prize winners, yet they do not treat academic achievement as a betrayal of one's *race*.

Employment Discrimination. Another theory is that employment discrimination leads students to "expect little gain from their effort and achievement in school."[85] Thus, because black students expect that they will face discrimination in the labor market at some future point, they have less reason to value education today.

Once again, the timing is all wrong. Employment discrimination certainly did not begin in the 1960s; it was obviously far worse during the days of Jim Crow laws and slavery. Indeed, it was in 1964 that the federal Civil Rights Act made racial discrimination in employment illegal on the federal level, for the first time in our nation's history. If employment discrimination caused the "acting white" criticism, it should have arisen *long* before the 1960s, and should have started to *decrease* at that time.

Moreover, students who expect to face employment discrimination don't necessarily shirk their duties in school.[86] Far from it: Many older blacks recall that their black teachers used to tell them that it was a "white man's world" out there, and that this meant they would have to work doubly hard in school.

Finally, it isn't true that black students expect job discrimination to undermine the value of their education. When Laurence Steinberg and his colleagues surveyed some twenty thousand students, they found—to their surprise—that there were "no ethnic differences in the extent to which youngsters believe that getting a good education pays off." "Although African-American and Hispanic youth earn lower grades in school than their Asian-American and White counterparts, they are *just as likely as their peers* to believe that doing well in school will benefit them occupationally."[87]

Concentration of Poverty. Another explanation for "acting white" is that a high concentration of poverty causes students to devalue academic achievement.[88] But just as with racial discrimination, poverty did not begin in the 1960s. To the contrary, serious *anti*-poverty efforts began for the first time with President Johnson's Great Society and its accompanying welfare expansions. To be sure, poverty became more *concentrated* in certain inner cities in the mid-twentieth century.[89] Yet, as we saw in Chapter 3, blacks in the Jim Crow era (including former slaves) pursued education eagerly even in the presence of far more dire poverty. If poverty of any concentration caused the "acting white" criticism, it surely would have shown up long before the 1960s.

One counterargument would be that "acting white" might be caused by a potent combination of poverty, the breakdown of the family, and the rise of inner-city gangs and crime since the 1960s. To be sure, I can imagine that all of those factors might make children less likely to pursue their schoolwork for a variety of reasons. Still, those factors do not have any obvious connection to why students would view education in *racial* terms. Why would the breakdown of the family make black students think that education was "acting white"?

Involuntary Minorities. John Ogbu's theory of "acting white" rests on a distinction between two types of minorities in America: involuntary and voluntary. *Voluntary* minorities came to America of their own free will— recent Caribbean immigrants, for example. These people find it easier to place their "trust" in the school system and its demands.[90] *Involuntary* minorities are those whose ancestors were forcibly brought to America as slaves, and who "developed their collective identity under oppression and in opposition to . . . their White oppressors."[91] In the school setting, such an "oppositional" identity shows up for two reasons: Black students perceive the school culture or curriculum as an "imposition," and their experience is "negative" because the white curriculum and language "communicate the message that Black people are inferior to White people."[92]

But in light of the fact that "acting white" did not show up until the 1960s, Ogbu's explanation is unconvincing. If "involuntary" presence in America has anything to do with it, "acting white" should have been *far* more common in the 1700s and 1800s—the generations that actually were brought to America involuntarily—rather than appearing several generations later.

Black Nationalism. Another theory is that "acting white" was caused by the black nationalist or "black power" movements that arose toward the end of the 1960s. As Henry Louis Gates said, "In the '50s, the blackest thing you could be was a doctor or lawyer. But after the '60s, 'genuine' blackness was equated with rebellious identity, the hip-hop ideal. That's a travesty of our tradition."[93] Or as John McWhorter told NPR, "It's something that starts in the late '60s with post–civil rights, black power, ideological atmosphere. And where it came from, I believe, is a sense that came in, in black culture around that time, that white culture was an evil that it was no longer worth trying to integrate towards. The idea at this time was that integration was folly and that separatism was a better path. . . . [I]t's not an accident that it's around that time when the separatist current was at its strongest, that black kids began teasing each other in that way."[94]

This theory is very plausible, and I think that black separatism did indeed play a role in the rise of "acting white" in education. At the same time, I think that black separatism would have played a role *precisely* because of the concurrent push for integration.

After all, there is something of a mystery here. As I have explained in Chapter 3, there was a long history of black pursuit of education. Indeed, black power activists of the 1960s themselves placed a high value on education. Why would black separatism have given rise to the feeling that education was something meant for whites? Why wouldn't those ideas lead black kids to pursue education in order to benefit themselves and increase black power?

I suspect that black power or black separatist attitudes could have played a role *only* insofar as schools were integrated and run by whites. One theme of the black power movement was that blacks needed to be strong, united, and forceful in asserting the rights of the black community. To the extent that children in an all-black school held separatist attitudes, there is no reason they would have engaged in the "acting white" criticism *as to education.* But in an integrated school—where a majority of school board members, teachers, administrators, and students in advanced classes were white—the black power attitude could have strengthened the "acting white" criticism. Anyone going off to join the white students in the advanced classes, or who was perceived as currying favor with white teachers, would have come under suspicions for being disloyal to the black community.

In fact, black power activists often claimed that *integration itself* was nothing more than trying to be white. Carol Taylor, who helped found "Negro Women on the March," told a newspaper in 1997 that "Our motto was, '*Integration is the quiet conviction of the white man that all blacks want to be white.*' We were not for busing. We thought it better to send the best teachers to the black schools, and then, look out."[95] Likewise, Stokely Carmichael and Charles Hamilton consistently mocked integrationists for trying too desperately (as they saw it) to fit in with an unfriendly white society. They claimed that when white people allowed "even token integration, it applies only to black people like themselves: as 'white' as possible."[96] They contended that integration "is based on the assumption that there is nothing of value in the black community and that little of value could be created among black people. The thing to do is siphon off the 'acceptable' black people into the surrounding middle-class white community."[97] Even more starkly, they claimed that "implicit [in integration] is the idea that the closer you get to whiteness, the better you are." Thus they concluded, "The real need at present is not integration but quality education."[98]

As Malcolm X said in 1964, "I just can't see where if white people can go to a white classroom and there are no Negroes present and it doesn't affect the academic diet they're receiving, then I don't see where an all-black classroom can be affected by the absence of white children. . . . So, what the integrationists, in my opinion, are saying, when they say that whites and blacks must go to school together, is that the whites are so much superior that just their presence in a black classroom balances it out."[99] Similarly, Nathan Wright, the chairman of the 1967 National Black Power Conference, wrote, "Negroes should long ago have perceived that enforced 'integration' as a goal is a compromise of black Americans on its face. Negroes do not need the presence of white people either to give them worth or to learn."[100]

In short, it does make sense that black separatism or black nationalism would have bolstered the "acting white" criticism in an integrated school.

9

WHERE DO WE GO FROM HERE?

"When you speak proper English and don't use Ebonics or slang, they say, 'Why are you acting white?' . . . They say, 'Yo, what's up?' I say my name's not Yo."

—Student from Binghamton, New York, 2007

This book will be controversial in some circles, if only because I say that "acting white" exists and should be taken seriously. To some people, it is borderline racist to suggest that any cultural factors might contribute to the fact that black students lag far behind white students. What's more, if you say that some black students think of studiousness as "acting white," it is as if you have accused black students of bizarre and nonsensical behavior. These critics appear to believe that "acting white" must be downplayed or denied at all costs, because if it did exist, it would be an inexcusable form of stupidity.

As it happens, I think that those critics are wrong all the way around. They are wrong in claiming that "acting white" is a myth. But they are also wrong in assuming that "acting white" is nonsensical and inexcusable behavior. Indeed, I would *defend* the "acting white" criticism as entirely normal.

To be sure, *normal* does not mean *beneficial*. Rather, it is normal in the sense that eating too much sugar is normal—it is behavior that arises from deeply rooted and commonplace desires that made sense throughout our history, but that, unfortunately, can be destructive if given full rein today.

Thus, in order to have an idea how the "acting white" criticism might be reduced, we need to understand the powerful psychological forces that generate it in the first place.

Humans Are Tribal

What do I mean by saying that the "acting white" criticism is "normal"?

Human beings are usually tribal. We like to associate with people who are similar to ourselves. As Gordon Allport says in his classic work *The Nature of Prejudice,* "Everywhere on earth we find a condition of separateness among groups."[1] Thus, we have the proverb, "Birds of a feather flock together." Sociologists call this tendency "homophily," from the Greek "homo" (or "same") and "phileo" (or "friendship"). Homophily is particularly strong in the area of race: Sociologists have found "strong homophily on race and ethnicity in a wide array of relationships, ranging from the most intimate bonds of marriage and confiding, to the more limited ties of schoolmate friendships and work relations, to the limited networks of discussion about a particular topic, to the mere fact of appearing in public together or 'knowing about' someone else."[2] Indeed, scientists are beginning to trace homophily to specific areas of the brain.[3]

Not only do we humans associate with others who are like ourselves; we also tend to pit our own group in competition against other groups. The entire history of the world shows that people of different races and nationalities are often hostile toward one another, even over cultural or ethnic differences that are completely imperceptible to outsiders.[4] This shows up at the earliest age: As Judith Rich Harris points out, "Babies around the world begin to show a wariness of strangers at around six months of age."[5]

Examples abound from every possible aspect of life. Fans of one sports team cordially (or not so cordially) despise the fans of the opposing team. Fans of alternative rock music roll their eyes at the thought that anyone still listens to Bon Jovi. Gourmet cooks and organic gardeners pity the rest of us for eating at McDonald's. Avant-garde artists sneer at Norman Rockwell paintings. American Baptists dislike the more fundamentalist Southern Baptists. Managers versus union workers; waiters versus diners; Southerners versus Yankees; people who shop at Nordstrom's versus people who shop at Gap versus people who get their clothes on sale at K-Mart;

Hummer drivers versus Prius drivers; chess club members versus cheerleaders. We love to bask in the feeling that our own little coterie is different from everyone else.

In fact, the human drive to categorize is so strong that people will differentiate themselves from another group even based on very slight differences that have no rational basis at all. There is a large social psychology literature on this phenomenon, stretching back several decades.

In one experiment, for example, Henri Tajfel and two colleagues had ninety-six children rate their favorites from several pairs of pictures that were supposedly drawn by other children in one of two schools: the Red School and the Blue School. They then told the children that "we have found something quite amazing: about half of you preferred pictures from the Red School and about half preferred pictures from the Blue School." This wasn't actually true; it was just a way of getting the children to believe that they were part of a group that had chosen similar pictures.

The researchers then gave the children little cards with pairs of numbers, and had the children take turns assigning money to the "Blue" group and the "Red" group by choosing one of the options on the cards. For example, one of the cards had these three choices: three coins for your group and four for the other group; two coins for each group; or one coin for your group and zero coins for the other. Thus, the first option would lead to the maximum payoff for both groups, while the last option would allow your own group to have more money than the other group. The researchers discovered that the children showed a large preference for the latter result—giving your own group the advantage, even if it effectively cost money to do so. This showed the "ease" with which "discriminatory social acts" can be "triggered in children as young as seven years of age."[6]

Similarly, the mere act of dressing people in white versus red coats causes them to dislike each other more. In one experiment, two groups of people had to complete tasks such as devising a plan to rehabilitate a juvenile delinquent and coming up with an advertising slogan for toothpaste. People liked their own group more than the other group, even when the two groups were being graded together. They had an even stronger preference for their own group when the two groups were graded competitively, and the strongest preference for their own group occurred when one group was made to wear white coats and the other wore red coats.[7]

In another pair of similar experiments, Tajfel and his colleagues were able to get a group of teenagers to engage in "deliberate discriminatory behavior" in awarding money to themselves and another group of teenagers, even though they thought that the groups had been chosen based on a fairly meaningless characteristic (that is, in one experiment, the groups were told that they had been chosen based on whether members had overestimated or underestimated the number of dots on a piece of paper; in the other experiment, groups were told that they had been chosen based on their own preference for Klee versus Kandinsky). Amazingly, the groups showed discriminatory behavior even though the groups were *completely anonymous*—no one knew who else was in his own "group."[8]

As Tajfel and Michael Billig said, "it seems that the mere mention of 'groups' by the experimenters was sufficient to produce strong intergroup discrimination."[9]

How Group Interactions Cause "Acting White"

So we divide ourselves into groups. What of it?

Groups often enforce the boundaries between themselves and another group—especially one that appears threatening—by demanding that same-group members comply with the right social norms.[10] If you belong to a group of hardcore punk rockers who think that mainstream music has sold out to corporate interests, and you start waxing eloquent about your love for *American Idol* or Britney Spears, you are in for some skepticism. If you show up to the typical university faculty meeting wearing a cowboy hat and carrying a rifle, expect some odd stares. If you attend a revival at a Pentecostal church wearing a perfectly modest swimsuit, people will not approve.

Why? Because by the way that you act, talk, and dress, you are *signaling* something to other people.[11] By doing something that is contrary to the group's typical behavior, you are signaling that you do not care about the group's opinion, and ultimately that you do not care about belonging to the group. The theory of signaling, as Eric Posner points out, "shows why schoolchildren and the rest of us devote so much energy and worry to what always seem in the grand scheme of things to be trivial—clothes, hygiene, appearance, manners, forms of speech, and all the other attributes which, because of their salience, present opportunities for others to discriminate against us."[12]

Just as groups tend to be wary of other groups, they dislike group members who flout group norms and signal that they would rather resemble another group. *More* so, in fact: people usually resent a dissenting member of their own group even more than a complete outsider. Heretics are more of a threat than nonbelievers. The nonbeliever merely shows that there are people who never believed in your religion in the first place, while the heretic is trying to undermine and even ditch your religion altogether.

The same is true in the racial context. As Posner observes, the reason that blacks have traditionally despised "Uncle Toms" is because they "submitted more readily to white racism," and "special venom is directed to the insider who breaks ranks and treats outsiders with respect."[13]

How do group norms play out in schools? In integrated schools, the two relevant groups are blacks and whites (other ethnicities exist, of course, but they are not the subject of this book). As we know from the studies of social psychologists, even if children were *randomly* assigned to be "black" or "white," you would expect to see group competition or animosity emerge. But children are obviously not randomly assigned. Instead, they arrive at the middle or high school having lived their entire lives as either black or white, and as we saw in Chapter 1, the middle school years are the first time when children truly become aware of racial issues.

Why "acting white"? What is the signal being sent there? Why would other black students resent this signal?

For hundreds of years, blacks were forced into a position of subservience to white people—most dramatically in the case of slavery, but also in the years of legally mandated segregation and Jim Crow laws. As a result, the black community in America has tended to be of two minds toward the white community. On the one hand, whites were viewed as the oppressors, as the slave owners, as the privileged. On the other hand, whites were often envied for their superior wealth, clothes, education, station in society, and innumerable other advantages. This created a deep and historic antagonism toward those blacks who sought to advance their own privilege by associating with oppressive whites, such as "house slaves" or "Uncle Toms."[14]

The same antagonism was present at the time of desegregation, and it lingers to some extent today. An integrated school can often appear to black students to be controlled by whites, or to be run in a way that benefits white students. Thus, the black student who tries to curry favor with the white authorities is seen as saying, "I'm better than you."

Indeed, in one of the earliest scholarly accounts of "acting white," one of the poorer black students was remarkably frank about how he viewed the more accomplished black students in his class: "There're just a few of these Uncle Toms at school, these are the goody-goody guys. Maybe I say this, though, because they're doing a little bit better than I am. And maybe I'm a little bit ashamed of myself because I'm not doing as good as they are in school, and I'm jealous. Maybe that's why I think of them as Uncle Toms."[15] Similarly, another poor black student said, "Well, the type of Negro that joins that type of thing [a certain club] are Negroes who look down on other Negroes anyway, and conform to the white ways. . . . Their idea is to get a good education and try to be as white as possible. They're what we call 'white Negroes.'"[16] The same sentiments are expressed today, as can be seen in a story from Cincinnati: "Since she began achieving high grades as a freshman three years ago, the Mount Auburn teen has endured a stream of verbal harassment from some of her African-American peers. 'It was always, "Why are you trying to be white? Are you trying to be better than us?"' Carrie says. . . ."[17]

The fear of trying to be "better" than your peers could cause an "acting white" effect even *without* express peer pressure. As Ronald Ferguson of Harvard points out, "Students who have the skills to perform at high levels sometimes hold back [voluntarily] because their friends are struggling and they want to fit in . . . . Consider two friends walking on the street, urgently en route to an important destination. The slower walker is not in good physical condition. He does not appear to be able to keep up if the friend who is more fit were to accelerate. A decision by the faster friend to hold back in this situation—to keep walking slowly—would seem completely reasonable based on feelings of empathy and social attachment. Active peer pressure, stigmas, or stereotypes are not required for such voluntary inclinations toward accommodation to operate."[18] In other words, "acting white" is just another way in which people change their behavior so as to send the right signal to their friends.

Also recall from Chapter 1 that "acting white" is strongest by far in schools that are most evenly balanced and integrated—with neither huge white majorities nor huge black majorities. This is consistent with Martin Patchen's finding (in a large study of desegregation in Indianapolis) that in schools where blacks were a tiny minority, they got along well with whites, as they had no other choice. Similarly, where blacks were an overwhelming majority, they also got along with whites, because they felt comfortable and didn't have to worry about "possible rejection or domination by whites." But race relations (as well as academic achievement) were the worst in well-integrated schools, where there were substantial numbers of both blacks and whites. Why was this? Because this was where blacks "often felt disliked and unwelcome," but also had enough of a critical mass to form a "separate 'black society.'"[19] Another study similarly found that "at the extremes of the racial composition dimension (our one virtually all-black school and the most highly-white schools)" blacks were more likely to identify themselves as "students" than "in the more racially-balanced schools."[20]

The same thing, incidentally, is true of religion. In looking at a wide variety of countries around the world, economists at Harvard have found that religious strife tends to be highest when around half the country is religious. It's at that point that there are struggles for dominance. When a religion already is overwhelmingly dominant, the people in that religion feel more comfortable and can afford to be a bit more tolerant; when a religion is an overwhelming minority, its adherents realize that their best option is to play nice.[21]

In short, when we feel that we are part of a beleaguered group that is caught in a struggle for dominance, it becomes all the more important to stick together as a group and to punish group members who seem disloyal. That is what the "acting white" charge does. It is a perfectly normal human reaction, akin to the group solidarity felt by all types of minority groups (whether involving religion, sexual orientation, or anything else).

What Can Be Done?

As I have noted in previous chapters, many people have agreed that when a school is all-black, it never even occurs to the black students to associate academic achievement with the way that "whites" behave at school. And the "acting white" criticism is most likely to emerge in racially balanced schools—not in all-black schools (where the opportunity rarely arises) or in mostly white schools (where no black students are in a position to criticize someone else for associating too often with whites).

As I have reiterated many times, I am not arguing for the return of segregation in any fashion. Integration does have many advantages—most importantly, bringing black children into the American mainstream, and potentially forcing legislatures to fund schools on a more equitable basis. These advantages almost certainly outweigh any of the detrimental effects of "acting white."

That said, it may be the case that some students would thrive if allowed to choose an all-black environment that includes black teachers and principals. As John McWhorter points out, "Black children often can be weaned off of that acting white tendency in small all-minority schools. . . . When you have a school with, you know, at most a few hundred students, most of them or all of them black, and you have teachers who are deeply committed and set high standards, then you see that there is a representative number of excellent black students and a lot less of the idea that to do well in school is to step outside of your culture, because after all, in such schools there are no white people to define yourself against."[22]

Thus, we should be tolerant of educational experimentation; it's not as if our nation's inner-city public schools have a stunning record of success that would thereby be jeopardized. Take, for example, the occasional black entrepreneur wishes to start up a black charter school with the aim of providing a nurturing environment for black achievement, or the voucher programs that allow mostly black inner-city children to choose a school best suited to their needs and aspirations. These educational opportunities may allow at least some black children to enter schools that place a higher value on academic achievement.

For another example, take the growing movement to offer single-sex schools—including regular public schools and charter schools—aimed at poor minorities.[23] Such schools are often viewed with suspicion; in the 1990s, for example, the ACLU successfully sued to shut down a few planned schools for black males in Detroit, where the black male dropout rate was approaching two-thirds. If such legal pressures were not an issue, single-sex schools might be able to make a difference for at least some vulnerable young black males, who are especially hard hit by negative peer pressure. (Recall that in Chapter 1, we saw that "acting white" is strongest for black males.) One researcher found from national data that blacks who attended single-sex high schools later earned far higher salaries than blacks who attended coed schools, and that this effect was greater for blacks than for whites.[24] When the U.S. Department of Education exhaustively reviewed hundreds of studies, 35 percent showed that single-sex education improved academic achievement (53 percent showed no difference, 10 percent were mixed, and a mere 2 percent favored coed schools), while a full 45 percent of studies showed that single-sex education improved students' attitudes (only 10 percent of studies favored schooling males and females together here).[25]

We should also do more to recruit and encourage blacks—and especially black males—to go into teaching. This could include privately funded scholarships and recruitment efforts aimed at getting black males to study education.

In addition, school boards should consider hiring teachers without being hamstrung by the usual certification requirements, which have not been shown to affect student achievement.[26] To the contrary, teacher certification requirements tend to keep out black teachers who would otherwise do a good job. Recent statistics on a nationwide certification test show that 83.5 percent of whites pass the test, compared with 52.1 percent of blacks.[27] In light of this fact, Dan Goldhaber and a colleague recently studied eleven years of data on every student in North Carolina. Strikingly, they found that while black teachers had lower licensure test scores, black teachers were so much more effective with black students that "black teachers in the lower end of the teacher test distribution are estimated to perform at approximately the same level as white teachers at the upper end of the distribution." Thus, "removing the lowest of performers on the exam would necessarily remove some of the more-effective teachers for [black students]."[28]

Although black achievement could be better across the board, black males are more likely than females to drop out, to flunk out, to get in trouble with the law, and to fail to go to college.[29] These young black males may tend to be better off if they have an adult black male role model in their lives. But for all the reasons discussed in Chapter 6, black boys tend to be alienated from a teaching workforce made up mostly of white females.

For many black boys in America—those who virtually never come in contact with the military or with the world of business—seeing a black male teacher or principal could be the *only* time they ever see someone like themselves in a position of authority and success. As a black educational leader said in 1976, lamenting the loss of black principals in Mississippi, "young blacks in the community . . . want and need someone that they can emulate. And without that symbol there—it's just like having a father in a home is that symbol. It makes the difference."[30] As well, the presidency of Barack Obama might have an impact on the lives of some young black males who previously might have disdained the world of academic achievement in which Obama excelled.

Within existing schools, special programs might be able to counteract bad peer pressure. For example, Cleveland High School in Los Angeles created a program called "The Village" a few years ago. The program was aimed exclusively at the three hundred or so black students at a high school with a student body of over four thousand; the black students met regularly with black faculty and staff to discuss racial issues and academic achievement. A black teacher noted that the white principal of the school approved the program when he realized "that as African Americans we could say things to these kids that he as a white man couldn't."

Although the results are somewhat anecdotal, they are initially impressive: According to the *Los Angeles Times,* "scores on the Academic Performance Index jumped 95 points in two years, from 569 in 2003 to 664 in 2005, according to the California Department of Education. The districtwide average among all students in 2005 was 649, department statistics show. In 2003, 36 percent of black students at Cleveland passed the math portion of the California High School Exit Examination. The figure rose to 81 percent in 2006."[31]

Another recent example comes from Rev. Eugene Rivers in the Boston area. Rivers and his wife Jacqueline established the Du Bois Society, in which black youth meet to discuss academic topics. Rev. Rivers told the *Boston Globe* that "one of the developments of the last 40 years has been the evolution of an anti-intellectual culture that . . . rejected academic achievement as at best corny and at worst white. What we are really dealing with in the Du Bois Society is not others' opinions of our kids, but their opinions of themselves, of each other, and of their culture. Our objective is to transform their image of themselves. . . . The fact that between 25 and 30 black students come together on a Saturday morning to study the work of such a distinguished collection of scholars is in and of itself revolutionary."[32]

To be sure, scalability is always a huge problem for any education reform. Something that looks promising when implemented by a small group of highly dedicated people may turn out to be a flop when implemented on a wide scale. Thus, it remains to be seen how well such programs can be replicated everywhere. Still, they offer at least a small sign of hope.

A more radical idea—one that I will describe in some detail here—springs from the sociology literature. The idea is to eliminate individual grades; instead, students would compete against other schools in academic competitions.

As far as I can tell, this idea originated from the eminent sociologist James Coleman.[33] Coleman observed the striking fact that while students regularly cheer for their school's football or basketball team, they will poke fun or jeer at other students who study too hard or are too eager in class: "the boy who goes all-out scholastically is scorned and rebuked for working too hard; the athlete who *fails* to go all-out is scorned and rebuked for not giving his all."[34]

But this is odd, is it not? Why are attitudes toward academics and athletics so different? Sports are more fun than classwork, of course, but that does not explain why success would actually be *discouraged* in class.

Coleman's explanation was disarmingly simple: The students on the athletic teams are not competing against other students from their own school. Instead, they are competing against another school. And when they win a game, they bring glory to their fellow students, who get to feel like they too are victors, if only vicariously.

But the students in the same class are competing against one another for grades and for the teacher's attention. Naturally, that competition gives rise to resentment against other children who are too successful (just as students will hate the football team from a crosstown rival). In Coleman's words, the scholar's "victories are purely personal ones, often at the expense of his classmates, who are forced to work harder to keep up with him. Small wonder that his accomplishments gain little reward, and are often met by such ridicule as 'curve raiser' or 'grind,' terms of disapprobation having no analogues in athletics."[35]

Indeed, going back to the first study that found the "acting white" criticism, Frank Petroni pointed out that "athletes are exempt from the 'Uncle Tom' label because athletic achievement brings credit to the whole group while intellectual achievement does not."[36]

Coleman's suggestion, therefore, was that if you want the students' attitudes toward their studies to resemble their attitudes toward sports, you should minimize the role of grades—which involve competition against one's classmates. In his words, we need to get rid of the "notion that each student's achievement must be continually evaluated or 'graded' in every subject."[37] Instead, such grades should be "infrequent or absent," and should be replaced by "contests and games" between schools, such as "debate teams, music contests, drama contests, science fairs, . . . math tournaments, speaking contests," and so on.[38] Then, the students in any one class or school would have a greater incentive to encourage their fellow students to study hard, and to take pride in their fellow students' success. In Coleman's words, "I suspect that the impact upon student motivation would be remarkably great—an impact due to the fact that the informal social rewards from community and fellow-students would reinforce rather than conflict with achievement."[39]

A recent paper titled "Why We Harass Nerds and Freaks" similarly proposes that academic extracurricular activities would "harness the energy and school spirit that inter-school rivalry and public performance generate."[40] These "inter-scholastic team competitions in academic subjects" should include as "many students as possible," by having "separate competitions for each grade, increasing the size of teams, and allowing schools to field larger teams." These teams should begin as soon as the "first week of middle school," so as to create "academically oriented friendship networks" while the "social order is still fluid."

Finally, the sociologist Seymour Spilerman once proposed the payment of cash rewards for grades on a *group* basis.[41] He pointed out that if we give cash rewards to individual students, everyone would have an incentive to enforce a group norm against achieving too highly, and that several studies in the area of industrial research found this phenomenon among workers.[42] But if cash payments were made to groups, then the whole group would have an incentive to encourage their teammates to perform their best. Again, Spilerman spotted a parallel in industrial research on payment plans that allowed the entire work force to share "in the profits which result from a reduction in labor costs": "Formerly, a man who expressed his achievement motivation by working harder endangered his bonds of solidarity with his co-workers. . . . [Now] no matter when the saving was accomplished everyone in the force benefits and so a man who tries to achieve an improvement helps the entire group."[43] In short, with group rewards in sight, "peer pressure can be expected to encourage individual attainment and foster an interest in mutual assistance and cooperation."[44]

Thus, the radical idea would be a combination of tactics: Let grades be replaced by regular interschool competitions, supplemented by small rewards for the winners on a group basis. (Alternatively, various classrooms in the same school could compete against each other on a regular basis.) Just as in athletics, schools would probably have to be divided up into leagues based on ability levels, so that more accomplished schools would not completely dominate the competitions. In such an atmosphere, students would have every incentive—both because of money and because of school spirit—to support their peers' academic aspirations, and to cheer for those students who win an academic award on behalf of their classmates.

Why might this idea help with the "acting white" problem? We must again look to social psychologists, who have long found that when groups can be persuaded to *cooperate* at some task, they like each other more than when they are directly in competition.[45] Muzafer and Carolyn Sherif's famous Robbers' Cave experiment showed that a "superordinate goal" can bring opposing groups together. They sent twenty-four boys around twelve years old to the Robbers' Cave campsite, and split them into two groups of twelve, which lived and played separately. The Sherifs then introduced competitive situations—such as bean toss contests, baseball, or football—and the boys unsurprisingly showed solidarity and friendship within their own group, but hostility toward the other group.

Having created competition between the groups, the Sherifs now tried to figure out how to get rid of it. One option was having the boys engage in collective activities—such as "eating together in the same dining room, watching a movie in the same hall," and the like. But this didn't work: "Such occasions of contact were utilized as opportunities to engage in name-calling and in abuse of each other to the point of physical manifestations of hostility." Sherif points out more broadly that "intergroup contact without superordinate goals is not likely to produce lasting reduction of intergroup hostility."

What *did* work? Giving the groups tasks that could be completed only by cooperating with each other. For example, the researchers blocked up the camp's water supply, and the boys had to figure out what was wrong and fix it. On another occasion, the researchers took the boys to a lake to swim, but when lunchtime came, the truck that was going to fetch the food was deliberately stalled on a hill, and the hungry boys had to find a way to get it started again. Eventually, about twenty of them used a tug-of-war rope to pull the truck up the hill a couple of times, whereupon the driver started the truck. After such cooperative tasks, there was a "sharp decrease in the name-calling and derogation of the out-group," and the "blatant glorification and bragging about the in-group" diminished. More boys starting making friends with the other group.

Sherif also points out that stereotypes can be reduced by such superordinate goals. Without such goals, "favorable information about a disliked out-group tends to be ignored, rejected, or reinterpreted to fit prevailing stereotypes. But, when groups are pulling together toward superordinate goals, true and even favorable information about the out-group is seen in a new light."[46] One analysis of several dozen studies found that, in most cases, when students are asked to cooperate with one another (as opposed to competing against), blacks and whites are more likely to get along.[47]

Groups are even more likely to set aside their differences when they have a common *enemy*. Early in the twentieth century, progressive journalist Randolph Bourne famously wrote that "war is the health of the state." In Bourne's words: "Psychologists recognize the gregarious impulse as one of the strongest primitive pulls which keeps together the herds of the different species of higher animals. Mankind is no exception. Our pugnacious evolutionary history has prevented the impulse from ever dying out.

This gregarious impulse is the tendency to imitate, to conform, to coalesce together, and is most powerful when the herd believes itself threatened with attack. Animals crowd together for protection, and men become most conscious of their collectivity at the threat of war."[48] Similarly, Gordon Allport observed: "The threat from a common enemy is not the *only* basis of human association, but it is a strong cement. A nation is never so cohesive as in wartime."[49]

America recently experienced this phenomenon right after 9/11, when for a brief period political divisions seemed to drop away as the country was unified in making war on the Taliban. In a less significant arena, researchers found that when black and white interviewers tried to talk to football fans about their food preferences, whites were substantially more likely to agree to be interviewed by a black person who was wearing clothing with their favored team's logo (as opposed to the other team's logo).[50]

Based on the way humans tend to think, it is a good guess that at least some students within the same school would be more tolerant (or even encouraging) toward academic achievement if the high-achieving students were winning competitions on behalf of the entire school, rather than merely winning individual grades for themselves.

Eliminating grades in favor of interschool competitions would not be any panacea, of course. For example, racial tensions could emerge if the academic teams are perceived as a "white" activity. One researcher's field notes (from a study of an integrated school) describe what happened when the all-white academic team competed in an academic bowl against an all-white team from another school: "Marian (black) has been rather unruly all during class today. When the teacher tells her to sit down and watch the TV, Marian mutters in an undertone, 'That's not Wexler School . . . might as well call it White School.'"[51] Thus, teachers may have to make special efforts to include black students in any academic competitions.

In writing this final chapter, I do not wish to mislead anyone into thinking that I have a pat ten-step solution for "solving" the problem of "acting white." I have offered tentative suggestions here, nothing more. As this entire book should have made clear by now, "acting white" is a problem with deep cultural roots, both in human psychology and in American history.

Even if my suggestions in this chapter are unavailing, anyone who wants to address the achievement gap in America should carefully consider these cultural roots. More importantly, we should all be aware that policies carried out with the best of intentions and goals may nonetheless have unintended consequences that can partly unravel the good we hope to do.

NOTES

Introduction

1. Leon F. Litwack, *Trouble in Mind: Black Southerners in the Age of Jim Crow* (New York: Knopf, 1998), p. 154.

2. Charles Stearns, *The Black Man of the South and the Rebels; or, the Characteristics of the Former, and the Recent Outrages of the Latter* (New York: American News, 1872; reprint, New York: Kraus, 1969), p. 484.

3. Molly McDonough, "Making Brown Real: A North Carolina Family Fought Threats and Intimidation After Suing to Integrate Schools," *ABA Journal* 90 (2004): 45.

4. Beverly Daniel Tatum, *"Why Are All the Black Kids Sitting Together in the Cafeteria?"* (New York: Basic, 1997), pp. 64–65.

5. John McWhorter, *Winning the Race: Beyond the Crisis in Black America* (New York: Gotham, 2006), p. 268.

6. Tatum, *"Why Are All the Black Kids Sitting Together in the Cafeteria?"* pp. 64–65. I did not come across Tatum's passage until a year or so after conceiving the idea for this book.

7. Martin Luther King, Jr., *Stride Toward Freedom: The Montgomery Story* (New York: Harper, 1958).

8. Brad Christerson, Korie L. Edwards, and Michael O. Emerson, *Against All Odds: The Struggle for Racial Integration in Religious Organizations* (New York: New York University Press, 2004).

Chapter 1. Does "Acting White" Occur?

Epigraphs: Philip Walzer, "Students, Researchers Debate the 'Acting White' Stigma for Blacks," *Virginian-Pilot,* 17 June 2006; Christina Vanoverbeke, "School Club Calls for an End to Racial Slurs," *East Valley Tribune,* 22 Feb. 2008.

1. Michael Eric Dyson, *Is Bill Cosby Right?* (New York: Basic Civitas, 2005), pp. 84–88.

2. Paul Tough, "The 'Acting White' Myth," *New York Times Magazine,* 12 Dec. 2004.

3. This speech is recounted in Edmund T. Hamann, "Lessons from the Interpretation/Misinterpretation of John Ogbu's Scholarship," *Intercultural Education* 15, no. 4 (2004): 405–6. Hamann observes that he found himself pulled off a federally funded education research project merely because he had written a draft paper that cited and relied on John Ogbu—famous for writing about the "acting white" phenomenon—even while making clear that he had several "caveats" with Ogbu's scholarship. At a national meeting related to the research project, Hamann's supervisor got "blasted" for allowing a paper to rely on Ogbu in any way. Hamann concludes that "Ogbu was not just controversial; he was taboo," and that "citing Ogbu's ideas is a route to a kneejerk and jarring dismissal."

4. Quotations are taken from the short version of the study: Roland G. Fryer, "Acting White," *Education Next,* Jan. 2006, http://media.hoover.org/documents /ednext20061_52.pdf. A much longer version of the same study, with the supporting mathematics, is available online at http://post.economics.harvard.edu/faculty/fryer /papers/fryer_torelli.pdf. For more on Fryer's biography and research, see generally Stephen J. Dubner, "A Unified Theory of Black America," *New York Times,* 20 Mar. 2005, www.nytimes.com/2005/03/20/magazine/20HARVARD.html?ei=5090&en =e9727 ddcbbbd4431&ex=1268974800&partner=rssuserland&page wanted=all. The National Longitudinal Study of Adolescent Health data can be obtained by following the instructions at www.cpc.unc.edu/addhealth.

5. Fryer, "Acting White," p. 54. Interestingly, Fryer found that Hispanic students experience an even sharper drop-off in popularity with higher grade-point averages.

6. Harold B. Gerard, Terrence D. Jackson, and Edward S. Conolley, "Social Contact in the Desegregated Classroom," in *School Desegregation: A Long-Term Study,* ed. Harold B. Gerard and Norman Miller (New York: Plenum, 1975), pp. 214, 230–31. Granted, this study may have missed the sort of drop-off that Fryer found—increased popularity up to a GPA of 3.5 and decreasing popularity after that. Baughman and Dahlstrom also found in their 1960s study of North Carolina rural children that black children who were smarter and more achievement-oriented were also the most popular; E. Earl Baughman and W. Grant Dahlstrom, *Negro and White Children: A Psychological Study in the Rural South* (New York: Academic, 1968), pp. 331–37.

7. Signithia Fordham and John Ogbu, "Black Students' School Successes: Coping with the Burden of Acting White," *Urban Review* 18, no. 3 (1986): 176–206.

8. Signithia Fordham, *Blacked Out: Dilemmas of Race, Identity, and Success at Capital High* (Chicago: University of Chicago Press, 1996), pp. 22, 314. Capital was almost all black: about 99 percent (p. 31). But whites were "generally" the "teachers of the more advanced or 'difficult' courses—e.g., physics, chemistry, and advanced placement courses in English and mathematics," as well as the teachers who sponsored the academic clubs for high-achieving students (pp. 32–33). This could have led some stu-

dents to view their high-achieving peers as trying to please or imitate the white teachers.

9. Donna Y. Ford, "An Investigation of the Paradox of Underachievement Among Gifted Black Students," *Roeper Review* 16, no. 2 (1993): 78–84; see also Donna Y. Ford, "Determinants of Underachievement as Perceived by Gifted, Above-Average, and Average Black Students," *Roeper Review* 14, no. 3 (1992): 130–36.

10. Donna Y. Ford, "Underachievement Among Gifted and Non-Gifted Black Females," *Journal of Secondary Gifted Education* (Winter 1994–95): 165–75.

11. Donna Y. Ford, Tarek C. Grantham, and Gilman W. Whiting, "Another Look at the Achievement Gap," *Urban Education* 43, no. 2 (2008): 216–39.

12. Jan Collins-Eaglin and Stuart A. Karabenick, "Devaluing of Academic Success by African-American Students: On 'Acting White' and 'Selling Out,'" Paper presented at Annual Meeting of the American Educational Research Association, Atlanta, Georgia, 12–16 Apr. 1993, http://eric.ed.gov/ERICDocs/data/ericdocs2sql/content_storage_01/0000019b/80/13/1e/01.pdf.

13. Laurence Steinberg, *Beyond the Classroom: Why School Reform Has Failed and What Parents Need To Do* (New York: Touchstone, 1996).

14. Roslyn Arlin Mickelson and Anne E. Velasco, "Bring It On! Diverse Responses to 'Acting White' Among Academically Able Black Adolescents," in *Beyond Acting White: Reframing the Debate on Black Student Achievement,* ed. Erin McNamara Horvat and Carla O'Connor (Lanham, Md.: Rowman and Littlefield, 2006).

15. Ronald F. Ferguson, "New Evidence on Why Black High Schoolers Get Accused of 'Acting White,'" p. 2, http://agi.harvard.edu/events/download.php?id=104.

16. See Annette Hemmings, "The 'Hidden' Corridor," *High School Journal,* 83, no. 2 (1 Dec. 1999): 1; Angela M. Neal-Barnett, "Being Black: New Thoughts on the Old Phenomenon of Acting White," in *Forging Links: African American Children, Clinical Developmental Perspectives,* ed. Angela M. Neal-Barnett, Josefina M. Contreras, and Kathryn A. Kerns (Westport, Conn.: Praeger, 2001), p. 82; Tarek C. Grantham and Donna Y. Ford, "A Case Study of the Social Needs of Danisha: An Underachieving Gifted African-American Female," *Roeper Review,* 21, no. 2 (1998); Grace Kao, "Group Images and Possible Selves Among Adolescents: Linking Stereotypes to Expectations by Race and Ethnicity," *Sociological Forum* 15, no. 3 (2000): 407–30; Amanda Datnow and Robert Cooper, "Peer Networks of African American Students in Independent Schools: Affirming Academic Success and Racial Identity," *Journal of Negro Education* 66, no. 1 (1997): 56–72.

17. Frank A. Petroni, Ernest Hirsch, and C. Lillian Petroni, *2, 4, 6, 8: When You Gonna Integrate?* (New York: Behavioral, 1970), pp. 8–9.

18. Petroni et al., *2, 4, 6, 8,* p. 254.

19. Petroni et al., *2, 4, 6, 8,* p. 132 (emphasis added).

20. Karolyn Tyson, "The Making of a 'Burden': Tracing the Development of a 'Burden of Acting White' in Schools," in *Beyond Acting White: Reframing the Debate on Black Student Achievement,* ed. Erin McNamara Horvat and Carla O'Connor (Lanham, Md.: Rowman and Littlefield, 2006), p. 57.

21. Tyson, "The Making of a 'Burden,'" pp. 61, 73.

22. Amy Stuart Wells and Robert L. Crain, *Stepping Over the Color Line: African-American Students in White Suburban Schools* (New Haven: Yale University Press, 1997), p. 240.

23. David A. Bergin and Helen C. Cooks, "High School Students of Color Talk About Accusations of 'Acting White,'" *Urban Review* 34, no. 2 (2002): 113–34.

24. Bergin and Cooks, "High School Students of Color," p. 131. Bergin and Cooks are a bit skeptical of the "acting white" phenomenon; they report that none of the students in the study "avoid[ed] academic achievement in order to avoid accusations of acting white" (p. 130). This, however, is probably because the study involved only those students who had applied to an academic-enrichment program, and who were therefore likely to value academic achievement already. The real question would be whether any of the hundreds of *other* students in these schools avoided academic achievement.

25. Richard Morin, "Unconventional Wisdom," *Washington Post,* 5 June 2005, www.washingtonpost.com/wp-dyn/content/article/2005/06/04/AR2005 060400126_2.html.

26. See Jay P. Greene and Marcus A. Winters, "The Boys Left Behind: The Gender Graduation Gap," *National Review,* 19 Apr. 2006 ("Notably, while females of all racial groups graduate at higher rates than their male counterparts, the size of this gap differs substantially by race. The difference in graduation rates between females and males was about 5 percentage points for white students and only 3 percentage points for Asian students. Among Hispanic and black female students the graduation rates are 58 percent and 59 percent, respectively, compared to 49 percent for Hispanic males and 48 percent for black males. Thus, the gender gap is twice as large for minority students as for white students.").

27. Fryer, "Acting White," p. 56.

28. Roslyn Arlin Mickelson and Anthony D. Greene, "Connecting Pieces of the Puzzle: Gender Differences in Black Middle School Students' Achievement," *Journal of Negro Education* 75, no. 1 (2006): 34–48. Researchers who studied a rural county in North Carolina in the 1960s similarly found that boys were "more alienated from school than are the girls with respect to both motivation and performance"; Baughman and Dahlstrom, *Negro and White Children,* pp. 158–59.

29. Ron Suskind, *A Hope in the Unseen: An American Odyssey from the Inner City to the Ivy League* (New York: Broadway, 1998), p. 127. John Ogbu found the same sort of phenomenon among black males; John U. Ogbu and Astrid Davis, *Black American Students in an Affluent Suburb: A Study of Academic Disengagement* (Mahwah, N.J.: Lawrence Erlbaum, 2003), pp. 192, 201.

30. See, e.g., Gary Alan Fine, "Friends, Impression Management, and Preadolescent Behavior," in *The Development of Children's Friendships,* ed. Steven R. Asher and John M. Gottman (Cambridge: Cambridge University Press, 1981), p. 41.

31. Steinberg, *Beyond the Classroom,* p. 141. Penelope Eckert points out that the distinction between "jocks" and "burnouts" arose "overnight" as soon as kids entered

junior high school; Penelope Eckert, *Jocks and Burnouts: Social Categories and Identity in the High School* (New York: Teachers College Press, 1989), p. 76. As she puts it, "suddenly, in junior high school, a population differentiated by what had been perceived in elementary school as individual differences became organized into two major categories." At the junior high school level, "students felt the greatest pressure to affiliate and to conform with one or the other category, and at that time hostility between the categories was at its height" (p. 92).

32. Correspondents of the New York Times, *How Race Is Lived in America* (New York: Times, 2001), pp. 154–55.

33. Correspondents of the New York Times, *How Race Is Lived,* pp. 156, 159.

34. Datnow and Cooper, "Peer Networks," pp. 56–72.

35. Walt Harrington, "Black and White and the Future," *Washington Post,* 24 Nov. 1991.

36. Mickelson and Velasco, "Bring It On!" pp. 40–41; see also Tyson, "The Making of a 'Burden,'" pp. 77–80; Neal-Barnett, "Being Black," p. 84. Compare Karolyn Tyson, "Weighing In: Elementary-Age Students and the Debate on Attitudes Toward School Among Black Students," *Social Forces* 80, no. 4 (2002): 1157–89.

37. Ogbu and Davis, *Black American Students in an Affluent Suburb,* pp. 196, 204.

38. Ogbu and Davis, *Black American Students in an Affluent Suburb,* p. 198.

39. Neal-Barnett, "Being Black," p. 82.

40. Ferguson, "New Evidence," p. 5. See also Prudence Carter, "Intersecting Identities: 'Acting White,' Gender, and Academic Achievement," in *Beyond Acting White: Reframing the Debate on Black Student Achievement,* ed. Erin McNamara Horvat and Carla O'Connor (Lanham, Md.: Rowman and Littlefield, 2006), p. 121.

41. Tyson, "The Making of a 'Burden,'" pp. 61–62. Similarly, in the Bergin and Cooks study, the "acting white" accusation arose if blacks spoke "proper" English or if they spent "too much time with white students," as was the case if they "enrolled in college preparation or honors courses that tended to be mostly white"; Bergin and Cooks, "High School Students of Color," p. 121.

42. McWhorter, *Winning the Race,* p. 280.

43. McWhorter, *Winning the Race,* p. 281.

44. Stephanie Esters, "When Black Kids Are Accused of 'Acting White,' Grades Can Suffer as They Try to Maintain Popularity," *Kalamazoo Gazette,* 23 Apr. 2006.

45. Leslie Postal and Dave Weber, "'Achievement Gap' Vexes Schools; Black Students—and Hispanics—Lag Behind White Classmates," *Orlando Sentinel,* 16 May 2004.

46. Rhonda Stewart, "Long-Distance Learner: After Logging Many Miles as a Metco Student, She's a Documentary Star," *Boston Globe,* 4 Aug. 2005.

47. Tracey Early, "Triangle Educators Debate Racial Issues at Conference," *News14 Carolina,* 28 Oct. 2005.

48. Correspondents of the New York Times, *How Race Is Lived,* p. 163.

49. Correspondents of the New York Times, *How Race Is Lived,* p. xvii.

50. John Ogbu points to a researcher who claimed that for black children, "read-

ing and spelling" are "artificial, contrived and arbitrary" requirements; John U. Ogbu, "The Consequences of the American Caste System," in *The School Achievement of Minority Children: New Perspectives,* ed. Ulric Neisser (Hillsdale, N.J.: Lawrence Erlbaum, 1986), p. 26. Barbara J. Shade refers to the alleged "preference of African American students for an intuitive, holistic-integrative thinking style that often stands in contrast to the logical-mathematical style required by most traditional academic tasks"; B. J. Shade, "Understanding the African American Learner," in *Teaching Diverse Populations: Formulating a Knowledge Base,* ed. E. Hollins, J. E. King, and W. Hayman (Albany: State University of New York Press, 1994), pp. 175–89, quoted in Avi Kaplan and Martin L. Maehr, "Enhancing the Motivation of African American Students: An Achievement Goal Theory Perspective," *Journal of Negro Education* 68, no. 1 (1999): 23–41. Or consider Jay MacLeod's complaint that when lower-class children do poorly in school, the real problem is "the definitions and standards of the school"; Jay MacLeod, *Ain't No Makin' It: Aspirations and Attainment in a Low-Income Neighborhood* (Boulder, Colo.: Westview, 1987), p. 100.

51. John U. Ogbu, "Foreword," in R. Patrick Solomon, *Black Resistance in High School: Forging a Separatist Culture* (Albany: State University of New York Press, 1992), p. xi.

52. Steinberg, *Beyond the Classroom,* p. 97.

53. Ogbu and Davis, *Black American Students in an Affluent Suburb,* pp. 40–41, 48.

54. Karolyn Tyson, William Darity, Jr., and Domini R. Castellino, "It's Not 'a Black Thing': Understanding the Burden of Acting White and Other Dilemmas of High Achievement," *American Sociological Review* 70 (2005): 582–605.

55. Prudence Carter, "Intersecting Identities: 'Acting White,' Gender, and Academic Achievement," in *Beyond Acting White: Reframing the Debate on Black Student Achievement,* ed. Erin McNamara Horvat and Carla O'Connor (Lanham, Md.: Rowman and Littlefield, 2006), pp. 115–16.

56. Roseana Auten, "Acting Right, Not White," *Austin Chronicle,* 7–13 Nov. 1997, www.austinchronicle.com/issues/vol17/issue10/pols.tales.html.

57. One sociologist found that although black students had positive *abstract* attitudes toward education (for example, they agreed in the abstract that "education is the key to success in the future"), they had much more negative *concrete* attitudes (for example, they agreed that "when our teachers give us homework, my friends never think of doing it"); Roslyn Arlin Mickelson, "The Attitude-Achievement Paradox Among Black Adolescents," *Sociology of Education* 63, no. 1 (1990): 44–61.

58. Darity et al., "It's Not 'a Black Thing,'" p. 599n.16.

59. James W. Ainsworth-Darnell and Douglas B. Downey, "Assessing the Oppositional Culture Explanation for Racial/Ethnic Differences in School Performance," *American Sociological Review* 63, no. 4 (1998): 536–53; Philip J. Cook and Jens Ludwig, "The Burden of 'Acting White': Do Black Adolescents Disparage Academic Achievement?" in *The Black-White Test Score Gap,* ed. Christopher Jencks and Meredith Phillips (Washington, D.C.: Brookings Institution Press, 1998).

60. Ainsworth-Darnell and Downey, "Assessing the Oppositional Culture," pp. 541–42, 545. An earlier paper making a similar point from the National Education Longitudinal Study data is Eugene Kennedy, "Correlates of Perceived Popularity Among Peers: A Study of Race and Gender Differences Among Middle School Students," *Journal of Negro Education* 64, no. 2 (1995): 186–95.

61. See, e.g., Nathan R. Kuncel, Marcus Credé, and Lisa L. Thomas, "The Validity of Self-Reported Grade Point Averages, Class Ranks, and Test Scores: A Meta-Analysis and Review of the Literature," *Review of Educational Research* 75, no. 1 (2005): 63–82.

62. This is why Roland Fryer's research is superior: It does not rely on whether John thinks of himself as popular or hard-working. Instead, Fryer examines whether *other black* students specifically name John as a personal friend, and compares that to John's GPA.

63. Ainsworth-Darnell and Downey, "Assessing the Oppositional Culture," p. 549.

64. Ainsworth-Darnell and Downey, "Assessing the Oppositional Culture," p. 549. Another set of researchers similarly found that "blacks who consider themselves not a troublemaker or a 'very good student' earn lower grades than white students who evaluate themselves similarly"; Grace Kao, Marta Tienda, and Barbara Schneider, "Racial and Ethnic Variation in Academic Performance," *Research in Sociology of Education and Socialization* 11 (1996), p. 290.

65. Ainsworth-Darnell and Downey, "Assessing the Oppositional Culture," p. 549 (emphasis added).

66. Cook and Ludwig, "The Burden of 'Acting White,'" pp. 382–83.

67. Cook and Ludwig, "The Burden of 'Acting White,'" p. 383.

68. Fordham, *Blacked Out,* p. 293.

69. Fordham, *Blacked Out,* pp. 306–7.

70. Cook and Ludwig, "The Burden of 'Acting White,'" p. 383.

71. Cook and Ludwig, "The Burden of 'Acting White,'" pp. 385–86.

72. Angel L. Harris, "I (Don't) Hate School: Revisiting Oppositional Culture Theory of Blacks' Resistance to Schooling," *Social Forces* 85, no. 2 (Dec. 2006): 797–833.

73. Harris, "I (Don't) Hate School," p. 809.

74. Harris, "I (Don't) Hate School," p. 816.

75. Harris, "I (Don't) Hate School," p. 817.

76. Harris, "I (Don't) Hate School," p. 819.

77. Harris, "I (Don't) Hate School," pp. 817, 819.

78. For a bit of the research on this, see Paul Willis, *Learning to Labor: Working-Class Kids Get Working-Class Jobs* (New York: Columbia University Press, 1981); Eckert, *Jocks and Burnouts;* MacLeod, *Ain't No Makin' It;* Rochelle Manor-Bullock, Christine Look, and David N. Dixon, "Is Giftedness Socially Stigmatizing? The Impact of High Achievement on Social Interactions," *Journal of Education of the Gifted* 18, no. 3 (1995): 319–38; John H. Bishop et al., "Why We Harass Nerds and Freaks: A Formal Theory of Student Culture and Norms," *Journal of School Health* 74, no. 7 (2004): 235–51; Tiffani Chin and Meredith Phillips, "The Ubiquity of Oppositional

Culture," working paper (May 2005); David A. Kinney, "From Nerds to Normals: The Recovery of Identity Among Adolescents from Middle School to High School," *Sociology of Education* 66, no. 1 (1993): 21–40.

79. James S. Coleman, *The Adolescent Society: The Social Life of the Teenager and Its Impact on Education* (New York: Free Press, 1961), pp. 50–51.

80. Coleman, *The Adolescent Society,* p. 51.

81. Coleman, *The Adolescent Society,* p. 265.

82. Steinberg, *Beyond the Classroom,* p. 19. Indeed, a form of "acting white" is sometimes present in the Hispanic community as well; Elaine Jarvik, "Coloring with 'Brown,'" *Deseret Morning News,* 16 May 2004.

83. Neal-Barnett, "Being Black," pp. 75, 79–81, 87.

Chapter 2. Why Should We Care?

Epigraphs: Juan Castillo, "African Americans Hear Self-Empowering Message," *Austin American-Statesman,* 23 July 2006.

1. Lawrence C. Stedman, "An Assessment of the Contemporary Debate over U.S. Achievement," in *Brookings Papers on Education Policy, 1998,* ed. Diane Ravitch (Washington, D.C.: Brookings Institution Press, 1998), p. 72.

2. Charts available at http://nces.ed.gov/nationsreportcard/.

3. "A Large Black-White Scoring Gap Persists on the SAT," *Journal of Blacks in Higher Education* (2007), www.jbhe.com/features/53_SAT.html.

4. Roland G. Fryer, Jr., and Steven D. Levitt, "Understanding the Black-White Test Score Gap in the First Two Years of School," *Review of Economics and Statistics* 86, no. 2 (2004): 447–64. Fryer and Levitt found that the achievement gap in young students went away by controlling for age, birth weight, socioeconomic status, WIC participation, mother's age, and number of children's books in the home. But these variables themselves are likely to be correlated with student achievement.

5. Derek A. Neal and William R. Johnson, "The Role of Premarket Factors in Black-White Wage Differences," *Journal of Political Economy* 104, no. 5 (1996): 869–95.

6. See Coleman, *Equality and Achievement in Education,* p. 123; Madhabi Chatterji, "Reading Achievement Gaps, Correlates, and Moderators of Early Reading Achievement: Evidence from the Early Childhood Longitudinal Study (ECLS) Kindergarten to First Grade Sample," *Journal of Educational Psychology* 98, no. 3 (2006): 489–507; National Center for Education Statistics, *From Kindergarten Through Third Grade: Children's Beginning School Experiences,* U.S. Department of Education, NCES 2004-007 (2004), p. x, http://nces.ed.gov/pubs2004/2004007.pdf.

7. Compare Keith E. Stanovich, "Matthew Effects in Reading: Some Consequences of Individual Differences in the Acquisition of Literacy," *Reading Research Quarterly* 21, no. 4 (Autumn 1986): 360–407.

8. Ogbu and Davis, *Black American Students in an Affluent Suburb,* p. 189.

9. See, e.g., Pedro Carneiro, James J. Heckman, and Dimitriy V. Masterov, "Labor Market Discrimination and Racial Differences in Premarket Factors," *Journal of Law*

and Economics 48 (2005): 10–14; Roy Wilkins Center for Human Relations and Social Justice, University of Minnesota, "Analysis of the 1996 Minnesota Basic Standards Test Data" (Mar. 1997), p. 24; Nancy A. Gonzales, Ana Mari Cauce, Ruth J. Friedman, and Craig A. Mason, "Family, Peer, and Neighborhood Influences on Academic Achievement Among African-American Adolescents: One-Year Prospective Effects," *American Journal of Community Psychology* 24, no. 3 (1996): 365–87.

10. Michael J. Puma, "The 'Prospects' Study of Educational Growth and Opportunity: Implications for Policy and Practice," paper presented at Annual Meeting of American Educational Research Association (Apr. 1999), p. 11.

11. Laurence Steinberg, Sanford M. Dornbusch, and B. Bradford Brown, "Ethnic Differences in Adolescent Achievement: An Ecological Perspective," *American Psychologist* 47, no. 6 (1992): 723–29; see also Sanford M. Dornbusch, Philip I. Ritter, and Laurence Steinberg, "Community Influences on the Relation of Family Statuses to Adolescent School Performance: Differences Between African Americans and Non-Hispanic Whites," *American Journal of Education* 99, no. 4 (1991): 543–67.

12. Kao, Tienda, and Schneider, "Racial and Ethnic Variation in Academic Performance." See also Larry V. Hedges and Amy Nowell, "Changes in the Black-White Gap in Achievement Test Scores," *Sociology of Education* 72, no. 2 (1999): 111–35. See Ogbu and Davis, *Black American Students in an Affluent Suburb*, p. 35.

13. Eric A. Hanushek and Alfred A. Lindseth, *Schoolhouses, Courthouses, and Statehouses: Solving the Funding-Achievement Puzzle in America's Public Schools* (Princeton: Princeton University Press, 2009), p. 68.

14. James S. Coleman, U.S. Department of Health, Education, and Welfare, *Equality of Educational Opportunity* (1966), p. 304.

15. Coleman, *Equality and Achievement in Education*, p. 73.

16. Coleman, *Equality and Achievement in Education*, p. 77.

17. See Eric A. Hanushek, "The Failure of Input-Based Schooling Policies," *Economic Journal* 113 (2003): F64–F98; Eric A. Hanushek, "The Economics of Schooling: Production and Efficiency in Public Schools," *Journal of Economic Literature* 24, no. 3 (1986), p. 1162; Eric A. Hanushek, Steven G. Rivkin, and Lori L. Taylor, "Aggregation and the Estimated Effects of School Resources," *Review of Economics and Statistics* 78 (1996), p. 625.

18. William G. Howell and Paul E. Peterson, *The Education Gap: Vouchers and Urban Schools* (Washington, D.C.: Brookings Institution Press, revised paperback ed., 2006), p. 91.

19. See, e.g., Alan Krueger's rebuttal of Eric Hanushek in *The Class Size Debate*, ed. Lawrence Mishel and Richard Rothstein (Washington, D.C.: Economic Policy Institute, 2002); R. L. Greenwald, L. V. Hedges, and R. D. Laine, "The Effect of School Resources on Student Achievement," *Review of Educational Research* 66, no. 3 (1996): 361–96.

20. For a summary of several research papers on this subject, see Robert Gordon, Thomas J. Kane, and Douglas O. Staiger, *Identifying Effective Teachers: Using Performance on the Job,* Brookings Institution White Paper 2006-01 (Apr. 2006), pp. 8–

9; Steven G. Rivkin, Eric A. Hanushek, and John F. Kain, "Teachers, Schools, and Academic Achievement," *Econometrica* 73, no. 2 (2005): 417–58.

21. See Heather G. Peske and Kati Haycock, *Teaching Inequality: How Poor and Minority Students Are Shortchanged on Teacher Quality* (Education Trust, 2006).

22. See, e.g., Hamilton Lankford, Susanna Loeb, and James Wyckoff, "Teacher Sorting and the Plight of Urban Schools: A Descriptive Analysis," *Educational Evaluation and Policy Analysis* 24, no. 1 (2002): 37–62.

23. See Ronald F. Ferguson, "Paying for Public Education: New Evidence on How and Why Money Matters," *Harvard Journal on Legislation* 28 (1991): 488–89. Nonetheless, programs to increase teacher salaries have not historically had much benefit; Hanushek, Rivkin, and Taylor, "Aggregation and the Estimated Effects of School Resources," p. 625.

24. See Leanna Stiefel, Amy Ellen Schwartz, and Ingrid Gould Ellen, "Disentangling the Racial Test Score Gap: Probing the Evidence in a Large Urban School District," *Journal of Policy Analysis and Management* 26, no. 1 (2007): 7–30; Meredith Phillips, James Crouse, and John Ralph, "Does the Black-White Test Score Gap Widen After Children Enter School?" in *The Black-White Test Score Gap,* ed. Christopher Jencks and Meredith Phillips (Washington, D.C.: Brookings Institution Press, 1998), p. 256.

25. See Claude Steele and Joshua Aronson, "Stereotype Threat and the Test Performance of Academically Successful African Americans," in *The Black-White Test Score Gap,* ed. Christopher Jencks and Meredith Phillips (Washington, D.C.: Brookings Institution Press, 1998), p. 401.

26. Paul Sackett, Chaitra Hardison, and Michael Cullen, "On Interpreting Stereotype Threat as Accounting for African American–White Differences in Cognitive Tests," *American Psychologist* 59 (2004): 7–13.

27. Carneiro, Heckman, and Masterov, "Labor Market Discrimination," pp. 17–19.

28. Geoffrey L. Cohen, Julio Garcia, Nancy Apfel, and Allison Master, "Reducing the Racial Achievement Gap: A Social-Psychological Intervention," *Science* 313 (2006): 1307–10.

29. Geoffrey L. Cohen et al., "Recursive Processes in Self-Affirmation: Intervening to Close the Minority Achievement Gap," *Science* 324 (17 April 2009): 400–403.

30. Jenessa R. Shapiro and Steven L. Neuberg, "From Stereotype Threat to Stereotype Threats: Implications of a Multi-Threat Framework for Causes, Moderators, Mediators, Consequences, and Interventions," *Personality and Social Psychology Review* 11 (2007): 107.

31. Betty Hart and Todd R. Risley, *Meaningful Differences in the Everyday Experience of Young American Children* (Baltimore: Brookes, 1995).

32. Erwin H. Epstein, "Social Class, Ethnicity, and Academic Achievement: A Cross-Cultural Approach," *Journal of Negro Education* 41, no. 3 (1972): 205.

33. This is a fairly commonplace observation. See Annette Lareau, "Invisible Inequality: Social Class and Childrearing in Black Families and White Families," *Amer-*

ican Sociological Review 67, no. 5 (2002): 747–76; Ann L. Brown, Annemarie Sullivan Palincsar, and Linda Purcell, "Poor Readers: Teach, Don't Label," in *The School Achievement of Minority Children: New Perspectives,* ed. Ulric Neisser (Hillsdale, N.J.: Lawrence Erlbaum, 1986), pp. 106–12; MacLeod, *Ain't No Makin' It,* pp. 17–18 (discussing research of Shirley Brice Heath); Celia B. Stendler-Lavatelli, "Environmental Intervention in Infancy and Early Childhood," in *Social Class, Race, and Psychological Development,* ed. Martin Deutsch, Irwin Katz, and Arthur R. Jensen (New York: Holt, Rinehart, and Winston, 1968), p. 352 (noting that in many of the poor homes observed, there were few infant toys and the adults did not play traditional games such as "peek-a-boo" with babies).

34. Baughman and Dahlstrom, *Negro and White Children,* p. 209.

35. Coleman, *Equality and Achievement in Education,* p. 96.

36. Coleman, *Equality and Achievement in Education,* p. 109.

37. Roland G. Fryer, Jr., and Paul Torelli, "Measuring the Prevalence and Impact of 'Acting White,'" Paper presented at Annual Meeting, Allied Social Science Associations, Boston, Jan. 2006, p. 36.

38. Fryer and Torelli, "Measuring the Prevalence and Impact of 'Acting White,'" p. 37.

39. Mickelson and Velasco, "Bring It On!" pp. 42–43, 52–53.

40. Ferguson, "New Evidence," p. 6. An earlier study looked at four high schools with an average enrollment of 1,700, in which the black/white ratio was 30/70. It found that black students perceived a gap between how they themselves viewed school and how their peers perceived schools, and that the "perception of a hostile peer environment could negatively affect academic performance" because academic achievement might cause "separation from a particular peer group"; John Rhodes Trotter, "Academic Attitudes of High Achieving and Low Achieving Academically Able Black Male Adolescents," *Journal of Negro Education* 50, no. 1 (1981): 60–61.

41. See, e.g., Eric A. Hanushek, John F. Kain, Jacob M. Markman, and Steven G. Rivkin, "Does Peer Ability Affect Student Achievement?" *Journal of Applied Econometrics* 18, no. 5 (2003): 527–44; Jane Cooley, "Desegregation and the Achievement Gap: Do Diverse Peers Help?" working paper (6 May 2009), www.ssc.wisc.edu/~jcooley/CooleyDeseg.pdf; Weili Ding and Steven F. Lehrer, "Do Peers Affect Student Achievement in China's Secondary Schools?" NBER Working Paper 12305 (June 2006); Kathryn R. Wentzel and Kathryn Caldwell, "Friendships, Peer Acceptance, and Group Membership: Relations to Academic Achievement in Middle School," *Child Development* 68, no. 6 (1997): 1198–1209; Allison Ryan, "The Peer Group as a Context for the Development of Young Adolescent Motivation and Achievement," *Child Development* 72, no. 4 (2001): 1135–50; Donald Robertson and James Symons, "Do Peer Groups Matter? Peer Group Versus Schooling Effect on Academic Achievement," *Economica* 70 (2003): 31–53; Caroline Hoxby, "Peer Effects in the Classroom: Learning from Gender and Race Variation," NBER Working Paper 7867 (2000), www.nber.org/papers/w7867.

42. Coleman, *The Adolescent Society,* pp. 262–65. Why does it matter whether high-

IQ students get good grades? If the student culture does not reward good grades, then the students who try to get good grades may not be those with the most ability. As an analogy, Coleman pointed out that if no one in the school cares about the volleyball team, it's rather unlikely that the few people who try out for volleyball are the ones with the most talent.

43. Coleman, *The Adolescent Society,* p. 265.

44. See David J. Zimmerman, "Peer Effects in Academic Outcomes: Evidence from a Natural Experiment," *Review of Economics and Statistics* 85, no. 1 (2003): 15–23; Bruce Sacerdote, "Peer Effects with Random Assignment: Results for Dartmouth Roommates," *Quarterly Journal of Economics* 116, no. 2 (2001): 681–704. Of course, this finding probably underestimates peer effects; after all, the overwhelming majority of college students have a peer group that extends far beyond a single roommate, and I remember from college that some students don't even *like* their roommates.

45. Scott E. Carrell, Richard L. Fullerton, Robert N. Gilchrist, and James E. West, "Peer and Leadership Effects in Academic and Athletic Performance," working paper (2 May 2007), www.rand.org/labor/seminars/adp/pdfs/2007_carrell.pdf. Indeed, it strikes me that scholars of both education and medicine (diet in particular) could design all sorts of useful experiments—humane, of course—to be deployed in military academies or prisons.

46. Steinberg, Dornbusch, and Brown, "Ethnic Differences in Adolescent Achievement," p. 726.

47. Steinberg, *Beyond the Classroom,* p. 147.

48. Steinberg, *Beyond the Classroom,* pp. 147–48.

49. Steinberg, *Beyond the Classroom,* pp. 84–87.

50. Steinberg, *Beyond the Classroom,* p. 136.

51. Steinberg, *Beyond the Classroom,* p. 134.

52. Steinberg, *Beyond the Classroom,* p. 137.

53. Steinberg, *Beyond the Classroom,* p. 157.

54. Steinberg, *Beyond the Classroom,* p. 158.

55. Steinberg, *Beyond the Classroom,* p. 161.

56. Steinberg, Dornbusch, and Brown, "Ethnic Differences in Adolescent Achievement," p. 726.

57. See Grace Kao and Marta Tienda, "Optimism and Achievement: The Educational Performance of Immigrant Youth," *Social Science Quarterly* 76, no. 1 (1995): 1–19. As Laurence Steinberg and his colleagues found, "foreign-born students—who, incidentally, report significantly more discrimination than American-born youngsters and significantly more difficulty with the English language—nevertheless earn higher grades in school," and they "outscore" native-born Americans of whatever race on "virtually every factor we know to be correlated with school success." Moreover, "the longer a student's family has lived in this country, the worse the youngster's school performance and mental health." Steinberg, *Beyond the Classroom,* p. 97.

58. Stiefel, Schwartz, and Ellen, "Disentangling the Racial Test Score Gap."

59. While some people have suggested that black immigrants do especially well in

school only because of selection effects (that is, because they come from families that are particularly motivated and driven to succeed), that excuse doesn't work as well where the comparison is to white immigrants (who presumably are subject to the same selection effects).

60. Stiefel, Schwartz, and Ellen, "Disentangling the Racial Test Score Gap."

61. Suskind, *A Hope in the Unseen*, p. 3.

62. Janita Poe, "A Black-on-Black Education Barrier; Achievers Told Success Is a Sellout," *Chicago Tribune,* 1 Jan. 1994; Mark Curnutte, "For Some Black Students, Failing Is Safer; Many Who Strive to Do Well Often Face Peers Who Call Them 'Too White,'" *Cincinnati Enquirer,* 28 May 1998; see also Sophfronia Scott Gregory, "The Hidden Hurdle: Talented Black Students Find that One of the Most Insidious Obstacles to Achievement Comes from a Surprising Source: Their Own Peers," *Time,* 16 Mar. 2002, p. 44; Esters, "When Black Kids Are Accused of 'Acting White.'"

Chapter 3. The History of Black Education in America

1. See U.S. Department of Education, National Center for Education Statistics, *A First Look at the Literacy of America's Adults in the 21st Century,* NCES 2006-470 (2006), http://nces.ed.gov/NAAL/PDF/2006470.PDF.

2. See Ruth Wallis Herndon, "Literacy Among New England's Transient Poor, 1750–1800," *Journal of Social History* 29, no. 4 (Summer 1996): 963–65.

3. Of course, we can look at other clues too, such as the fact that today's politicians would never write something as dense and intricately argued as the Federalist Papers in an essay aimed at a general audience (even if they had the ability to write at that level).

4. For a useful discussion of the problems that historians face in dealing with biased and nonrepresentative sources, see generally Martha C. Howell and Walter Prevenier, *From Reliable Sources: An Introduction to Historical Methods* (Ithaca: Cornell University Press, 2001).

5. I make no pretense of doing professional historical research here, and have relied mostly on secondary literature rather than original historical sources. A few indispensable works are Carter G. Woodson, *The Education of the Negro Prior to 1861* (1919); James D. Anderson, *The Education of Blacks in the South, 1860–1935* (Chapel Hill: University of North Carolina Press, 1988); Horace Mann Bond, *The Education of the Negro in the American Social Order* (Octagon, 1966); Henry Allen Bullock, *The History of Negro Education in the South from 1619 to the Present* (New York: Praeger, 1967); Thomas L. Webber, *Deep Like the Rivers: Education in the Slave Quarter Community, 1831–1865* (New York: W. W. Norton, 1978); Arnold Cooper, *Between Struggle and Hope: Four Black Educators in the South, 1894–1915* (Ames: Iowa State University Press, 1989); Janet Duitsman Cornelius, *When I Can Read My Title Clear: Literacy, Slavery, and Religion in the Antebellum South* (Columbia: University of South Carolina Press, 1991); James L. Leloudis, *Schooling the New South: Pedagogy, Self, and Society in North Carolina, 1880–1920* (Chapel Hill: University of North Carolina Press, 1996); and

Heather Andrea Williams, *Self-Taught: African American Education in Slavery and Freedom* (Chapel Hill: University of North Carolina Press, 2007).

6. As Heather Andrea Williams points out, "Teachers were further motivated to tell only of improvements out of fear that any negative remarks would fuel opposition to black education"; Williams, *Self-Taught*, p. 163.

7. You might object that there are selection effects here: most people in the nineteenth century—whether black or white—never finished high school in the first place. Therefore, students in the smaller percentage who attended school in the nineteenth century were more likely to be enthusiastic about school. By the same token, if you had forced all of the sixteen-year-olds in 1880 to attend school, perhaps many of them would have had a negative attitude. On the other hand, it is not as if the average sixteen-year-old in 1880 would have been hanging out at the mall if she were not in school. Instead, many teenagers in that time would have been working on a farm or at some other manual job, and might well have loved to have the chance to go to school instead.

8. Donnie D. Bellamy, "The Education of Blacks in Missouri Prior to 1861," *Journal of Negro History* 59, no. 2 (1974): 150.

9. See, e.g., Sing-nan Fen, "Notes on the Education of Negroes in North Carolina During the Civil War," *Journal of Negro Education* 36, no. 1 (1967): 24; David Freedman, "African-American Schooling in the South Prior to 1861," *Journal of Negro History* 84, no. 1 (1999): 12–13; Cornelius, *When I Can Read My Title Clear*, pp. 32–33.

10. See, e.g., Cornelius, *When I Can Read My Title Clear*, pp. 64–66; Webber, *Deep Like the Rivers*, pp. 29–30, 131–37; Samuel L. Horst, *Education for Manhood: The Education of Blacks in Virginia During the Civil War* (Lanham, Md.: University Press of America, 1987), pp. 50–51; Jacqueline Jones, *Soldiers of Light and Love: Northern Teachers and Georgia Blacks, 1865–1873* (Athens: University of Georgia Press, 1992; originally published Chapel Hill: University of North Carolina Press, 1980), p. 60; Bullock, *History of Negro Education in the South*, p. 43; Williams, *Self-Taught*, pp. 14–18.

11. William Henry Singleton, *Recollections of My Slavery Days* (Raleigh: North Carolina Department of Cultural Resources, 1999), p. 41.

12. Webber, *Deep Like the Rivers*, p. 100. On the other hand, it's possible that abolitionists laid a bit too much emphasis on the stories of blacks being forbidden to learn to read; Cornelius, *When I Can Read My Title Clear*, p. 62.

13. Eugene D. Genovese, *Roll, Jordan, Roll: The World the Slaves Made* (New York: Vintage, 1976), p. 565.

14. Bellamy, "The Education of Blacks in Missouri Prior to 1861," pp. 145–46, citing John Mason Peck, *Forty Years of Pioneer Life: Memoir of John Mason Peck, Edited from His Journals and Correspondence by Rufus Babcock* (Philadelphia, 1864), pp. 93–94.

15. Bellamy, "The Education of Blacks in Missouri Prior to 1861," p. 146, citing Timothy Flint, *Recollection of the Last Ten Years, Passed in Occasional Residences and Jorneyings in the Valley of the Mississippi* (Boston, 1826), p. 345.

16. Bellamy, "The Education of Blacks in Missouri Prior to 1861," p. 156.

17. Webber, *Deep Like the Rivers,* p. 135.

18. Freedman, "African-American Schooling in the South Prior to 1861," pp. 11–15; Horst, *Education for Manhood,* p. 61; Edmund L. Drago, *Initiative, Paternalism, and Race Relations; Charleston's Avery Normal Institute* (Athens: University of Georgia Press, 1990), pp. 14–15; Williams, *Self-Taught,* pp. 20–21.

19. Christopher M. Span, "'I Must Learn Now or Not at All': Social and Cultural Capital in the Educational Initiatives of Formerly Enslaved African Americans in Mississippi, 1862–1869," *Journal of African American History* 87 (2002): 200–201.

20. Freedman, "African-American Schooling in the South Prior to 1861," p. 6.

21. See Anderson, *Education of Blacks in the South,* p. 281. One such school in the swamps of Louisiana came to a tragic end:

> Cyrille, having been a pupil in the "nocturnal schools" already mentioned, had thereby obtained just a sufficiency of the forbidden fruit to create an intense longing for more, and every moment he could wrest from labor was diligently applied to the attainment of this earnestly desired result. In due time, believing himself qualified to become a teacher of his fellow slaves, he took a few of the most trustworthy into his confidence and twice or thrice in each week they regularly met on a small island in the midst of one of the great Cypress swamps. . . . [After he told his wife, Eulalie, of the school, she would go with him to the island], then they would, if they were the first across the morass, build a fire which served the double purpose of lighting their "rural academy" and driving away the swarming mosquitos. Finally, drawing forth their "child's First Primer," each dusky scholar would pour [*sic*] again and again over its soiled pages, until the "we small hours" bade them prepare to depart on their homeward journey.

Their studies ended when, one night, Eulalie couldn't be found on the plantation. Whites deemed her and her companions to be fugitives, and ultimately tracked down her and her classmates and killed them. Freedman, "African-American Schooling in the South Prior to 1861," pp. 7–8.

22. Freedman, "African-American Schooling in the South Prior to 1861," p. 17.

23. Susie King Taylor, *Reminiscenses of My Life: A Black Woman's Civil War Memoirs* (orig. pub. 1902; reprint, New York: Wiener, 1988), pp. 29–30.

24. Taylor, *Reminiscenses of My Life,* pp. 37–38.

25. Laura S. Haviland, *A Woman's Life-Work, Labors, and Experiences* (1881), www.gutenberg.org/dirs/etext05/wlwrk10.txt.

26. Anderson, *Education of Blacks in the South,* p. 16; Genovese, *Roll Jordan Roll,* p. 563. This average rate was occasionally exceeded, of course. In Missouri, the 1860 census revealed that 2,687 out of 3,572 free Missouri blacks could read and write; Bellamy, "The Education of Blacks in Missouri Prior to 1861," p. 156.

27. During the Civil War as well. The chaplain of a Union black regiment wrote, "I am sure I never witnessed greater eagerness for study; and all, who have examined the writing books and listened to the recitations in the schools, have expressed their as-

tonishment and admiration. A majority of the men seem to regard their books as an indispensable portion of their equipments, and the cartridge box and spelling book are attached to the same belt." Anderson, *Education of Blacks in the South,* p. 282.

28. See, e.g., Webber, *Deep Like the Rivers,* pp. 137–38; Jones, *Soldiers of Light and Love,* pp. 3–4; Howard N. Rabinowitz, *Race Relations in the Urban South, 1865–1890* (Urbana: University of Illinois Press, 1980), pp. 156–61.

29. William J. Collins and Robert A. Margo, "Historical Perspectives on Racial Differences in Schooling in the United States," Vanderbilt University Working Paper no. 03-W13 (2003), Table 1.

30. The quotes above come from Span, "'I Must Learn Now or Not at All.'"

31. Thomas L. Johnson, *Twenty-Eight Years a Slave, or the Story of My Life in Three Continents* (Bournemouth: W. Math, 1909), p. 76, http://docsouth.unc.edu/johnson/johnson.html.

32. John B. Myers, "The Education of the Alabama Freedmen During Presidential Reconstruction, 1865–1867," *Journal of Negro Education* 40, no. 2 (1971), p. 163. For similar experiences in New York, see Carleton Mabee, *Black Education in New York State from Colonial to Modern Times* (Syracuse: Syracuse University Press, 1979), pp. 36–37.

33. See Kay Ann Taylor, "Mary S. Peake and Charlotte L. Forten: Black Teachers During the Civil War and Reconstruction," *Journal of Negro Education* 74, no. 2 (2005): 122–34.

34. For a history of the "missionary" school movement, see Jones, *Soldiers of Light and Love.* The "missionary" movement had its roots in the eighteenth century. See Shawn Comminney, "The Society for the Propagation of the Gospel in Foreign Parts and Black Education in South Carolina, 1702–1764," *Journal of Negro History* 84, no. 4 (1999): 360–69.

35. See, e.g., Drago, *Initiative, Paternalism, and Race Relations,* p. 57. These sorts of events occasionally occurred outside the South; Robert L. McCaul, *The Black Struggle for Public Schooling in Nineteenth-Century Illinois* (Carbondale: Southern Illinois University Press, 1987), p. 51.

36. Myers, "The Education of the Alabama Freedmen During Presidential Reconstruction," p. 169.

37. Myers, "The Education of the Alabama Freedmen During Presidential Reconstruction," pp. 169–70.

38. Joe M. Richardson, "The Freedmen's Bureau and Negro Education in Florida," *Journal of Negro Education* 31, no. 4 (1962): 464.

39. Litwack, *Trouble in Mind,* p. 87.

40. Freedman, "African-American Schooling in the South Prior to 1861," p. 3. For much more on this point, see Williams, *Self-Taught,* pp. 72–79.

41. Bellamy, "The Education of Blacks in Missouri Prior to 1861," p. 149, citing Kensinger Jones, *Freedom for Sale* (St. Louis, 1951), p. 17.

42. Robert G. Sherer, *Subordination or Liberation? The Development and Conflicting Theories of Black Education in Nineteenth-Century Alabama* (Tuscaloosa: Uni-

versity of Alabama Press, 1977), p. 134; see also Jones, *Soldiers of Light and Love*, pp. 3–4.

43. See Anderson, *Education of Blacks in the South*, pp. 22–23, 96–97; C. Calvin Smith, *Educating the Masses: The Unfolding History of Black School Administrators in Arkansas, 1900–2000* (Fayetteville: University of Arkansas Press, 2003), p. 2–3; Williams, *Self-Taught*, pp. 121–25, 149–50.

44. Quoted in Dorothy Granberry, "Black Community Leadership in a Rural Tennessee County, 1865–1903," *Journal of Negro History* 83, no. 4 (1998): 255.

45. Adah Ward Randolph, "Building upon Cultural Capital: Thomas Jefferson Ferguson and the Albany Enterprise Academy in Southeast Ohio, 1863–1886," *Journal of African American History* 87 (2002): 183.

46. Richardson, "The Freedmen's Bureau," p. 464. See also Adam Fairclough, *Teaching Equality: Black Schools in the Age of Jim Crow* (Athens: University of Georgia Press, 2001), p. 61.

47. Leloudis, *Schooling the New South*, pp. 121, 178.

48. Anderson, *The Education of Blacks in the South, 1860–1935*, p. 5; see also Bullock, *The History of Negro Education in the South*), pp. 24–25 ("[Teachers] found in their Negro charges not only a desire for literacy but also a willingness to endure the hardships necessary to attain it. Years of servitude had generated an intense desire for knowledge among the freedmen."). Many examples can be found in Williams, *Self-Taught*, pp. 41–42, 69–70, 153–60.

49. Quoted in Anderson, *Education of Blacks in the South*, p. 6.

50. Anderson, *Education of Blacks in the South*, p. 10.

51. Heather Andrea Williams, "'Clothing Themselves in Intelligence': The Freedpeople, Schooling, and Northern Teachers, 1861–1871," *Journal of African American History* 87 (2002): 375, quoting John Alvord, Inspector's Report, *First Semi-Annual Report on Schools and Finances*, 1 Jan. 1866, p. 10.

52. Michael Goldhaber, "A Mission Unfulfilled: Freedmen's Education in North Carolina, 1865–1870," *Journal of Negro History* 77, no. 4 (1992): 206.

53. Booker T. Washington, *Up from Slavery: An Autobiography* (New York: Bantam, 1900), p. 56.

54. Horst, *Education for Manhood*, p. 129.

55. William Preston Vaughn, *Schools for All: The Blacks and Public Education in the South, 1865–1877* (Lexington: University of Kentucky Press, 1974), p. 42.

56. Stearns, *The Black Man of the South*, p. 67.

57. Stearns, *The Black Man of the South*, pp. 131–32; see also Charles Lee Smith, *The History of Education in North Carolina* (Government Printing Office, 1888), p. 157, http://docsouth.unc.edu/true/smith/smith.html#p157.

58. Myers, "The Education of the Alabama Freedmen During Presidential Reconstruction," p. 163.

59. Williams, "'Clothing Themselves in Intelligence,'" p. 375.

60. Williams, "'Clothing Themselves in Intelligence,'" p. 375.

61. Cornelius, *When I Can Read My Title Clear*, p. 143.

62. Sherer, *Subordination or Liberation?* p. 2.

63. Joe M. Richardson, "The Negro in Post Civil-War Tennessee: A Report by a Northern Missionary," *Journal of Negro Education* 34, no. 4 (1965): 420.

64. Jones, *Soldiers of Light and Love,* p. 59.

65. Jones, *Soldiers of Light and Love,* p. 63.

66. Williams, "'Clothing Themselves in Intelligence,'" pp. 377–78.

67. Williams, "'Clothing Themselves in Intelligence,'" p. 378.

68. Richardson, "The Freedmen's Bureau," p. 463.

69. See, e.g., Mabee, *Black Education in New York State,* p. 21; William E. Parrish, *A History of Missouri,* vol. 3: *1860–1875* (Columbia: University of Missouri Press, 1973), pp. 164–65 (the state superintendent of Missouri wrote in his 1869 annual report, "I have witnessed recitations in colored schools which were not inferior in enthusiasm, readiness and grasp in thought to any I ever saw in a white school, considering the time the pupils had studied").

70. See Anderson, *Education of Blacks in the South,* p. 26.

71. See Anderson, *Education of Blacks in the South,* p. 282.

72. Litwack, *Trouble in Mind,* p. 53.

73. Richardson, "The Freedmen's Bureau," p. 463.

74. Jones, *Soldiers of Light and Love,* p. 117.

75. Williams, *Self-Taught,* p. 153.

76. Williams, *Self-Taught,* pp. 160, 196.

77. See Adam Fairclough, *A Class of Their Own: Black Teachers in the Segregated South* (Cambridge: Harvard University Press, 2007), pp. 18, 43, 102.

78. See, e.g., Jones, *Soldiers of Light and Love,* p. 62.

79. Span, "'I Must Learn Now or Not at All,'" p. 200.

80. Henry S. Enck, "Black Self-Help in the Progressive Era: The 'Northern Campaigns' of Smaller Southern Black Industrial Schools, 1900–1915," *Journal of Negro History* 61, no. 1 (1976): 81.

81. Adam Fairclough, "'Being in the Field of Education and also Being a Negro . . . Seems . . . Tragic': Black Teachers in the Jim Crow South," *Journal of American History* 87, no. 1 (2000): 77.

82. Myers, "The Education of the Alabama Freedmen During Presidential Reconstruction," p. 164. Similar stories are described in Sherer, *Subordination or Liberation?* p. 132.

83. See Anderson, *Education of Blacks in the South,* p. 172.

84. See Anderson, *Education of Blacks in the South,* p. 184. See also Leloudis, *Schooling the New South,* pp. 226–27.

85. Bellamy, "The Education of Blacks in Missouri Prior to 1861," p. 157.

86. See Anderson, *Education of Blacks in the South,* p. 179. For more on the philanthropic activities of Julius Rosenwald, see J. Scott McCormick, "The Julius Rosenwald Fund," *Journal of Negro Education* 3, no. 4 (1934): 605–26.

87. Anderson, *Education of Blacks in the South,* p. 153.

88. Anderson, *Education of Blacks in the South,* p. 162.

89. Anderson, *Education of Blacks in the South,* p. 165.

90. Anderson, *Education of Blacks in the South,* p. 165.

91. I am speaking, of course, *only* of the "acting white" sentiment in the world of education. In earlier times, blacks sometimes thought of behavior in the business world or elsewhere as "white." In 1957, E. Franklin Frazier wrote: "When a Negro is competent and insists upon first-rate work it appears to this class that he is trying to be a white man, or that he is insisting that Negroes measure up to white standards. This is especially true where the approval of whites is taken as a mark of competence and first-rate performance." E. Franklin Frazier, *Black Bourgeoisie* (New York: Free Press, 1957), p. 217. Even earlier, people had litigated over whether they should be treated as "black" for purposes of Jim Crow laws, and accordingly claimed that they had "acted white"; Ariela J. Gross, "Litigating Whiteness: Trials of Racial Determination in the Nineteenth-Century South," *Yale Law Journal* 108 (1998): 135, 156–76.

Chapter 4. What Were Black Schools Like?

Epigraphs: Tracey Berry, "Inherently Unequal," *Missouri Resources* 17, no. 4 (2000–2001), www.dnr.mo.gov/magazine/2000-01-winter.pdf; National Public Radio, *All Things Considered,* "Teachers Weigh the Impact of *Brown* Decision," 13 Dec. 2003, www.npr.org/templates/story/story.php?storyId=1547570.

1. For good reviews of the literature on segregated schools, see Vanessa Siddle Walker, "Valued Segregated Schools for African American Children in the South, 1935–1969: A Review of Common Themes and Characteristics," *Review of Educational Research* 70, no. 3 (2000): 253–85, and Vanessa Siddle Walker, "African American Teaching in the South, 1940–1960," *American Educational Research Journal* 38, no. 4 (2001): 751–79.

2. The literature describing such deprivation is enormous. For just a few examples, see Carter Julian Savage, "Cultural Capital and African American Agency: The Economic Struggle for Effective Education for African Americans in Franklin, Tennessee, 1890–1967," *Journal of African American History* 87 (2002): 211–12; William M. Berg and David L. Colton, "Brown and the Distribution of School Resources," *New Directions for Testing and Measurement: Impact of Desegregation* 14 (June 1982): 83–97; Fairclough, *Teaching Equality,* p. 58; David Tyack and Larry Cuban, *Tinkering Toward Utopia: A Century of Public School Reform* (Cambridge: Harvard University Press, 1995), pp. 22–24.

3. Scott Henry, "Segregated, Again: Brown v. Board of Education Hasn't Delivered Integrated Schools, but That Doesn't Mean It Failed," *Creative Loafing,* 13 May 2004, http://atlanta.creativeloafing.com/gyrobase/Content?imageIndex=3&oid=oid %3A15606.

4. Parrish, *A History of Missouri,* p. 163.

5. University of North Carolina Television, Black Issues Forum, *50 Years After Brown,* Episode 1924 (2003–4), www.unctv.org/bif/transcripts/2003/transcript1924 .html.

6. Foster, *Black Teachers on Teaching,* pp. 57, 87, 94.

7. Jim Auchmutey and Gracie Bonds Staples, "Amid the Battle, a School Flourished," *Atlanta Journal-Constitution*, 16 May 2004.

8. Winfred E. Pitts, *A Victory of Sorts: Desegregation in a Southern Community* (Lanham, Md.: University Press of America, 2003), p. 34.

9. Smith, *Educating the Masses*, p. 10.

10. Monique Angle, "Dennis Gardner," *Hampton Daily Press*, 2 May 2004.

11. I heard this directly from a black woman who lived in such a boarding house in Fort Smith for her tenth-grade year, in 1953, and then moved back to Fayetteville, Arkansas (which, incidentally, is where I was born), to join the first integrated high school class in the entire South.

12. Vanessa Siddle Walker, *Their Highest Potential: An African American School Community in the Segregated South* (Chapel Hill: University of North Carolina Press, 1996), p. 219.

13. Jonathan Tilove, "In the Black Schools of America Before Brown, Keys to Renewing Success," Newhouse News Service, 28 Apr. 2004.

14. Irwin Katz, "Review of Evidence Relating to Effects of Desegregation on the Intellectual Performance of Negroes," *American Psychologist* 19, no. 6 (1964): 387.

15. See, e.g., Jerome E. Morris, "A 'Communally Bonded' School for African American Students, Families, and a Community," *Phi Delta Kappan* 84, no. 3 (2002): 230; Vivian Gunn Morris and David L. Morris, *Creating Caring and Nurturing Educational Environments for African-American Children* (Westport, Conn.: Bergin and Garvey, 2000), pp. 63–65, 91–115; George W. Noblit and Van O. Dempsey, *The Social Construction of Virtue: The Moral Life of Schools* (Albany: State University of New York Press, 1996), pp. 130–33; Anna Victoria Wilson and William E. Segall, *Oh, Do I Remember! Experiences of Teachers During the Desegregation of Austin's Schools, 1964–1971* (Albany: State University of New York Press, 2001), pp. 101–3; Thomas W. Collins, "From Courtrooms to Classrooms: Managing School Desegregation in a Deep South High School," in *Desegregated Schools: Appraisals of an American Experiment*, ed. Ray C. Rist (New York: Academic, 1979), pp. 98–99; Faustine Childress Jones, *A Traditional Model of Educational Excellence: Dunbar High School of Little Rock, Arkansas* (Washington, D.C.: Howard University Press, 1981), pp. 71–72; Afro-American Genealogy and History Society, *The Way We Were: Oral Histories of Four Former All-Black Public Schools in Two North Carolina Counties* (self-published, 1991); Maike Philipsen, *Values-Spoken and Values-Lived: Race and the Cultural Consequences of a School Closing* (Cresskill, N.J.: Hampton, 1999), pp. 49–53.

16. Frederick A. Rodgers, *The Black High School and Its Community* (Lexington, Mass.: Lexington, 1975), p. 46; see also Alvis Adair, *Desegregation: The Illusion of Black Progress* (Lanham, Md.: University Press of America, 1984), pp. 108–11.

17. Savage, "Cultural Capital and African American Agency," p. 230.

18. Peggy B. Gill, "Community, Commitment, and African American Education: The Jackson School of Smith County, Texas, 1925–1954," *Journal of African American History* 87 (2002): 261–62.

19. Maike Philipsen, "Values-Spoken and Values-Lived: Female African Americans'

Educational Experiences in Rural North Carolina," *Journal of Negro Education* 62, no. 4 (1993): 422.

20. Vivian Gunn Morris and David L. Morris, *The Price They Paid: Desegregation in an African American Community* (New York: Teachers College Press, 2002), p. 7.

21. See, e.g., Audrey Schwitzerlette, "Stratton Legacy One of Strong Educators, Good Students," *Register-Herald,* 16 May 2004, www.wwhsalumni.org/stratton.html; Afro-American Genealogy and History Society, *The Way We Were.*

22. Philipsen, "Values-Spoken and Values-Lived," p. 422.

23. Bakari McClendon, "Graduates Remember Dunbar; Old All-Black School Brings Back Memories," *Florida Times-Union,* 26 July 2000.

24. Jennifer Booth Reed, "Dunbar High Still Home for Alumni," *The News-Press,* 6 Oct. 2001. See also Patricia A. Edwards, "Before and After School Desegregation: African American Parents' Involvement in Schools," in *Beyond Desegregation: The Politics of Quality in African American Schooling,* ed. Mwalimu J. Shujaa (Thousand Oaks, Calif.: Corwin, 1996), p. 147.

25. Foster, *Black Teachers on Teaching,* p. 112.

26. See, e.g., Afro-American Genealogy and History Society, *The Way We Were* (interview with Annye M. Wright, who recalls being the May Queen for Dudley High School in Greensboro, North Carolina).

27. Barbara Shircliffe, *The Best of That World: Historically Black High Schools and the Crisis of Desegregation in a Southern Metropolis* (Cresskill, N.J.: Hampton, 2006), p. 166.

28. Dana Banker, "History Classes; Dillard Grads Reuniting in Tribute to Broward's First Black High School," *Fort Lauderdale Sun-Sentinel,* 30 June 1995.

29. To be clear, this is not intended as any criticism of today's teachers, most of whom care deeply about their childrens' academic success as well.

30. In all of the following books, articles, and interviews, black people who experienced segregated schooling describe the nurturing and caring environment that their teachers provided. Fairclough, *A Class of Their Own,* pp. 287–88; Afro-American Genealogy and History Society, *The Way We Were;* Unified Committee for Afro-American Contributions, *In Relentless Pursuit of an Education: African American Stories from a Century of Segregation, 1865–1967* (Lexington Park, Md.: Unified Committee for Afro-American Contributions, 2006), www.ucaonline.org, pp. 77, 92–93; Morris and Morris, *Creating Caring and Nurturing Educational Environments,* pp. 45–60; Philipsen, *Values-Spoken and Values-Lived,* pp. 56–60; Walker, *Their Highest Potential,* pp. 148–58; Noblit and Dempsey, *The Social Construction of Virtue,* pp. 128–33, 186–90; Wilson and Segall, *Oh, Do I Remember!* pp. 101–3; David S. Cecelski, *Along Freedom Road: Hyde County, North Carolina, and the Fate of Black Schools in the South* (Chapel Hill: University of North Carolina Press, 1994), pp. 34–35; Charlayne Hunter-Gault, *In My Place* (New York: Vintage, 1992), pp. 53–54; Jacqueline Scherer and Edward J. Slawski, "Color, Class, and Social Control in an Urban Desegregated School," in *Desegregated Schools: Appraisals of an American Experiment,* ed. Ray C. Rist (New York: Academic, 1979), pp. 150–51; Morgan Freeman, "Home," in *America Behind*

the Color Line, ed. Henry Louis Gates, Jr. (New York: Warner, 2004), p. 141; Jesse L. Jackson, "Restitution, Reinvestment," in *America Behind the Color Line,* ed. Henry Louis Gates, Jr. (New York: Warner, 2004), pp. 352–53; Brenda Joyce Burrell, "Bear Witness: African American Teachers' Perspectives of Their Teaching Practices in Segregated and Desegregated Schools" (Ph.D. diss., University of Texas at Austin, 2005); Jake Jacobs, "Progression out of Depression; Former Students During '30s Segregation Recall Schools Fondly," *Macon Telegraph,* 26 Feb. 2007; "Dunbar Remembered as 'Extension of Home' Half Century After Integration Closed School," *Tecumseh Countywide News,* 1 Feb. 2007; Denise Smith Amos, "Segregated Black Students 'Looked Adversity in the Eye,'" *Cincinnati Enquirer,* 13 Jan. 2007; Christina M. Woods, "All-Black Dunbar School Plans Reunion," *Wichita Eagle,* July 2006; Kenneth W. Livingston, "Clark Helped Change the Face of America," *Los Angeles Times,* 6 May 2005; Phuong Ly, "New Chapter for an Emblem of Exclusion; As Black School Reopens as Museum, Students Recall Segregation Era," *Washington Post,* 17 Feb. 2005; Ruth Ann Gaines, "Home-Styled Pride," *Des Moines Register,* 19 Feb. 2005; Angela Dawson, "'Coach Carter' Makes the Grade with Jackson," *Chicago Sun-Times,* 21 Jan. 2005; Jennifer Torres, "At the Head of the Class," *Florida Today,* 9 Aug. 2004; Connie Nogas, "Brown Verdict at 50; Tier Residents Recall Time Before, After Segregation," *Press and Sun-Bulletin (Binghamton, N.Y.),* 17 May 2004; Sam Scott, "Painful Process with Mixed Results," *Wilmington (N.C.) Star News,* 17 May 2004; Thomas C. Tobin and Denise Watson Batts, "Reading, Writing, Race: A Special Report on the Achievement Gap," *St. Petersburg Times,* 17 May 2004; Robin Farmer, "A Ruling on Race That Is Still Reverberating," *Richmond Times Dispatch,* 17 May 2004; Sara Neufeld, "Recovering a 'Positive Culture,'" *Baltimore Sun,* 16 May 2004; Kevin McKenzie, "Separate, Unequal—Schools Emerge Worlds Apart, Seeking an Ideal," *Memphis Commercial Appeal,* 16 May 2004; Sandra Yin, "Integration's Legacy; Community Leaders Believe the Brown v. Board Decision Had Mixed Results," *Newport News (Va.) Daily Press,* 16 May 2004; Jerry Barca, "Still Learning Lessons in Racial Equality," *East Brunswick (N.J.) Home News Tribune,* 16 May 2004; Joseph A. Slash, "Schools Strengthened the Black Community," *Indianapolis Star,* 16 May 2004; Jay Hamburg, "Ruling that Integrated Schools Brought Vital Gains, Some Loss," *The Tennessean,* 16 May 2004; Gregory Kane, "High-Quality Teachers Transcended Brown Case," *Baltimore Sun,* 8 May 2004; Tamara Dietrich, "It Kind of Made Me Blossom," *Newport News Daily Press,* 2 May 2004; Meredith Moss, "Black Women's Accomplishments Noted at Luncheon," *Dayton Daily News,* 11 Apr. 2004; Sean Carter, "Luncheon Celebrates History," *Hilltop Times,* 4 Mar. 2004; Monique Fields, "Historic Hopes Still Aren't Fully Realized, Professor Says," *St. Petersburg Times,* 18 Feb. 2004; Gary R. Kremer, "'Just Like the Garden of Eden': African-American Community Life in Kansas City's Leeds," *Missouri Historical Review* 98, no. 2 (2003): 135; Jack Hicks, "Lincoln-Grant Still a Fond Memory," *Cincinnati Enquirer,* 28 Oct. 2003; Chris Richburg, "The Legacy of Elizabeth Heights Lives On," *Rock Hill (S.C.) Herald,* 24 Feb. 2003; Talibah Chikwendu, "Public School Integration: Did We Lose?" *Baltimore Afro-American,* 14 Feb. 2003; Tim Simmons, "A Sense of Estrangement," *Raleigh (N.C.)*

News and Observer, 29 Sept. 2002; Mike Adams, "Finding the Limits of Integration; In Topeka, Questions About Racial Progress," *Baltimore Sun,* 6 Jan. 2002; Texas Council for the Humanities, Interview with William C. Akins, 2001, www.humanities texas.org/programs/past/crossover/hustontillotson/akins.php; Texas Council for the Humanities, Interview with Ada M. Hardin, 2001, www.humanitiestexas.org/programs /past/crossover/houston/hardin.php; University of North Carolina, Oral History Interview with Fran Jackson, 23 Mar. 2001, Interview K-0208, Southern Oral History Program Collection (no. 4007), http://docsouth.unc.edu/sohp/K-0208/K-0208 .xml; Kentucky Historical Society, Civil Rights Movement in Kentucky, Interview with Howard Bailey, 13 Dec. 2000; Kentucky Historical Society, Civil Rights Movement in Kentucky, Interview with George Esters, 6 June 2000; Kentucky Historical Society, Civil Rights Movement in Kentucky, Interview with Eleanor Jordan, 3 Feb. 1999; Berry, "Inherently Unequal"; Carlos Vega, "Telling It Like It Was," *Charleston Gazette,* 18 Feb. 2000; Theotis Robinson, Jr., "School Desegregation Was Weighty Issue," *Knoxville News-Sentinel,* 6 Dec. 1999; Will Molineux, "Carver Students Took Home Lessons for Life," *Newport News Daily Press,* 21 Feb. 1999; Stephanie Barrett, "Teachers Did More . . . They Taught the Whole Person," *Newport News Daily Press,* 21 Feb. 1999; Jonathan Harris, "Reunion: Alumni of Old School for Negroes to Gather," *Atlanta Journal-Constitution,* 12 Nov. 1998; Waveney Ann Moore, "Educating by Segregating," *St. Petersburg Times,* 13 Sept. 1998; Yvette Kimm, "Black Educators Recall Time Before Integration," *Sarasota Herald-Tribune,* 20 Aug. 1998; Dale Fuchs, "'Miss McCoy' Gave Pupils Hope in Troubled Times," *Palm Beach Post,* 4 Feb. 1998; Stan Swofford, "Separate but Equal," *Greensboro (N.C.) News and Record,* 25 May 1997; University of Southern Mississippi, Center for Oral History and Cultural Heritage, Interview with Reuben Anderson, 1997, www.lib.usm.edu/~spcol /crda/oh/anderson.htm; Dana Banker, "History Classes"; Joseph H. Brown, "Busing Has Run Out of Gas," *Tampa Tribune,* 22 Jan. 1995; Gregory P. Kane, "Segregated Schools Not Such a Bad Thing," *Buffalo News,* 29 May 1994; Suzanne Jeffries, "Reid Revisited," *Charlotte Observer,* 2 Apr. 1995; Virginia Black History Archives, Interview with James E. Washington, 1992, www.library.vcu.edu/jbc/speccoll/vbha /school/washj.html; Stephen Hegarty, "One Teacher Molds Generations," *St. Petersburg Times,* 24 Feb. 1991; James Scudder, "Families Gave These Two an Educational Head Start," *Arkansas Democrat-Gazette,* 19 Mar. 1989.

31. Foster, *Black Teachers on Teaching,* p. 102.

32. Auchmutey and Bonds Staples, "Amid the Battle, a School Flourished."

33. Vega, "Telling It Like It Was.

34. Phil Walzer and Matthew Bowers, "The Downside of Desegregation," *Virginian-Pilot,* 18 Apr. 2004.

35. Morris and Morris, *The Price They Paid,* p. 68.

36. Morris and Morris, *The Price They Paid,* p. 74.

37. Shircliffe, *The Best of That World,* p. 55. Lenwood Davis recounts that the black high school teachers were "strict disciplinarians," and that they "cared for their students and had a genuine interest in their educational, moral, and social well-being."

"In many instances," said one former student, "I remember teachers taking money out of their own pockets to buy construction paper and other school supplies that they did not have. They did what was necessary to make sure that the students would learn." Lenwood G. Davis, *A History of Beaufort/Queen Street High School, 1928–1968* (Kingston, N.Y.: Tri State Services, 1996), pp. 113–26.

38. See, e.g., Davis, *A History of Beaufort/Queen Street High School,* pp. 118–27.

39. Alice McCullough-Garrett, "Reclaiming the African American Vision for Teaching: Toward an Educational Conversation," *Journal of Negro Education* 62, no. 4 (1993), p. 438.

40. Booth Reed, "Dunbar High Still Home for Alumni."

41. Jeff Zeigler, "Trailblazers," *Virginian-Pilot,* 25 Feb. 1996.

42. Paul Riede, "Dean Mines His Past for Youths' Future," *Syracuse (N.Y.) Post-Standard,* 20 Jan. 1992.

43. Kim McCoy Vann, "Alumni Reunite to Remember; SAIL Stages Tribute to Former School," *Tallahassee Democrat,* 1 Feb. 2005; see also Chalmers Archer, Jr., *Growing Up Black in Rural Mississippi* (New York: Walker, 1992), pp. 114–15.

44. Joan I. Duffy, "'Separate But Equal' Had a Powerful Message that Resounds Even Today," *Memphis Commercial Appeal,* 21 Sept. 1997.

45. Pat Mitchell, "A Flawed Effort to Attain Equality," *Tampa Tribune,* 16 May 2004.

46. Angle, "Dennis Gardner."

47. Unified Committee for Afro-American Contributions, *In Relentless Pursuit,* p. 77.

48. See *Brown v. Board of Education,* 347 U.S. 483, 494 and n.11 (1954).

49. As Roy Brooks notes, Clark's research actually showed that there was a "lesser percentage of out-group preference among southern children who attended segregated schools than among northern children who attended racially mixed schools. Thirty-seven percent of segregated children, compared to 28 percent of integrated children, preferred to play with the brown doll; 46 percent of the segregated children, compared to 30 percent of the integrated children, believed that the brown doll was nice; 49 percent of the segregated children, compared to 71 percent of the integrated children, said that the brown doll looked bad; and 40 percent of the segregated children, compared to 37 percent of the integrated children, felt that the brown doll had a nice color." Brooks, *Integration or Separation?* p. 13.

50. Benjamin J. Hodgkins and Robert G. Stakenas, "A Study of Self-Concepts of Negro and White Youth in Segregated Environments," *Journal of Negro Education* 38, no. 4 (1969): 370–77; James E. Greene, Sr., "A Comparison of the 'School Morale' of White and Negro Students in a Large Southeastern School System," *Journal of Negro Education* 31, no. 2 (1962): 132–38; Baughman and Dahlstrom, *Negro and White Children,* pp. 417, 445–47; Gloria J. Powell, *Black Monday's Children: A Study of the Effects of School Desegregation on Self-Concepts of Southern Children* (New York: Appleton-Century-Crofts, 1973), pp. 255–61.

51. Darrel W. Drury, "Black Self-Esteem and Desegregated Schools," *Sociology of Education* 53, no. 2 (1980): 88–103.

52. Afro-American Genealogy and History Society, *The Way We Were* (interview with Annye M. Wright, p. 9).

53. Interview with the author.

54. Walker, *Their Highest Potential.*

55. Foster, *Black Teachers on Teaching*, p. 55.

56. Van Dempsey and George Noblit, "Cultural Ignorance and School Desegregation: A Community Narrative," in *Beyond Desegregation: The Politics of Quality in African American Schooling*, ed. Mwalimu J. Shujaa (Thousand Oaks, Calif.: Corwin, 1996), p. 123.

57. George W. Noblit, *Particularities: Collected Essays on Ethnography and Education* (New York: Peter Lang, 1999), p. 189.

58. Noblit and Dempsey, *The Social Construction of Virtue*, pp. 132–33.

59. Jerome E. Morris, "A Pillar of Strength: An African American School's Communal Bonds with Families and Community Since *Brown*," *Urban Education* 33, no. 5 (1999): 595–96.

60. Elizabeth Wright, "The Greatest School Under the Sun," *Issues and Views*, Winter 1994, www.issues-views.com/index.php/sect/1000/article/1017.

61. Richburg, "The Legacy of Elizabeth Heights Lives On."

62. Rodgers, *The Black High School*, pp. 63–64.

63. Marilyn Marks, "A Lifetime of Going Against the Flow: Lawyer Fought Segregation," *Miami Herald*, 13 Aug. 1995.

64. See, e.g., Drago, *Initiative, Paternalism, and Race Relations*, pp. 119–20.

65. See Bullock, *The History of Negro Education in the South*, pp. 74–85, for a discussion of Washington.

66. Washington, *Up from Slavery*, p. 56.

67. Washington, *Up from Slavery*, p. 86.

68. Fleming, "The Plight of Black Educators in Postwar Tennessee, 1865–1920," *Journal of Negro History* 64, no. 4 (1979): 357, quoting Tennessee, *Annual Report of the State Superintendent of Public Instruction for Tennessee for the Scholastic Year Ending June 30, 1901*, p. 34.

69. See generally Anderson, *Education of Blacks*, pp. 28–29.

70. Fanny Jackson-Coppin, *Reminiscences of School Life, and Hints on Teaching* (Philadelphia: L. J. Coppin, 1913), pp. 17–18, http://docsouth.unc.edu/jacksonc/jackson.html.

71. Jackson-Coppin, *Reminiscences of School Life*, pp. 19–20.

72. William J. Edwards, *Twenty-Five Years in the Black Belt* (Boston: Cornhill, 1918), p. 36.

73. See Anderson, *Education of Blacks in the South*, p. 142.

74. See Anderson, *Education of Blacks in the South*, pp. 198–99; Morris and Morris, *The Price They Paid*, p. 96.

75. See Anderson, *Education of Blacks in the South*, p. 132.

76. Foster, *Black Teachers on Teaching*, p. 13.

77. Litwack, *Trouble in Mind*, p. 84.

78. Quoted in Tilove, "In the Black Schools of America Before Brown." A former

student from West Virginia similarly recalls, "We read Shakespeare and studied the classics. I can still remember poems we had to memorize, . . . lines from 'Hamlet.'" Schwitzerlette, "Stratton Legacy."

79. Leloudis, *Schooling the New South*, p. 200.

80. See Anderson, *Education of Blacks in the South*, p. 142.

81. See Anderson, *Education of Blacks in the South*, p. 198.

82. See Anderson, *Education of Blacks in the South*, p. 85.

83. See Anderson, *Education of Blacks in the South*, p. 97.

84. See Anderson, *Education of Blacks in the South*, p. 223 (emphasis added).

85. See, e.g., Davis, *A History of Beaufort/Queen Street High School*, pp. 32–36; Foster, *Black Teachers on Teaching*, p. 38; Morris and Morris, *The Price They Paid*, p. 51.

86. Clifton L. Taulbert, *When We Were Colored* (New York: Penguin, 1989), p. 35.

87. Jill Nelson, "Retired Educators Recall 50 Years of Change in D.C. Schools," *Washington Post*, 22 Apr. 1989.

88. For examples from Tennessee, Kentucky, Mississippi, Florida, Delaware, and Louisiana, see Sonya Ramsey, "'We Will Be Ready Whenever They Are': African American Teachers' Responses to the Brown Decision and Public School Integration in Nashville, Tennessee, 1954–1966," *Journal of African American History* 90 (2005): 29; Winson Hudson and Constance Curry, *Mississippi Harmony: Memoirs of a Freedom Fighter* (New York: Palgrave Macmillan, 2002), p. 48; David R. Goldfield, *Black, White, and Southern: Race Relations and Southern Culture, 1940 to the Present* (Baton Rouge: Louisiana State University Press, 1990), p. 256; University of South Florida, Olive B. McLin Community History Project, www.nelson.usf.edu/mclin/photo .1.9.html#schools; Kentucky Historical Society, Interview with George Esters; Raymond Wolters, *The Burden of Brown: Thirty Years of School Desegregation* (Knoxville: University of Tennessee Press, 1984), p. 202. There were exceptions, of course. See Charles C. Bolton, "Mississippi's School Equalization Program, 1945–1954: 'A Last Gasp to Try to Maintain a Segregated Educational System,'" *Journal of Southern History* 66, no. 4 (2000): 781–814.

89. Carolyn Carter Modlin, "The Desegregation of Southampton County, Virginia, Schools, 1954–1970" (Ph.D. diss., Virginia Polytechnic Institute and State University, 1998, http://scholar.lib.vt.edu/theses/available/etd-121098-154942/ unrestricted/DISSERTATION.PDF), p. 55.

90. Michael Berryhill, "What's Wrong with Wheatley?" *Houston Press*, 17 Apr. 1997.

91. Anthony J. Badger, "The White Reaction to *Brown*: Arkansas, the Southern Manifesto, and Massive Resistance," in *Understanding the Little Rock Crisis: An Exercise in Remembrance and Reconciliation*, ed. Elizabeth Jacoway and C. Fred Williams (Fayetteville: University of Arkansas Press, 1999), pp. 86–87.

92. Shircliffe, *The Best of That World*, p. 88.

93. Harry S. Ashmore, *The Negro and the Schools* (Chapel Hill: University of North Carolina Press, 1954), pp. 61–63.

94. Ashmore, *The Negro and the Schools*, p. 159; Rodgers, *The Black High School*, p. 32. Mississippi was the outlier: black teachers there earned only 51 percent as much as whites in 1952, far lower than any other Southern state.

95. Marshall S. Smith, "Equality of Educational Opportunity: The Basic Findings Reconsidered," in *On Equality of Educational Opportunity,* ed. Frederick Mosteller and Daniel P. Moynihan (New York: Vintage, 1972), p. 313.

96. David Card and Alan B. Krueger, "School Quality and Black-White Relative Earnings: A Direct Assessment," *Quarterly Journal of Economics* 107, no. 1 (1992): 151–200.

97. Berryhill, "What's Wrong with Wheatley?"

Chapter 5. The Closing of Black Schools

Epigraphs: Collins, "From Courtrooms to Classrooms," pp. 96–97; Auchmutey and Bonds Staples, "Amid the Battle, a School Flourished"; Tilove, "In the Black Schools of America Before Brown"; Morris and Morris, *Creating Caring and Nurturing Educational Environments,* p. 131; Rodgers, *The Black High School,* p. 73.

1. *Brown v. Board of Education,* 349 U.S. 294 (1955).

2. Gerald Rosenberg, *The Hollow Hope: Can Courts Bring About Social Change?* (Chicago: University of Chicago Press, 1991), p. 52; see also *Civil Rights '63,* Report of the United States Commission on Civil Rights, p. 65, www.law.umaryland.edu /marshall/usccr/documents/cr11963a.pdf; Davison M. Douglas, *Reading, Writing, and Race: The Desegregation of the Charlotte Schools* (Chapel Hill: University of North Carolina Press, 1995), p. 26.

3. See Rosenberg, *Hollow Hope,* pp. 53–54, 97–100.

4. Harrell R. Rodgers, Jr., and Charles S. Bullock III, "School Desegregation: A Policy Analysis," *Journal of Black Studies* 2, no. 4 (1972): 416–17.

5. *Green v. County School Board,* 391 U.S. 430, 438, 441 (1968).

6. Steven G. Rivkin, "Residential Segregation and School Integration," *Sociology of Education* 67, no. 4 (1994): 284.

7. Rivkin, "Residential Segregation and School Integration," p. 281.

8. Rosenberg, *Hollow Hope,* p. 50.

9. Coleman, *Equality and Achievement in Education,* pp. 166–67. The way that sociologists treated James Coleman brings to mind the Galileo incident, which was also caused by "rivalry, jealousy, and vindictiveness from other scientists and philosophers"; Robert Nisbet, *Prejudices: A Philosophical Dictionary* (Cambridge: Harvard University Press, 1982), pp. 190–96.

10. Rivkin, "Residential Segregation and School Integration," pp. 286–88.

11. By another measure, however—the Gini index—the amount of segregation in Atlanta *decreased* over the same time period; Rivkin, "Residential Segregation and School Integration," p. 289. How is this possible? The Gini index looks at how closely the typical school comes to having a representative number of whites and blacks, and in 1988, the few white students still in Atlanta were not as concentrated in a "white" school. This goes to show how much depends on your definition of "segregation."

12. Erica Frankenberg, *The Segregation of American Teachers* (Cambridge: Civil Rights Project at Harvard University, 2006), p. 15, www.civilrightsproject.ucla.edu/ research/deseg/segregation_american_teachers12-06.pdf.

13. Sean P. Corcoran and William N. Evans, "The Role of Inequality in Teacher Quality," in *Steady Gains and Stalled Progress: Inequality and the Black-White Test Score Gap,* ed. Katherine Magnuson and Jane Waldfogel (New York: Russell Sage Foundation, 2008), pp. 212–49.

14. Virginia Causey, "Mostly Separate and Still Not Equal: A History of Desegregation in Muscogee County Schools," *Columbus Ledger-Enquirer,* 23 June 2002.

15. In the few instances when judges or school boards did attempt to assign white students to formerly black schools, white students and their parents typically rebelled. For a brief period in 1970 in Tampa, Florida, a judge attempted to assign white children to black schools. But "on the first day of classes, only one of the anticipated 280 White students attended Blake." Most of the whites eventually moved or changed schools by some hook or crook. Shircliffe, *The Best of That World,* pp. 127–28.

16. *Green v. County School Board,* 391 U.S. 430, 437–38 (1968); *Swann v. Charlotte-Mecklenburg Board of Education,* 402 U.S. 1 (1971).

17. Shircliffe, *The Best of That World,* p. 70.

18. See *Brown v. Board of Education,* 671 F. Supp. 1290, 1299 (D. Kan. 1987).

19. Rodney Bowers, "Built on a Strong Foundation," *Arkansas Democrat-Gazette,* 2 Feb. 2003.

20. Mac Bentley, "Proud Pioneers; Black Schools Thrived in '50s," *Daily Oklahoman,* 21 July 2002; Timothy M. Phelps, "A View from the West Side," *Newsday,* 15 May 1994; Foster, *Black Teachers on Teaching,* p. xxxvii.

21. Paula F. Kelly, "One Dream, Many Lives," *Wilmington (Del.) News Journal,* 12 Jan. 2007.

22. Adair, *Desegregation,* pp. 93–108.

23. Many specific examples are discussed throughout this chapter. Other examples include:

- Duval County, Florida: Tonyaa Weathersbee, "So Much Progress Through Brown, but Still So Far to Go," *Florida Times-Union,* 17 May 2004.
- Martin County, Florida: Rani Gupta, "Transition Difficult in Martin Schools," *Palm Beach Post,* 16 May 2004, www.palmbeachpost.com/news/content/news/special_reports/brown_v_board/m14a_mcbrown_0516.html.
- Lafayette, Louisiana: Sebreana Domingue, "Deseg Could End Today in Lafayette," *Opelousas (La.) Daily World,* 22 Dec. 2004.
- Conway, Arkansas: Jay Meisel, "Ex-Teacher, Others Keep Alive Memories of Segregated School," *Arkansas Democrat-Gazette,* 5 July 1999.
- Virginia: Barrett, "Teachers Did More . . . They Taught the Whole Person"; Foster, *Black Teachers on Teaching,* p. 56.
- North Carolina: Carrie Smith Johnson Washington, "A Study of Former Negro High School Students, Teachers, and Administrators in the Piedmont Area of North Carolina" (Ph.D. diss., East Tennessee State University, 2002), p. 73, http://etd-submit.etsu.edu/etd/theses/available/etd-0531102-163233/unrestricted /Washington062302.pdf.

- West Virginia: Rick McCann, "Herd Greats Tee It Up," *Huntington (W.Va.) Herald-Dispatch,* 3 June 2003; Vega, "Telling It Like It Was."
- Lafayette, Indiana: Michelle Grovak, "Lafayette Black Schools Helped Shape Generation," *Lafayette (Ind.) Journal and Courier,* 3 Feb. 1999.
- Kentucky: Denise Smith Amos, "Segregated Black Students 'Looked Adversity in the Eye,'" *Cincinnati Enquirer,* 13 Jan. 2007; Linda B. Blackford, "Fayette schools Eye Race-Based Admissions Case," *Lexington Herald Leader,* 6 Dec. 2006.

24. Carl L. Bankston III and Stephen J. Caldas, *A Troubled Dream: The Promise and Failure of School Desegregation in Louisiana* (Nashville, Tenn.: Vanderbilt University Press, 2002), pp. 138–39.

25. Ronald Roach, "A Rich, but Disappearing Legacy: Remembering Black Boarding Schools; A Tradition Obscured by Desegregation's Impact," *Black Issues in Higher Education,* 14 Aug. 2003.

26. McCullough-Garrett, "Reclaiming the African American Vision for Teaching," p. 438.

27. Henry, "Segregated, Again."

28. Foster, *Black Teachers on Teaching,* pp. 57–58.

29. Interview with the author.

30. Pitts, *A Victory of Sorts.*

31. Pitts, *A Victory of Sorts,* p. xi.

32. Pitts, *A Victory of Sorts,* p. ix.

33. Pitts, *A Victory of Sorts,* p. xviii.

34. Pitts, *A Victory of Sorts,* p. xviii.

35. Pitts, *A Victory of Sorts,* p. 130.

36. Pitts, *A Victory of Sorts,* p. xix.

37. Pitts, *A Victory of Sorts,* p. xix.

38. Pitts, *A Victory of Sorts,* p. xix.

39. Pitts, *A Victory of Sorts,* p. 170.

40. Pitts, *A Victory of Sorts,* p. 171.

41. Pitts, *A Victory of Sorts,* p. xx.

42. Pitts, *A Victory of Sorts,* p. 165.

43. Pitts, *A Victory of Sorts,* p. 175.

44. Pitts, *A Victory of Sorts,* p. 175.

45. Pitts, *A Victory of Sorts,* p. 180.

46. Pitts, *A Victory of Sorts,* p. 180.

47. Pitts, *A Victory of Sorts,* p. 173.

48. Pitts, *A Victory of Sorts,* p. 177.

49. Pitts, *A Victory of Sorts,* p. 177.

50. See Morris and Morris, *Creating Caring and Nurturing Educational Environments,* p. 169; Barbara Shircliffe, "'We Got the Best of That World': A Case for the Study of Nostalgia in the Oral History of School Segregation," *Oral History Review*

2, no. 28 (2001): 59; Donald O. Leake and Christine J. Faltz, "Do We Need to Desegregate All of Our Black Schools?" *Educational Policy* 7, no. 3 (1993): 370–87.

51. Foster, *Black Teachers on Teaching,* p. 116.

52. Rodgers, *The Black High School,* p. 48.

53. Rodgers, *The Black High School,* p. 48.

54. Rodgers, *The Black High School,* pp. 48–49.

55. Brent Spodek, "Community Mulls Effects of Integration on Schools," *Chapel Hill Herald,* 11 Oct. 1998.

56. Lee V. Fowler, "School Integration: A Case Study of the 1971–1972 School Year at Indian River High School" (Ph.D. diss., Virginia Polytechnic Institute and State University, 1997), p. 73.

57. Interview with the author, 24 Aug. 2006.

58. Auchmutey and Bonds Staples, "Amid the Battle, a School Flourished."

59. Adair, *Desegregation,* p. 100.

60. McCullough-Garrett, "Reclaiming the African American Vision for Teaching," p. 433.

61. Berryhill, "What's Wrong with Wheatley?"

62. National Public Radio, *All Things Considered,* "Birmingham's A. H. Parker High School and Its Role in the Civil Rights Movement," 4 May 2004.

63. Nelson, "Retired Educators Recall 50 Years of Change."

64. Burrell, *Bear Witness,* p. 94.

65. See, e.g., Washington, "A Study of Former Negro High School Students," p. 74.

66. Rodgers, *The Black High School,* pp. 46–48.

67. Rodgers, *The Black High School,* p. 47.

68. Rodgers, *The Black High School,* p. 47.

69. Rodgers, *The Black High School,* p. 47. See also Gupta, "Transition Difficult in Martin Schools."

70. Powell, *Black Monday's Children,* p. 75.

71. Morris and Morris, *The Price They Paid,* pp. 11, 57.

72. Morris and Morris, *The Price They Paid,* p. 72.

73. See Fairclough, *A Class of Their Own,* p. 397.

74. Harrell R. Rodgers, Jr., and Charles S. Bullock, III, *Law and Social Change: Civil Rights Laws and Their Consequences* (New York: McGraw-Hill, 1972), p. 94.

75. University of North Carolina, Oral History Interview with Fran Jackson.

76. Afro-American Genealogy and History Society, *The Way We Were* (interview with Stanley Harley).

77. Adair, *Desegregation,* pp. 93–94. See also Lanita Withers, "Black Piedmont High School Alumni Hope to Reclaim Its Legacy," *Associated Press,* 29 Sept. 2004.

78. Adair, *Desegregation,* p. 107, quoting "Racial Tensions and Fears Cloud Integration at Louisiana School," *Washington Post,* 27 Sept. 1970.

79. Schwitzerlette, "Stratton Legacy." The same was true across all of West Virginia; John Raby, "Sports Memorabilia from Former Black Schools Tough to Find," *Associated Press,* 30 July 2005.

80. Virginia Causey, "Color Lines: A History of Desegregation in Muscogee County Schools," *Columbus Ledger-Enquirer,* 23 June 2002. For another example from Florida, see DeMorris A. Lee, "Forever United by Segregation," *St. Petersburg Times,* 25 May 2008.

81. Lee, "Forever United by Segregation."

82. Florence Hamlish Levinsohn and Benjamin Drake Wright, eds., *School Desegregation: Shadow and Substance* (Chicago: University of Chicago Press, 1976), p. 188.

83. Pamela Grundy, "The Way We Live Now: 9–15–02: Segregation Revisited," *New York Times Magazine,* 15 Sept. 2002.

84. You can see more photos of Second Ward at www.cmstory.org/aaa2/places /brook_oo6.htm#. Another good Web site devoted to the history of Second Ward is www.unctv.org/acoloredschool/wwilike.html. The Second Ward High School National Alumni Foundation is here: www.charlottecultureguide.com/organization .php?id=16.

85. University of North Carolina at Chapel Hill, Southern Oral History Program, Race and Desegregation: West Charlotte High School (Interview Collage 2), formerly at http://sohp.org/research/lfac/lfac_31b.html.

86. WFAE, "Charlotte Talks," 15 Feb. 1999, part two, formerly at http://sohp.org /research/lfac/lfac_31b.html (around 5:12 of the sound file).

87. Morris and Morris, *Creating Caring and Nurturing Educational Environments,* p. 147.

88. Morris and Morris, *Caring and Nurturing Educational Environments,* p. 151.

89. Morris and Morris, *Caring and Nurturing Educational Environments,* p. 153.

90. Morris and Morris, *The Price They Paid,* p. 79.

91. Tilove, "In the Black Schools of America Before Brown."

92. Savage, "Cultural Capital and African American Agency," p. 229.

93. Andrew Dunn, "School Integration Revisited," *Tallahassee Democrat,* 18 Feb. 2001.

94. Tilove, "In the Black Schools of America Before Brown."

95. Tilove, "In the Black Schools of America Before Brown."

96. Tilove, "In the Black Schools of America Before Brown."

97. Shircliffe, "We Got the Best of That World," p. 59.

98. Fowler, *School Integration,* p. 61.

99. Fowler, *School Integration,* p. 92.

100. Fowler, *School Integration,* p. 25.

101. Dempsey and Noblit, "Cultural Ignorance and School Desegregation," pp. 134–35.

102. Rita Lee Pettiford, "The Effects of Closing an All-Black School," *Greensboro (N.C.) News and Record,* 6 Oct. 1997.

103. Clarke Morrison, "Desegregation Stressful but Opened up Avenues," *Asheville Citizen-Times,* 16 May 2004.

104. McCoy Vann, "Alumni Reunite to Remember."

105. Wilson and Segall, *Oh, Do I Remember!* p. 104.

106. Texas Council for the Humanities, Interview with William C. Akins, 2001, www.public-humanities.org/programs/past/crossover/hustontillotson/akins.php.

107. Texas Council for the Humanities, Interview with Cynthia Sauls Houston, 2001, www.public-humanities.org/programs/past/crossover/hustontillotson/houston .php.

108. Shircliffe, *The Best of That World.*

109. Shircliffe, *The Best of That World,* p. 1.

110. Shircliffe, *The Best of That World,* p. 1.

111. Shircliffe, *The Best of That World,* p. 6.

112. Shircliffe, *The Best of That World,* p. 149.

113. Shircliffe, *The Best of That World,* p. 167.

114. Shircliffe, *The Best of That World,* p. 162.

115. Shircliffe, *The Best of That World,* p. 10.

116. Shircliffe, *The Best of That World,* p. 187.

117. Interview with the author, 14 Aug. 2006.

118. Here are numerous stories about defunct black schools that have had reunions in Arizona, South Carolina, Florida, Texas, North Carolina, Mississippi, Alabama, Virginia, Kansas, Georgia, and West Virginia: Eric Swedlund, "Dunbar Restoration Advancing: Old Segregated School to Relate Black History," *Arizona Daily Star,* 16 Jan. 2004, www.azstarnet.com/sn/printDS/6024; Woods, "All-Black Dunbar School Plans Reunion"; Richburg, "The Legacy of Elizabeth Heights Lives On"; McClendon, "Graduates Remember Dunbar"; Lee, "Forever United by Segregation"; Texas Council for the Humanities, Interview with Clara Henry-Kay, 2001, www.humanities texas.org/programs/past/crossover/jarvis/henrykay.php; Cecelski, *Along Freedom Road,* pp. 163–64; "Black Schools Will Hold Reunion," *Sun Herald,* 2 July 2003; Molineux, "Carver Students Took Home Lessons for Life"; Morris and Morris, *Creating Caring and Nurturing Educational Environments,* pp. 178–79; Holly Hollman, "Trinity High School Graduates Planning Reunion in Athens," *Decatur Daily,* 9 Aug. 2006; Tammy Shriver and Tom Shumate, "I Just Love to See My Classmates: Smiles All Around as About 380 Former Dunbar Students Gather for Reunion," *Times West Virginian,* 2 July 2006, www.timeswv.com/intodayspaper/local_story_183000203.html; Liz Fabian, "Pearl Stephens Students and Teachers Reunite," *Macon Telegraph,* 11 June 2006.

119. This is the case for several old black schoolhouses in Maryland, Alabama, and Tennessee. See Joshua Partlow and Amit R. Paley, "Area's Black Schoolhouses Still Have a Lesson to Teach," *Washington Post,* 17 Feb. 2005; Elgin L. Klugh, "Reclaiming Segregation-Era, African American Schoolhouses: Building on Symbols of Past Cooperation," *Journal of Negro Education* 74 (Summer 2005): 246–59; Joseph D. Bryant, "Old School Revival Once All-Black Facility Gets Life as Community Center," *Birmingham News,* 17 Mar. 2004; "Historic School in Murfreesboro Restored as African American Museum and Community Center," *Tennessee Tribune,* 3 May 2000.

120. Here are three memorial Web sites for the Douglass School from Kingsport, Tennessee, which closed in 1966: www.sonsanddaughtersofdouglass.org/history.html,

http://rivervieworalhistories.blogspot.com, and http://douglassteachermemories.blog spot.com. Here are three Web sites devoted to the Stratton High School in Beckley, West Virginia: www.wwhsalumni.org/stratton.html, http://community-2.webtv.net /Renaldo36/SHS50thREUNION2004/page2.html, and www.geocities.com/stratton high1960/index.html. Here's the Web site for an Alabama black school: www.bham wiki.com/w/Dunbar-Abrams_Community_Center. Here's another Web site for the alumni association that wants to rebuild the old black high school in Huntsville, Alabama: www.whcaa.org/index.htm.

121. All of the quotes in this paragraph are from Withers, "Black Piedmont High School Alumni."

122. Withers, "Black Piedmont High School Alumni."

123. Cynthia Jeffries, "Memorabilia from What Used to Be the County's All-Black High School Has Been Lovingly Assembled in a 'Mini Museum,'" *Greensboro (N.C.) News and Record,* 6 Nov. 2005.

124. Booth Reed, "Dunbar High Still Home for Alumni."

125. C. J. Clemmons, "Flashback to School: Alumni Remember an Educational Experience as Special to Them as It Was Important to the Community," *Wilmington Star-News,* 25 Feb. 2001.

126. Wright, "The Greatest School Under the Sun."

127. Eileen LeBlanc, "Chorale Group Continues After High School Does Not," National Public Radio, *Morning Edition,* 12 Dec. 1994 (transcript no. 1496-13).

128. Wright, "The Greatest School Under the Sun."

129. Jeffries, "Reid Revisited."

130. Cecelski, *Along Freedom Road.*

131. Walzer and Bowers, "The Downside of Desegregation."

132. Tilove, "In the Black Schools of America Before Brown."

133. Walzer and Bowers, "The Downside of Desegregation."

134. Fowler, *School Integration,* p. 62.

135. Walzer and Bowers, "The Downside of Desegregation." A similar story: John Stamper, "Award Was Tossed in Trash After Integration Closed All-Black School," *Lexington Herald Leader,* 19 Aug. 2002.

136. Causey, "Color Lines."

137. Douglas, *Reading, Writing, and Race,* p. 154.

138. Douglas, *Reading, Writing, and Race,* p. 154.

139. Shircliffe, *The Best of That World,* p. 124.

140. Shircliffe, *The Best of That World,* p. 130.

141. Auchmutey and Bonds Staples, "Amid the Battle, a School Flourished."

142. Interview with the author.

143. Raymond L. Calabrese, "The Public School: A Source of Alienation for Minority Parents," *Journal of Negro Education* 59, no. 2 (1990): 148–54.

144. Kenneth L. Wilson, "The Effect of Integration and Class on Black Educational Attainment," *Sociology of Education* 52, no. 2 (1979): 96.

145. Goldfield, *Black, White, and Southern,* p. 268.

146. Morris and Morris, *The Price They Paid*, p. 78.

147. Adair, *Desegregation*, p. 123.

148. Noblit and Dempsey, *The Social Construction of Virtue*, p. 189.

149. Vivian Gussin Paley, *Kwanzaa and Me: A Teacher's Story* (Cambridge: Harvard University Press, 1995), p. 79.

150. Foster, *Black Teachers on Teaching*, p. 60.

151. Tim Simmons, "Brown Ends Era—In Two Ways," *Raleigh (N.C.) News and Observer*, 17 May 2004.

152. Bell Hooks, *We Real Cool: Black Men and Masculinity* (New York: Routledge, 2004), pp. 38–39.

153. Philipsen, *Values-Spoken and Values-Lived*, p. 45.

154. Fowler, *School Integration*, p. 93.

155. Fowler, *School Integration*, p. 96.

Chapter 6. The Loss of Black Teachers and Principals

1. Phil W. Petrie, "The Triumph of Excellence," *New Crisis* (Mar.–Apr. 2000).

2. Claudia Sanchez, "Weekend Edition," *National Public Radio*, 15 May 1994 (transcript no. 1071-2).

3. Frederick Rodgers reprints a table from a 1973 *Urban Review* article that performed a simple calculation: Take the number of black students in each individual Southern state in 1970. Calculate how many black teachers *would have been* teaching those students (assuming the average student-teacher ratio) if those students had still been in all-black schools. Then compare that figure to the *actual* numbers of black teachers in 1970. Just in the South, there should have been about 31,500 additional black teachers in 1970. Rodgers, *The Black High School*, pp. 95–96. I do not give too much credibility to that calculation, however, given that it assumes that the percentage of black teachers should have remained constant.

4. See Robert W. Hooker, "Displacement of Black Teachers in the Eleven Southern States," *Afro-American Studies* 2 (1971): 165–80.

5. McCullough-Garrett, "Reclaiming the African American Vision for Teaching," pp. 433–34.

6. National Public Radio, *All Things Considered*, "Teachers Weigh the Impact of *Brown* Decision," 13 Dec. 2003, www.npr.org/templates/story/story.php?storyId =1547570.

7. Alice E. Carter, "Segregation and Integration in the Appalachian Coalfields: McDowell County Responds to the *Brown* Decision," *West Virginia History* 54 (1995): 78–104, www.wvculture.org/HISTORY/journal_wvh/wvh54-5.html.

8. National Education Association, "Task Force Survey of Displacement in Seventeen Southern States" (Washington, D.C., 1965), quoted in Foster, *Black Teachers on Teaching*, p. xxviii.

9. Foster, *Black Teachers on Teaching*, pp. xvi, xxxvi–xxxviii.

10. Foster, *Black Teachers on Teaching*, p. 86.

11. Ken Flynn, "Tough but Fair; Undaunted by Racial Barriers, Teacher Has Demanded Excellence for Decades," *El Paso Times,* 28 May 2002.

12. African American Contributions: Preserving Our Footprints in History, "Folkways—Education," interview with James Neal, http://www.ucaconline.org/education.html.

13. The table showing these figures is reprinted in John W. Smith and Bette M. Smith, "Desegregation in the South and the Demise of the Black Educator," *Journal of Social and Behavioral Sciences* 20, no. 1 (1974): 33–40.

14. Adair, *Desegregation,* p. 15. Adair provides many more details on pages 91–108.

15. Rodgers, *The Black High School,* p. 70.

16. Rodgers, *The Black High School,* p. 70; Unified Committee for Afro-American Contributions, *In Relentless Pursuit,* p. 92.

17. Tillman, "(Un)Intended Consequences," p. 293, quoting C. C. Yeakey, G. S. Johnston, and J. A. Adkison, "In Pursuit of Equity: A Review of Research on Minorities and Women in Educational Administration," *Educational Administration Quarterly* 22, no. 3 (1986): 122; see also Vanessa Siddle Walker, "The Architects of Black Schooling in the Segregated South: The Case of One Principal Leader," *Journal of Curriculum and Supervision* 19, no. 1 (2003): 54–72; Dunn, "School Integration Revisited."

18. Davis, *A History of Beaufort/Queen Street High School,* p. 111.

19. Thomas H. Buxton and Keith W. Prichard, "The Power Erosion Syndrome of the Black Principal," *Integrated Education* 15, no. 3 (May–June 1977): 9–14.

20. Kentucky Historical Society, Civil Rights Movement in Kentucky, Interview with John Johnson, http://www.ket.org/civilrights/bio_jjohnson.htm.

21. Michael Fultz, "The Displacement of Black Educators Post-Brown: An Overview and Analysis," *History of Education Quarterly* 44 (2004): 11–45. The percentage of black teachers dropped on a nationwide basis too, from 8 percent in 1971 to 7 percent in 1986; Gary Orfield, Susan E. Eaton, and the Harvard Project on School Desegregation, *Dismantling Desegregation: The Quiet Reversal of Brown v. Board of Education* (New York: New Press, 1996), p. 85.

22. Fairclough, *A Class of Their Own,* pp. 302–3, 406.

23. Dina L. Doolen, "A Half-Century Of," *Tucson Citizen,* 6 Mar. 2002; Carolyn Bower and Alexa Aguilar, "Teachers, Students Remember All-Black Segregated Schools," *St. Louis Post-Dispatch,* 17 May 2004.

24. Pat Antonio Goldsmith, "Schools' Racial Mix, Students' Optimism, and the Black-White and Latino-White Achievement Gaps," *Sociology of Education* 77 (Apr. 2004): 121–47.

25. As Leon Hall of the Southern Regional Council wrote, "I am convinced that they have chosen the most disruptive, discouraging and damaging means to incorporate black children and black educators. . . . [I]s it worth it? Many black parents are forced to raise this question when they look into the eyes of their children, eyes that once held gaiety, spontaneity and joy and that now show sadness, frustration and anger." Quoted in Cecelski, *Along Freedom Road,* p. 171. See also James E. Hedrick,

"A Case Study in the Desegregation of George Washington High School and Langston High School in Danville, Virginia, During the 1970–1971 School Year" (Ph.D. diss., Virginia Polytechnic Institute and State University, 2002), p. 119.

26. Hooker, "Displacement of Black Teachers," pp. 165–80.

27. Samuel G. Freedman, "Where School Desegregation Battle Began, Victory Casts a Shadow of Defeat," *New York Times,* 12 May 2004.

28. David K. Shipler, *A Country of Strangers* (New York: Alfred A. Knopf, 1997), pp. 96–97.

29. Buxton and Prichard, "The Power Erosion Syndrome of the Black Principal," pp. 9–14; see also Walker, *Their Highest Potential,* p. 195; Kara Miles Turner, "'Getting It Straight': Southern Black School Patrons and the Struggle for Equal Education in the Pre- and Post-Civil Rights Eras," *Journal of Negro Education* 72, no. 2 (2003): 225.

30. Banker, "History Classes." bell hooks writes, "Almost all our teachers at Booker T. Washington were black women. They were committed to nurturing intellect so that we could become scholars, thinkers, cultural workers. . . . Attending school then was sheer joy. . . . School changed utterly with racial integration. Gone was the messianic zeal to transform our minds and beings that had characterized teachers and their pedagogical practices in our all-black schools. . . . Bussed to white schools, we soon learned that obedience, and not a zealous will to learn was what was expected of us." bell hooks, *Teaching to Transgress* (New York: Routledge, 1984), pp. 2–4.

31. Cecelski, *Along Freedom Road,* pp. 34–35. See also Hedrick, *A Case Study in the Desegregation of George Washington High School,* pp. 118–19. Hedrick quotes a black teacher as saying, "With integration, we knew that home visits were not going to be feasible. I don't believe that the white teachers would have felt comfortable going to the homes of their African-American students and neither do I believe that the African-American teachers would have felt comfortable visiting the homes of their white students."

32. Carol A. Mickett, "History Speaks: Visions and Voices of Kansas City's Past," Charles N. Kimball Lecture, University of Missouri at Kansas City, 22 Oct. 2002, p. 13, web2.umkc.edu/whmckc/PUBLICATIONS/KIMBALL/CNKPDF/Mickett10-22-2002.pdf.

33. Shipler, *A Country of Strangers,* pp. 97–98.

34. Walzer and Bowers, "The Downside of Desegregation."

35. George C. Wright, "Growing Up Segregated," in *Understanding the Little Rock Crisis: An Exercise in Remembrance and Reconciliation,* ed. Elizabeth Jacoway and C. Fred Williams (Fayetteville: University of Arkansas Press, 1999), p. 48.

36. Wright, "Growing Up Segregated," p. 52.

37. Wright, "Growing Up Segregated," p. 52–53.

38. Wright, "Growing Up Segregated," p. 53.

39. Margo Harakas, "Being Black in America," *Fort Lauderdale Sun-Sentinel,* 28 Feb. 2000.

40. Beth Roy, *Bitters in the Honey: Tales of Hope and Disappointment Across Divides of Race and Time* (Fayetteville: University of Arkansas Press, 1999), p. 347.

41. Fryer and Levitt find that "Black children who have at least one black teacher

start out somewhat worse relative to their white peers on math, and slightly better on reading, than black students who have no black teachers. By the end of first grade, however, the black-white test score gap is greater across the board for students who have at least one black teacher. . . . This finding is exactly the opposite of what one would predict from a discrimination story." Fryer and Levitt, "Understanding the Black-White Test Score Gap," p. 459.

42. Sabrina Zirkel, "Is There a Place for Me? Role Models and Academic Identity Among White Students and Students of Color," *Teachers College Record* 104 (2002): 357–76.

43. Eric A. Hanushek, John F. Kain, Daniel M. O'Brien, and Steven G. Rivkin, "The Market for Teacher Quality," NBER Working Paper no. 11154 (2005), p. 20, www.nber.org/papers/w11154.

44. Thomas S. Dee, "Teachers, Race, and Student Achievement in a Randomized Experiment," *Review of Economics and Statistics* 86, no. 1 (Feb. 2004): 196.

45. Dee, "Teachers, Race, and Student Achievement," p. 206.

46. Kristin Klopfenstein, "Beyond Test Scores: The Impact of Black Teacher Role Models on Rigorous Math Taking," *Contemporary Economic Policy* 23, no. 3 (2005): 416–28.

47. Lawrence Otis Graham, *Our Kind of People: Inside America's Black Upper Class,* p. 240.

48. Virginia Black History Archives, Interview with Elizabeth Howlett (1992), www.library.vcu.edu/jbc/speccoll/vbha/school/howlett.html.

49. Causey, "Color Lines."

50. Postal and Weber, "'Achievement Gap' Vexes Schools."

51. University of North Carolina, Oral History Interview with Fran Jackson.

52. Interview with the author. Harold Sellars, who was one of the first black children to integrate a North Carolina school, said, "As I look at it, desegregation-integration, was something that had to be done, and it was the thing to do at the time. But it's like a person who is ill and a doctor prescribes you a medication, and you take it and you leave, but oh, by the way, let me tell you about these side effects that go along with it. And I don't think there was enough emphasis on the side effects, the things that we were giving up, having our own schools, having teachers that could relate to the students, not only for the color of their skin, but their background. They could give them guidance and support." University of North Carolina Television, Black Issues Forum, *50 Years After Brown,* Episode 1924 (2003–4), www.unctv.org/bif/transcripts /2003/transcript1924.html.

53. Foster, *Black Teachers on Teaching,* p. xxxiv.

54. Foster, *Black Teachers on Teaching,* p. xxxiv.

55. Foster, *Black Teachers on Teaching,* p. 89. For more interviews with former students and teachers who thought white teachers had lower expectations of black students, see Afro-American Genealogy and History Society, *The Way We Were.*

56. See, e.g., Gerald Grant, *The World We Created at Hamilton High* (Cambridge: Harvard University Press, 1988), pp. 30–31.

57. Roy L. Brooks, *Integration or Separation? A Strategy for Racial Equality* (Cambridge: Harvard University Press, 1996), p. 227.

58. Petroni et al., *2, 4, 6, 8*, p. 120.

59. Lisa Delpit, *Other People's Children: Cultural Conflict in the Classroom* (New York: New Press, 2006), pp. 45–46, citing G. C. Massey, M. V. Scott, and S. M. Dornbusch, "Racism Without Racists: Institutional Racism in Urban Schools," *The Black Scholar* 7, no. 3 (1975): 2–11.

60. Michael W. Homel, *Down from Equality: Black Chicagoans and the Public Schools, 1920–1941* (Urbana: University of Illinois Press, 1984), p. 110.

61. Foster, *Black Teachers on Teaching*, p. 48.

62. Foster, *Black Teachers on Teaching*, p. 61.

63. Foster, *Black Teachers on Teaching*, p. 121. A teacher from Florida noted, "One of the main criticisms of today's integrated schools is that the black youngsters do not get pushed enough" (p. 98).

64. Morris and Morris, *The Price They Paid*, p. 93.

65. Berryhill, "What's Wrong with Wheatley?" A black teacher from Virginia noted that "one of the negative things about integration" is that there are white teachers "who do not push Black students like they push the White students." Similarly, a Virginia teacher said, "It's something about White teachers that are not reaching the little Black boys. When I was in school, Black teachers made everybody learn. It was no such thing as you couldn't learn. . . . I don't think that projected into the integrated school system. I don't think a White teacher is going to tell an Afro-American student, 'You can do it. Try a little harder.'" Turner, "'Getting It Straight,'" p. 225. And another black teacher points out, "I had a really second-rate education in junior high and high school. Most of my teachers were white. Their approach was to pat us on the back and tell us we were fine. Nothing was required. They just gave up on us. . . . Once I had a black teacher who was really tough—but I love her because she *cared*. She even dared to flunk people. She made us do difficult tasks, made us think hard about what we were doing." Delpit, *Other People's Children*, p. 119.

66. Foster, *Black Teachers on Teaching*, p. 99.

67. Washington, "A Study of Former Negro High School Students," p. 53.

68. See, e.g., Afro-American Genealogy and History Society, *The Way We Were* (interview with N. Freeman Jones, Jr.).

69. Foster, *Black Teachers on Teaching*, pp. 6–7.

70. Foster, *Black Teachers on Teaching*, p. 9. Similarly, a former teacher at the Caswell County Training School in North Carolina recalled that the black principal had told the students, "You're going to have to be better. I don't care how many degrees you can go out and get. You are going to have to be better than that white man." Walker, *Their Highest Potential*, p. 110.

71. Foster, *Black Teachers on Teaching*, p. 128.

72. Turner, "'Getting It Straight,'" p. 225.

73. Tom Dent, *Southern Journey: A Return to the Civil Rights Movement* (Athens: University of Georgia Press, 2001), p. 219.

74. Washington, "A Study of Former Negro High School Students," p. 69. A former teacher from Birmingham points out in a National Public Radio story chronicling a former black school in Birmingham: "I just don't know if integration was a good thing after all. I think once we were allowed to integrate, if you will, we lost a lot of our self-respect. You know, we had a lot of pride because teachers said, 'You have to be better because you are black. You must work harder because you are black.' Nowadays we're taught, 'Oh, your skin color has nothing to do with it.' And I just don't think that's true." National Public Radio, *All Things Considered,* "Birmingham's A. H. Parker High School and Its Role in the Civil Rights Movement," 4 May 2004.

75. See Smith and Smith, "Desegregation in the South," p. 37; Banker, "History Classes"; Kentucky Oral History Commission, Interview with Audrey Grevious (13 Apr. 1999), www.ket.org/civilrights/restofstory.htm; University of Southern Mississippi, Center for Oral History and Cultural Heritage, Interview with Constance Baker (1995), www.lib.usm.edu/~spcol/crda/oh/baker.htm; Texas Council for the Humanities, Interview with Dorothy H. Orebo (2001), www.humanitiestexas.org/programs/past/crossover/hustontillotson/orebo.php. I heard the same point in an interview with John Stokes, an educator who worked in the Maryland school system from 1959 through 1994.

76. Berryhill, "What's Wrong with Wheatley?"

77. Buxton and Prichard, "The Power Erosion Syndrome of the Black Principal," pp. 9–14.

78. National Public Radio, "Birmingham's A. H. Parker High School."

79. Smith, *Educating the Masses,* p. 86.

80. Morris and Morris, *The Price They Paid,* p. 90.

81. Russell W. Irvine and Jacqueline Jordan Irvine, "The Impact of the Desegregation Process on the Education of Black Students: Key Variables," *Journal of Negro Education* 52, no. 4 (1983): 418.

82. See, e.g., Brenda L. Townsend, "The Disproportionate Discipline of African American Learners: Reducing School Suspensions and Expulsions," *Exceptional Children* 66, no. 3 (2000): 381; Douglas B. Downey and Shana Pribesh, "When Race Matters: Teachers' Evaluations of Students' Classroom Behavior," *Sociology of Education* 77 (2004): 267–82; Douglas, *Reading, Writing, and Race,* pp. 226–27.

83. There's some evidence that black students themselves might be better behaved for black teachers; Kenneth J. Meier, Joseph Stewart Jr., and Robert E. England, *Race, Class, and Education, The Politics of Second-Generation Discrimination* (Madison: University of Wisconsin Press, 1989), p. 33.

84. Greene, "A Comparison of the 'School Morale' of White and Negro Students," p. 137.

85. Rodgers, *The Black High School,* pp. 82–84.

86. Foster, *Black Teachers on Teaching,* pp. 59–60.

87. George W. Noblit, "Patience and Prudence in a Southern High School: Managing the Political Economy of Desegregated Education," in *Desegregated Schools: Appraisals of an American Experiment,* ed. Ray C. Rist (New York: Academic, 1979), p. 70.

88. James E. Greene, Sr., "Disciplinary Status of White and Negro High School Students in a Large Southeastern School System," *Journal of Negro Education* 31, no. 1 (1962): 28.

89. Patchen, *Black-White Contact in Schools*, p. 201.

90. Foster, *Black Teachers on Teaching*, p. 55.

91. Charles and Bonnie Remsberg, "Chicago Voices: Tales Told Out of School," in *Our Children's Burden: Studies of Desegregation in Nine American Communities*, ed. Raymond W. Mack (New York: Vintage, 1968), p. 330.

92. Virginia Causey, "Desegregation and Re-Segregation: A History of Desegregation in Muscogee County Schools," *Columbus Ledger-Enquirer*, 23 June 2002.

93. Mary Haywood Metz, *Classrooms and Corridors: The Crisis of Authority in Desegregated Secondary Schools* (Berkeley: University of California Press, 1978), p. 159.

94. Shipler, *A Country of Strangers*, p. 43. See also Cecelski, *Along Freedom Road*, p. 35 (noting similar suspicions on the part of black parents toward the integrated school).

95. Unified Committee for Afro-American Contributions, *In Relentless Pursuit*, p. 78.

Chapter 7. The Rise of Tracking

Epigraphs: Tanika White, "Douglass Still Struggling; Pre-Brown Alumni of Frederick Douglass High School Rue the Effects of Desegregation on Their Alma Mater," *Baltimore Sun*, 16 May 2004; Greg Winter, "Long After Brown v. Board of Education, Sides Switch," *New York Times*, 16 May 2004.

1. Some people use the term "tracking" to mean a rigid system wherein students are assigned to a track for all of their classes, while the term "ability grouping" refers to individual classes that have students of higher or lower ability in them. The distinction does not matter for my purposes, and for convenience' sake, I will use the term "tracking" to refer to both.

2. See, e.g., Charles T. Clotfelter, *After Brown: The Rise and Retreat of School Desegregation* (Princeton: Princeton University Press, 2004); Meier et al., *Race, Class, and Education*, p. 25; Angelia Dickens, "Revisiting Brown v. Board of Education: How Tracking Has Resegregated America's Public Schools," *Columbia Journal of Law and Social Problems* 29 (1996): 469, 472–73; "Note. Teaching Inequality: The Problem of Public School Tracking," *Harvard Law Review* 102 (1989): 1318.

3. See Kermit L. Hall, "The Constitutional Lessons of the Little Rock Crisis," in *Understanding the Little Rock Crisis: An Exercise in Remembrance and Reconciliation*, ed. Elizabeth Jacoway and C. Fred Williams (Fayetteville: University of Arkansas Press, 1999), pp. 134–35.

4. See, e.g., Katz, "Review of Evidence Relating to Effects of Desegregation," p. 387.

5. Texas Council for the Humanities, Interview with Vivian Howard (2001), www.humanitiestexas.org/programs/past/crossover/hustontillotson/howard.php.

6. Interview with the author, 22 Aug. 2006.

7. Interview with the author.

8. Foster, *Black Teachers on Teaching,* pp. 33–34.

9. Meier et al., *Race, Class, and Education,* p. 123 (citing several studies).

10. "Tracking," *Charleston Post and Courier,* 1 May 2004.

11. Causey, "Desegregation and Re-Segregation."

12. Nina H. Clarke and Lillian B. Brown, *History of the Black Public Schools of Montgomery County, Maryland, 1872–1961* (New York: Vantage, 1978), p. 149.

13. Dent, *Southern Journey,* p. 307.

14. Wells and Crain, *Stepping Over the Color Line,* p. 298.

15. Noblit, *Particularities,* pp. 148–49. See also Janet Ward Schofield and H. Andrew Sagar, "The Social Context of Learning in an Interracial School," in *Desegregated Schools: Appraisals of an American Experiment,* ed. Ray C. Rist (New York: Academic, 1979), p. 164.

16. Judith Preissle Goetz and E. Anne Rowley Breneman, "Desegregation and Black Students' Experiences in Two Rural Southern Elementary Schools," *Elementary School Journal* 88, no. 5 (1988): 493.

17. Goetz and Breneman, "Desegregation and Black Students' Experiences," p. 493.

18. Gerard et al., "Social Contact in the Desegregated Classroom," pp. 237–39.

19. Jomills Henry Braddock II and Marvin P. Dawkins, "Ability Grouping, Aspirations, and Attainments: Evidence from the National Educational Longitudinal Study of 1988," *Journal of Negro Education* 62, no. 3 (1993): 326.

20. Samuel R. Lucas and Mark Berends, "Race and Track Assignment in Public School," Presentation at the International Sociological Association Research Committee Number 28 Meeting, Tokyo, Japan, Mar. 2003, p. 23, http://web.iss.u-tokyo.ac.jp/~rc28/rc28hand.pdf.

21. Roslyn Arlin Mickelson, "Subverting Swann: First- and Second-Generation Segregation in the Charlotte-Mecklenburg Schools," *American Educational Research Journal* 38, no. 2 (2001): 233–34.

22. Mickelson, "Subverting Swann," p. 236. One scholar found a similar phenomenon in an integrated California high school in the 1960s; Nathaniel Hickerson, "Some Aspects of School Integration in a California High School," *Journal of Negro Education* 34, no. 2 (1965): 130–37.

23. Roslyn Arlin Mickelson and Damien Heath, "The Effects of Segregation on African American High School Seniors' Academic Achievement," *Journal of Negro Education* 68, no. 4 (1999): 568n.1.

24. Mickelson and Heath, "The Effects of Segregation," p. 568n.1. You might wonder whether tracking has any educational value. The widest-ranging study I could find says no. Eric Hanushek and Ludger Wößmann looked at data for about two dozen countries around the world. Their "most striking finding is that in no case do some students gain at the expense of others; *both high and low achievers lose . . . from tracking*"; Eric A. Hanushek and Ludger Wößmann, "Does Educational Tracking Affect Performance and Inequality? Differences-in-Differences Evidence Across Countries," *Economic Journal* 116 (2006): C63–C76. Other scholars, in more limited studies, have

suggested that tracking can become a self-fulfilling prophecy: students put into lower-ability classes can end up having a much different and less challenging classroom experience; Donna Eder, "Ability Grouping as a Self-Fulfilling Prophecy: A Micro-Analysis of Teacher-Student Interaction," *Sociology of Education* 54, no. 3 (1981): 151–62; Mieke Van Houtte, "Tracking Effects on School Achievement: A Quantitative Explanation in Terms of the Academic Culture of School Staff," *American Journal of Education* 110 (Aug. 2004): 354; William Carbonaro, "Tracking, Students' Effort, and Academic Achievement," *Sociology of Education* 78 (2005): 41. They can end up being less attentive to schoolwork, causing them to learn even less than they otherwise would. See Diane Felmlee and Donna Eder, "Contextual Effects in the Classroom: The Impact of Ability Groups on Student Attention," *Sociology of Education* 56, no. 2 (1983): 77–87. Still, like much in the realm of education, the scholarly literature is anything but unanimous. The argument in favor of tracking is that lower-ability children might benefit from having a curriculum and/or teaching style that is more geared to their ability level, rather than struggling to keep up with more advanced children. One recent paper —based on nationwide data and sophisticated economic techniques of analysis—finds that there is "no evidence that tracking harms low-ability students"; David N. Figlio and Marianne E. Page, "School Choice and the Distributional Effects of Ability Tracking: Does Separation Increase Inequality?" *Journal of Urban Economics* 51 (2002): 497–514; see also Adam Gamoran and Robert D. Mare, "Secondary School Tracking and Educational Inequality: Compensation, Reinforcement, or Neutrality?" *American Journal of Sociology* 94, no. 5 (1989): 1146–83.

25. Powell, *Black Monday's Children*, p. 216.

26. Metz, *Classrooms and Corridors*, p. 71.

27. Metz, *Classrooms and Corridors*, p. 108.

28. Powell, *Black Monday's Children*, p. 300.

29. George A. Akerlof and Rachel E. Kranton, "Identity and Schooling: Some Lessons for the Economics of Education," *Journal of Economic Literature* 40 (2002): 1193.

30. Doris Y. Wilkinson, "Integration Dilemmas in a Racist Culture," *Society* 33, no. 3 (1996): 27–31.

31. See, e.g., Sharon Fries-Britt, "Moving Beyond Black Achiever Isolation: Experiences of Gifted Black Collegians," *Journal of Higher Education* 69, no. 5 (1998): 556–76.

32. Petroni et al., *2, 4, 6, 8*, p. 162.

33. Petroni et al., *2, 4, 6, 8*, p. 14.

34. Petroni et al., *2, 4, 6, 8*, p. 9.

35. Janet Ward Schofield, "Complementary and Conflicting Identities: Images and Interaction in an Interracial School," in *The Development of Children's Friendships*, ed. Steven R. Asher and John M. Gottman (Cambridge: Cambridge University Press, 1981), pp. 74, 79–80.

36. Schofield, "Complementary and Conflicting Identities," p. 78.

37. Schofield, "Complementary and Conflicting Identities," p. 79.

38. Schofield, "Complementary and Conflicting Identities," p. 79.

39. Ogbu and Davis, *Black American Students in an Affluent Suburb*, p. 85.

40. Ronald F. Ferguson, "A Diagnostic Analysis of Black-White GPA Disparities in Shaker Heights, Ohio," in *Brookings Papers on Educational Policy, 2001*, ed. Diane Ravitch (2001).

41. Tyson, "The Making of a 'Burden,'" p. 57.

42. Tyson, "The Making of a 'Burden,'" p. 61.

43. Mickelson and Velasco, "Bring It On!" p. 41.

44. Esters, "When Black Kids Are Accused of 'Acting White.'"

45. Correspondents of the New York Times, *How Race Is Lived*, p. 161.

46. "Is School Integration Working?; Teens Talk About Race Relations," *Virginian-Pilot*, 20 May 1994.

47. See Samuel R. Lucas and Adam Gamoran, "Tracking and the Achievement Gap," in *Bridging the Achievement Gap*, ed. John E. Chubb and Tom Loveless (Washington, D.C.: Brookings Institution Press, 2002), pp. 186, 188.

48. Lucas and Berends, "Race and Track Assignment in Public School," p. 30.

49. Lucas and Berends, "Race and Track Assignment in Public School," p. 36.

50. Meier et al., *Race, Class, and Education*, pp. 95–99. Of course, it is possible that schools with more black teachers had fewer white students to put in the higher tracks in the first place.

51. Goetz and Breneman, "Desegregation and Black Students' Experiences," pp. 493–94.

52. Hugh Mehan, Irene Villanueva, Lea Hubbard, and Angela Lintz, *Constructing School Success: The Consequences of Untracking Low-Achieving Students* (Cambridge: Cambridge University Press, 1996), pp. 150–52.

53. For another example, see the description of a program that brought black students into expensive prep schools; Richard L. Zweigenhaft and G. William Domhoff, *Blacks in the White Establishment? A Study of Race and Class in America* (New Haven: Yale University Press, 1991), p. 26. The authors note that because they had a new group identity, these black students were "less likely to suffer conflict over allegedly 'acting white' by taking school seriously."

54. Ray C. Rist, "School Integration: Ideology, Methodology, and National Policy," in *School Desegregation: Shadow and Substance*, ed. Florence H. Levinsohn and Benjamin D. Wright (Chicago: University of Chicago Press, 1976), p. 117, quoting E. Cohen, "The Effects of Desegregation on Race Relations: Facts or Hypothesis," *Law and Contemporary Problems* 39 (1975).

55. See, e.g., Robert Cooper, "Detracking Reform in an Urban California High School: Improving the Schooling Experiences of African American Students," *Journal of Negro Education* 65, no. 2 (1996): 200–201.

Chapter 8. When Did "Acting White" Arise?

Epigraphs: Karla D. Shores, "Peer Pressure Shapes Student Performance," *South Florida Sun-Sentinel*, 9 May 2004.

1. See, e.g., Juan Williams, *My Soul Looks Back in Wonder: Voices of the Civil Rights*

Experience (New York: Sterling, 2005), pp. 65–67, 154–55; Powell, *Black Monday's Children*, p. 61, pp. 132–33, pp. 202–3; Timothy B. Tyson, *Blood Done Sign My Name* (New York: Crown, 2004), pp. 258–59.

2. See Melba Pattillo Beals, *Warriors Don't Cry* (New York: Archway, 1995).

3. Derrick Bell, *Silent Covenants: Brown v. Board of Education and the Unfulfilled Hopes for Racial Reform* (Oxford: Oxford University Press, 2004), p. 102.

4. James T. Patterson, *Brown v. Board of Education: A Civil Rights Milestone and Its Troubled Legacy* (Oxford: Oxford University Press, 2001), p. 165.

5. Patterson, *Brown v. Board of Education*, p. 166.

6. Kathryn Clark Gerken, "What Have We Been Doing? Black School Psychologists and the Desegregation Issue," *Journal of Negro Education* 47, no. 1 (1978): 87, citing M. A. Chesler and P. Segal, "Southern Negroes' Initial Experiences in School Desegregation," *Integrated Education* 6 (1968): 20–28; see also Ruth P. Simms, "The Savannah Story: Education and Desegregation," in *Our Children's Burden: Studies of Desegregation in Nine American Communities*, ed. Raymond W. Mack (New York: Vintage, 1968), pp. 123–24.

7. Kim Hackett, "A Mixed Legacy," *Sarasota Herald-Tribune*, 16 May 2004.

8. Leslie Baham Inniss, "Desegregation Pioneers: Casualties of a Peaceful Process," *International Journal of Contemporary Sociology* 31, no. 2 (1994): 253–72. A book chapter that's very similar: Leslie Baham Inniss, "Historical Footprints: The Legacy of the School Desegregation Pioneers," in *The Bubbling Cauldron: Race, Ethnicity, and the Urban Crisis*, ed. Michael Peter Smith and Joe R. Feagin (Minneapolis: University of Minneapolis, 1995).

9. Inniss, "Desegregation Pioneers," p. 259.

10. Inniss, "Desegregation Pioneers," p. 266.

11. Inniss, "Desegregation Pioneers," p. 266.

12. Inniss, "Desegregation Pioneers," p. 261.

13. Inniss, "Desegregation Pioneers," p. 263.

14. Inniss, "Desegregation Pioneers," p. 268.

15. Inniss, "Desegregation Pioneers," p. 267.

16. Inniss, "Desegregation Pioneers," pp. 267–68.

17. Inniss, "Desegregation Pioneers," p. 263.

18. Inniss, "Desegregation Pioneers," p. 264.

19. Wanda Lloyd, "Separate Didn't Always Mean Equal in a Pre-Integration School," Chipsquinn.org, 14 May 2004, www.chipsquinn.org/news/chipsnews/chips_news.aspx?id=338&printer-friendly=y.

20. Leonard Pitts, "The Color Line; Tracing Key Events Along the Road to Civil Rights," *Bergen County (N.J.) Record*, 12 Dec. 1999.

21. Clarissa T. Sligh, "It Wasn't Little Rock," 2005, http://clarissasligh.com/essays/rock.html.

22. W. E. B. DuBois, "Does the Negro Need Separate Schools?" *Journal of Negro Education* 4, no. 3 (1935): 335.

23. Bell, *Silent Covenants*, p. 105.

24. Bell, *Silent Covenants,* pp. 105, 121.

25. Derrick Bell, "A Model Alternative Desegregation Plan," in *Shades of Brown: New Perspectives on School Desegregation,* ed. Derrick Bell (New York: Teachers College Press, 1980), p. 138.

26. Homel, *Down from Equality,* p. 106. For more examples of "inattentive" black students in the 1800s, see Mabee, *Black Education in New York State,* p. 37.

27. Petroni et al., *2, 4, 6, 8,* p. 30.

28. Janet Ward Schofield, *Black and White in School: Trust, Tension, or Tolerance* (New York: Teachers College Press, 1989), p. 83.

29. Schofield, *Black and White in School,* pp. 93–94.

30. Noblit, *Particularities,* pp. 131–33; see also Collins, "From Courtrooms to Classrooms," p. 113.

31. Grant, *The World We Created at Hamilton High,* pp. 35, 59, 104.

32. Constance Curry, *Silver Rights* (New York: Harcourt Brace, 1995), pp. 122–23.

33. Wolters, *The Burden of Brown,* p. 176.

34. Wolters, *The Burden of Brown,* p. 180.

35. Thomas's story is recounted in Bill Torpy, "DeKalb Schools' 30-Year Struggle for Racial Balance Has Led to Resegregation, and the Question: What Was Gained?" *Atlanta Constitution,* 30 Sept. 1999.

36. Cox's story is told in Dunn, "School Integration Revisited."

37. Lorenzo Bowman, "Black and White Attorneys' Perspectives on Race, the Legal System, and Continuing Legal Education: A Critical Race Theory Analysis" (Ph.D. diss., University of Georgia, 2004, www.coe.uga.edu/leap/adulted/pdf/bowman_lorenzo_200405_phd.pdf), pp. 1–2.

38. Williams, *My Soul Looks Back in Wonder,* p. 103.

39. Postal and Weber, "'Achievement Gap' Vexes Schools."

40. Email to author, 22 Aug. 2006.

41. Interview with the author.

42. Shores, "Peer Pressure Shapes Student Performance," p. H5.

43. Interview with Leo Hamilton by Mary Hebert, 21 Aug. 1993, Tape 453, at Hill Memorial Library at Louisiana State University.

44. Judi Russell, "Teaching Change: 'Prof' Made Education His Life," *New Orleans Times-Picayune,* 14 Feb. 1993.

45. Unified Committee for Afro-American Contributions, *In Relentless Pursuit.*

46. Tracie Powell, "A Different World," *Atlanta Magazine,* Jan. 2007, p. 90.

47. Aimee Robinette, "Shaw Teacher Recalls Public School Integration," *Bolivar Commercial,* 2 Mar. 2005.

48. Washington, "A Study of Former Negro High School Students," p. 54.

49. Personal interview with the author.

50. James Walsh, "Tests of Time," *Minneapolis Star Tribune,* 9 May 2004.

51. Robert Coles, *Children of Crisis: A Study of Courage and Fear* (New York: Atlantic Monthly, 1964), p. 118.

52. Coles, *Children of Crisis,* p. 180.

53. Interview with the author.

54. Interview with the author.

55. Email to the author, 11 Dec. 2005.

56. Email to the author, 22 Aug. 2006.

57. *The NewsHour with Jim Lehrer,* 15 July 2004.

58. Courtland Milloy, "A Challenging Analysis of Black America," *Washington Post,* 21 Mar. 2004, www.washingtonpost.com/ac2/wp-dyn/A11831-2004Mar20?language =printer.

59. "Henry the First," *Guardian,* 6 July 2002, http://education.guardian.co.uk /higher/worldwide/story/0,9959,750264,00.html.

60. Tatum, *"Why Are All the Black Kids Sitting Together in the Cafeteria?"* p. 64.

61. Hooks, *We Real Cool,* p. 42.

62. Patrick Welsh, "The Black Talent Trap; Top High-School Students Are Caught Between White Racism and the Jealousy of Blacks," *Washington Post,* 1 May 1988.

63. Suzy Hansen, "Another Shade of Black" (interview with McWhorter), *Salon,* 14 Jan. 2003.

64. John H. McWhorter, "The End of Blackness: Returning the Souls of Black Folk to Their Rightful Owners," *Journal of Blacks in Higher Education* 43 (Spring 2004): 130–32.

65. John McWhorter, "Why the Black-White Test Gap Exists," *American Experiment Quarterly* (Spring 2002): 50; see also McWhorter, *Winning the Race,* p. 262.

66. Leonard Pitts, Jr., "With Gates, the Door Has Been Opened—Let's Walk In," *Houston Chronicle,* 24 Sept. 1999.

67. Stanley Crouch, "Role Models," in *Second Thoughts About Race in America,* ed. Peter Collier and David Horowitz (Lanham: Madison, 2000), p. 56, www.discover thenetwork.org/Articles/race.pdf.

68. Stanley Crouch, "Being a Dummy Makes One a Real Person: The Braining Down of the Education of African Americans," *Journal of Blacks in Higher Education,* no. 24 (Summer 1999): 104.

69. Matthew Daneman, "Spike Lee: Media Still Limit Minorities," *Rochester Democrat and Chronicle,* 24 Feb. 2006; Jim Kinney, "James Earl Jones Speaks at Saratoga Hotel for Teachers Convention," *The Saratogian (Saratoga Springs, N.Y.),* 11 Nov. 2007; Vernon Jordan, "Chairman of the Board," in *America Behind the Color Line,* ed. Henry Louis Gates, Jr. (New York: Warner, 2004), p. 31.

70. Harry Jaffe, "Avenging Angel," *Washingtonian,* Aug. 1995.

71. Leah Y. Latimer, "Will Integration Hurt My Black Son's Education?" *Washington Post,* 20 Apr. 1986.

72. Rick Badie, "Minister: Success Is an Open Book," *Orlando Sentinel* 30 Apr. 1994.

73. Ron Matus, "Studying's Reward: Stigma," *St. Petersburg Times,* 5 Dec. 2005.

74. Edwards, "Before and After School Desegregation," p. 152.

75. Trotter and Higgins, "King's Vision Evolves in Indiana—but Slowly."

76. Carter Modlin, "The Desegregation of Southampton County, Virginia, Schools," pp. 109–10.

77. Cecelski, *Along Freedom Road,* p. 9.

78. Sarah Lawrence of the Race and Place Project, Interview of Lorraine Paige (Feb. 2002), www2.vcdh.virginia.edu/afam/raceandplace/orals/paige.html.

79. Allison Davis, *Children of Bondage* (1940), pp. 226–27.

80. Davison M. Douglas, *Jim Crow Moves North: The Battle over Northern School Segregation, 1865–1954* (New York: Cambridge University Press, 2005). See also Max Wolff, "Segregation in the Schools of Gary, Indiana," *Journal of Educational Sociology* 36, no. 6 (1963): 251–61; Frank Herron, "The Pull of Magnet Schools: Racial Balance Still a Dream in City Schools," *Syracuse Post-Standard,* 22 Jan. 1992.

81. June Shagaloff, "A Review of Public School Desegregation in the North and West," *Journal of Educational Sociology* 36, no. 6 (1963): 292–96.

82. Homel, *Down from Equality,* p. 27.

83. "Bill Cosby's Cause," *Newsweek,* 21 Dec. 2004.

84. Felicia R. Lee, "Why Are Black Students Lagging," *New York Times,* 29 Nov. 2002.

85. See George Farkas, Christy Lleras, and Steve Maczuga, "Does Oppositional Culture Exist in Minority and Poverty Peer Groups," *American Sociological Review* 67 (2002): 148–55; Ogbu, "The Consequences of the American Caste System," pp. 46–47.

86. See, e.g., Mavis G. Sanders, "Overcoming Obstacles: Academic Achievement as a Response to Racism and Discrimination," *Journal of Negro Education* 66, no. 1 (1997): 83–93.

87. Steinberg, Dornbusch, and Brown, "Ethnic Differences in Adolescent Achievement," p. 726.

88. Sheryll D. Cashin, "American Public Schools Fifty Years After *Brown:* A Separate and Unequal Reality," *Howard Law Journal* 47 (2004): 341, 355.

89. See Douglas Massey, "American Apartheid: Segregation and the Making of the Underclass," *American Journal of Sociology* 96, no. 2 (1990): 329–57.

90. Ogbu and Davis, *Black American Students in an Affluent Suburb,* p. 175. Ogbu's theory is also laid out in John U. Ogbu, "Minority Education in Comparative Perspective," *Journal of Negro Education* 59, no. 1 (1990): 45–57.

91. Ogbu and Davis, *Black American Students in an Affluent Suburb,* p. 174.

92. Ogbu and Davis, *Black American Students in an Affluent Suburb,* p. 174.

93. "Henry the First," *Guardian,* 6 July 2002, http://education.guardian.co.uk/higher/worldwide/story/0,9959,750264,00.html.

94. National Public Radio, *Fresh Air,* 11 Mar. 2002.

95. Fred Kaplan, "Attack Backs Her 30 Rules," *Boston Globe,* 16 Aug. 1997.

96. Stokely Carmichael and Charles V. Hamilton, *Black Power: The Politics of Liberation in America* (New York: Vintage, 1967), p. 41.

97. Carmichael and Hamilton, *Black Power,* p. 53.

98. Carmichael and Hamilton, *Black Power,* p. 157.

99. Malcolm X, "Answers to Questions at the Militant Labor Forum," in *By Any Means Necessary: Speeches, Interviews, and a Letter,* ed. George Breitman (1970), p. 17.

100. Nathan Wright, Jr., *Black Power and Urban Unrest* (New York: Hawthorn, 1967), pp. 131–32.

Chapter 9. Where Do We Go From Here?

Epigraph: "For Black Students, Success Comes with a Price," *Binghamton Press and Sun-Bulletin,* 25 Feb. 2007.

1. Gordon Allport, *The Nature of Prejudice* (Boston: Beacon, 1954), p. 17.

2. Miller McPherson, Lynn Smith-Lovin, and James Cook, "Birds of a Feather: Homophily in Social Networks," *Annual Review of Sociology,* 27 (2001): p. 420.

3. Jason P. Mitchell, C. Neil Macrae, and Mahzarin R. Banaji, "Dissociable Medial Prefrontal Contributions to Judgments of Similar and Dissimilar Others," *Neuron* 50 (18 May 2006): 655–63.

4. An interesting paper on this subject is Timur Kuran, "Ethnic Norms and Their Transformation Through Reputational Cascades," *Journal of Legal Studies* 27 (1998): 623–59.

5. Judith Rich Harris, *No Two Alike: Human Nature and Human Individuality* (New York: W. W. Norton, 2006), p. 157.

6. Graham M. Vaughan, Henri Tajfel, and Jennifer Williams, "Bias in Reward Allocation in an Intergroup and an Interpersonal Context," *Social Psychology Quarterly* 44, no. 1 (1981): 37–42. Henri Tajfel and his colleagues found a similar result in J. C. Turner, R. J. Brown, and H. Tajfel, "Social Comparison and Group Interest in Ingroup Favouritism," *European Journal of Social Psychology* 9 (1979): 187–204. See also Henri Tajfel, "Experiments in Intergroup Discrimination," *Scientific American* 223 (1970): 96–102.

7. See Stephen Worchel, Danny Axsom, Frances Ferris, Gary Samaha, and Susan Schweizer, "Determinants of the Effect of Intergroup Cooperation on Intergroup Attraction," *Journal of Conflict Resolution* 22, no. 3 (1978): 429–39. For more examples, see Naomi Ellemers, Cathy van Dyck, Steve Hinkle, and Annelieke Jacobs, "Intergroup Differentiation in Social Context: Identity Needs Versus Audience Constraints," *Social Psychology Quarterly* 63, no. 1 (2000): 60–74; Thomas E. Ford and George R. Tonander, "The Role of Differentiation Between Groups and Social Identity in Stereotype Formation," *Social Psychology Quarterly* 61, no. 4 (1998): 372–84. On the other hand, some researchers have been able to reduce the amount of intergroup discrimination in such experiments by "priming" people to think about concepts such as "equality" or "fairness" (this is done by giving them a list of thirty words to remember, ten of which are words related to fairness); Guido Hertel and Norbert L. Kerr, "Priming In-Group Favoritism: The Impact of Normative Scripts in the Minimal Group Paradigm," *Journal of Experimental Social Psychology* 37 (2001): 316–24.

8. See Henri Tajfel, M. G. Billig, and R. P. Bundy, "Social Categorization and Intergroup Behaviour," *European Journal of Social Psychology* 1, no. 2 (1971): 149–77.

9. Michael Billig and Henri Tajfel, "Social Categorization and Similarity in Intergroup Behaviour," *European Journal of Social Psychology* 3 (1973): 27–52.

10. See Carmen G. Arroyo and Edward Zigler, "Racial Identity, Academic

Achievement, and the Psychological Well-Being of Economically Disadvantaged Adolescents," *Journal of Personality and Social Psychology* 69, no. 5 (1995): 903–14.

11. For a sophisticated mathematical analysis of how "acting white" is an example of signaling, see David Austen-Smith and Roland G. Fryer, Jr., "An Economic Analysis of 'Acting White,'" *Quarterly Journal of Economics* 102, no. 2 (2005): 551–83.

12. Eric Posner, *Law and Social Norms* (Cambridge: Harvard University Press, 2000), p. 25.

13. Posner, *Law and Social Norms*, p. 141.

14. See, e.g., Webber, *Deep Like the Rivers*, pp. 233–34; John U. Ogbu, "Collective Identity and the Burden of 'Acting White' in Black History, Community, and Education," *Urban Review* 36, no. 1 (2004): 1–35.

15. Petroni et al., *2, 4, 6, 8*, p. 173.

16. Petroni et al., *2, 4, 6, 8*, p. 44.

17. Curnutte, "For Some Black Students, Failing Is Safer."

18. Ferguson, "A Diagnostic Analysis of Black-White GPA Disparities."

19. Patchen, *Black-White Contact in Schools*, pp. 141–47. At least two other studies also found that race relations were worst in desegregated schools where the races were roughly balanced. See Janet Ward Schofield and H. Andrew Sagar, "Desegregation, School Practices, and Student Race Relations," in *The Consequences of School Desegregation*, ed. Christine H. Rossell and Willis D. Hawley (Philadelphia: Temple University Press, 1983), pp. 70–71.

20. Barry Wellman, "I Am a Student," *Sociology of Education* 44, no. 4 (1971): 422–37.

21. See Edward L. Glaeser, Giacomo A. M. Ponzetto, and Jesse M. Shapiro, "Strategic Extremism: Why Republicans and Democrats Divide on Religious Values," *Quarterly Journal of Economics* 120, no. 4 (2004): 1283–1330.

22. National Public Radio, *Fresh Air*, 11 Mar. 2002.

23. For examples, see Jack L. Perry, "Is Separate . . . More Equal? Tackle Boys' Learning Gap with Academic Focus," Delaware Online, 16 Mar. 2008, www.delaware online.com/apps/pbcs.dll/article?AID=2008803160325.

24. Sherrilyn M. Billger, "Reconstructing School Segregation: On the Efficacy and Equity of Single-Sex Schooling," IZA Discussion Paper no. 2037 (Mar. 2006), ftp://ftp.iza.org/dps/dp2037.pdf. Given that most single sex schools to date are private, the researcher attempted to control for selection effects in a variety of ways.

25. U.S. Department of Education, Office of Planning, Evaluation, and Policy Development, Policy and Program Studies Service, *Single-Sex Versus Secondary Schooling: A Systematic Review* (Washington, D.C., 2005), p. xiii.

26. See Dan Goldhaber, "Everyone's Doing It, but What Does Teacher Testing Tell Us About Teacher Effectiveness," Urban Institute Working Paper, 16 Oct. 2006, www.caldercenter.org/PDF/1001072_everyones_doing.PDF, p. 31.

27. Drew H. Gitomer, "Teacher Quality in a Changing Policy Landscape: Improvements in the Teacher Pool," Educational Testing Service Report, www.ets.org/Media /Education_Topics/pdf/TQ_full_report.pdf, pp. 17–18.

28. Dan D. Goldhaber and Michael Hansen, "Race, Gender, and Teacher Testing: How Objective a Tool Is Teacher Licensure Testing?" Center on Reinventing Public Education, University of Washington, Working Paper no. 2008-2 (2008), www.crpe .org/cs/crpe/view/csr_pubs/201, pp. 21–22.

29. For example, see Lionel Brown, "America's Black Male: Disadvantaged from Birth to Death," *Perspectives on Urban Education* 3, no. 2 (2005): 1–16, www.urbaned journal.org/notes/notes0016.pdf.

30. University of Southern Mississippi, Center for Oral History and Cultural Heritage, Interview with William A. Butts (1976), http://anna.lib.usm.edu/~spcol/crda /oh/ohbuttswp.html.

31. Carla Rivera, "Family-Like Program Opens Brave New Chapter for Black L.A. Students," *Los Angeles Times,* 6 July 2006.

32. Meghan Irons, "The New Cool Kids," *Boston Globe,* 22 Mar. 2009, www.boston .com/news/local/articles/2009/03/22/the_new_cool_kids?mode=PF.

33. Coleman, *The Adolescent Society,* pp. 306–10.

34. Coleman, *The Adolescent Society,* p. 309.

35. Coleman, *The Adolescent Society,* p. 309.

36. Frank A. Petroni, "Uncle Toms: White Stereotypes in the Black Movement," *Human Organization* 29, no. 4 (1970): 260–66.

37. Coleman, *The Adolescent Society,* p. 320.

38. Coleman, *The Adolescent Society,* p. 320.

39. Coleman, *The Adolescent Society,* p. 322.

40. Bishop et al., "Why We Harass Nerds and Freaks," pp. 235–51.

41. Seymour Spilerman, "Raising Academic Motivation in Lower-Class Adolescents: A Convergence of Two Research Traditions," *Sociology of Education* 44, no. 1 (1971): 103–18.

42. Spilerman, "Raising Academic Motivation," pp. 109–10.

43. Spilerman, "Raising Academic Motivation," p. 111, quoting Roger Brown, *Social Psychology* (1965), p. 472.

44. Spilerman, "Raising Academic Motivation," p. 114. Of course, a large literature suggests that when you give monetary rewards, children start to undertake the task solely for the reward and to have less *intrinsic* motivation to perform the task for its own sake. See, e.g., Edward L. Deci, Richard Koestner, and Richard M. Ryan, "Extrinsic Rewards and Intrinsic Motivation in Education: Reconsidered Once Again," *Review of Educational Research* 71, no. 1 (2001): 1–27. But the children that Spilerman was most worried about tend to have little intrinsic motivation to do well in school in the first place. The inimitable Roland Fryer is currently involved in a multiyear experiment in New York City involving financial rewards for grades, both on an individual and a group basis. Although this experiment does not involve the elimination of grades and their replacement by interschool competitions, I will be interested to see the results.

45. See, e.g., Dalmas A. Taylor and Beatrice F. Moriarty, "Ingroup Bias as a Function of Competition and Race," *Journal of Conflict Resolution* 31, no. 1 (1987): 192–

99; David W. Johnson, Roger T. Johnson, Margaret Tiffany, and Brian Zaidman, "Cross-Ethnic Relationships: The Impact of Intergroup Cooperation and Intergroup Competition," *Journal of Educational Research* 78, no. 2 (1984): 75–79.

46. The Robbers' Cave experiment is described in Muzafer Sherif, "Superordinate Goals in the Reduction of Intergroup Conflict," *American Journal of Sociology* 63 (1958): 349–56, and in more detail in Muzafer Sherif, O. J. Harvey, B. Jack White, William R. Hood, and Carolyn W. Sherif, *Intergroup Conflict and Cooperation: The Robbers Cave Experiment* (1954/1961).

47. See David W. Johnson, Roger Johnson, and Geoffrey Maruyama, "Goal Interdependence and Interpersonal Attraction in Heterogeneous Classrooms: A Metanalysis," in *Groups in Contact: The Psychology of Desegregation,* ed. Norman Miller and Marilynn B. Brewer (New York: Academic, 1984), pp. 187–212; see also Schofield and Sagar, "Desegregation, School Practices, and Student Race Relations," pp. 80–83.

48. For Bourne's essay, see http://struggle.ws/hist_texts/warhealthstate1918.html.

49. Allport, *The Nature of Prejudice,* p. 148.

50. Jason A. Nier, Samuel L. Gaertner, John F. Dovidio, Brenda S. Banker, Christine M. Ward, and Mary C. Rust, "Changing Interracial Evaluations and Behavior: The Effects of a Common Group Identity," *Group Processes and Intergroup Relations* 4, no. 4 (2001): 299–316.

51. Schofield, "Complementary and Conflicting Identities," p. 79.

BIBLIOGRAPHY

Abney, Everett E. "The Status of Florida's Black School Principals." *Journal of Negro Education* 43, no. 1 (1974): 3–8.

Adair, Alvis. *Desegregation: The Illusion of Black Progress.* Lanham, Md.: University Press of America, 1984.

Adams, Michelle. "Radical Integration." *California Law Review* 94 (2006): 261.

Afro-American Genealogy and History Society. *The Way We Were: Oral Histories of Four Former All-Black Public Schools in Two North Carolina Counties.* Self-published, 1991.

Ainsworth, James W. "Why Does It Take a Village? The Mediation of Neighborhood Effects on Educational Achievement." *Social Forces* 81, no. 1 (2002): 117–52.

Ainsworth-Darnell, James W., and Douglas B. Downey. "Assessing the Oppositional Culture Explanation for Racial/Ethnic Differences in School Performance." *American Sociological Review* 63, no. 4 (1998): 536–53.

Akerlof, George A., and Rachel E. Kranton. "Identity and Schooling: Some Lessons for the Economics of Education." *Journal of Economic Literature* 40 (2002): 1167–1201.

Akom, A. A. "Reexamining Resistance as Oppositional Behavior: The Nation of Islam and the Creation of a Black Achievement Ideology." *Sociology of Education* 76, no. 4 (2003): 305–25.

Alexander, Karl, and Bruce K. Eckland. "Contextual Effects in the High School Attainment Process." *American Sociological Review* 40, no. 3 (1975): 402–16.

Allen, Dwight W., and Jeffrey C. Hecht, eds. *Controversies in Education.* Philadelphia: W. B. Saunders, 1974.

Allport, Gordon. *The Nature of Prejudice.* Boston: Beacon, 1954.

Altonji, Joseph G., and Thomas A. Dunn. "Using Siblings to Estimate the Effect of School Quality on Wages." *Review of Economics and Statistics* 78, no. 4 (1996): 665–71.

Ambert, Anne-Marie. *Parents, Children, and Adolescents: Interactive Relationships and Development in Context.* New York: Haworth, 1997.

————. "A Qualitative Study of Peer Abuse and Its Effects: Theoretical and Empirical Implications." *Journal of Marriage and the Family* 56, no. 1 (1994): 119–30.

————. *The Rise in Problematic Behaviors Among Children and Adolescents, Part 2: Extra-Familial Causes* (2003), www.arts.yorku.ca/soci/ambert/writings/behavior _problems_pt2.html.

Ames, Mary. *From a New England Woman's Diary in Dixie in 1865*. Norwood, Mass.: Plimpton, 1906.

Amos, Robert T. "The Accuracy of Negro and White Children's Predictions of Teachers' Attitudes Toward Negro Students." *Journal of Negro Education* 21, no. 2 (1952): 125–35.

Anderson, Elijah. *Streetwise: Race, Class, and Change in an Urban Community*. Chicago: University of Chicago Press, 1990.

Anderson, James D. *The Education of Blacks in the South, 1860–1935*. Chapel Hill: University of North Carolina Press, 1988.

Angrist, Joshua D., and Kevin Lang. "Does School Integration Generate Peer Effects? Evidence from Boston's Metco Program." IZA Discussion Paper no. 976 (2004), http://ssrn.com/abstract=491482.

Archer, Chalmers, Jr. *Growing Up Black in Rural Mississippi*. New York: Walker, 1992.

Arendt, Hannah. "Reflections on Little Rock." *Dissent* 6 (1959): 45–56.

Armor, David J. *Forced Justice: School Desegregation and the Law*. New York: Oxford University Press, 1995.

Arnez, Nancy L. "Implementation of Desegregation as a Discriminatory Process." *Journal of Negro Education* 47, no. 1 (1978): 28–45.

Aronson, Elliot. "Busing and Racial Tension: The Jigsaw Route to Learning and Liking." *Psychology Today* 8, no. 9 (Feb. 1975): 43–50.

Arroyo, Carmen G., and Edward Zigler. "Racial Identity, Academic Achievement, and the Psychological Well-Being of Economically Disadvantaged Adolescents." *Journal of Personality and Social Psychology* 69, no. 5 (1995): 903–14.

Asch, Solomon. "Opinions and Social Pressure." *Scientific American* (1955): 31–35.

Ascik, Thomas R. "An Investigation of School Desegregation and Its Effects on Black Student Achievement." *American Education*, Dec. 1984, www.findarticles.com/p /articles/mi_m1011/is_v20/ai_3535945/print.

Ashenfelter, Orley, William J. Collins, and Albert Yoon. "Evaluating the Role of Brown vs. Board of Education in School Equalization, Desegregation, and the Income of African Americans." *American Law and Economics Review* 8, no. 2 (2006): 213–48.

Asher, Steven R., and John M. Gottman, eds. *The Development of Children's Friendships*. Cambridge: Cambridge University Press, 1981.

Ashmore, Harry S. *The Negro and the Schools*. Chapel Hill: University of North Carolina Press, 1954.

Austen-Smith, David, and Roland G. Fryer, Jr. "An Economic Analysis of 'Acting White.'" *Quarterly Journal of Economics* 102, no. 2 (2005): 551–83, http://post .economics.harvard.edu/faculty/fryer/papers/fryer_torelli.pdf.

Babcock, Philip. "From Ties to Gains? Evidence on Connectedness, Skill Acquisition, and Diversity." Working paper (1 Mar. 2006), www.econ.ucsb.edu/~babcock/TiestoGains.pdf.

Badger, Anthony J. "The White Reaction to *Brown*: Arkansas, the Southern Manifesto, and Massive Resistance." In *Understanding the Little Rock Crisis: An Exercise in Remembrance and Reconciliation,* ed. Elizabeth Jacoway and C. Fred Williams. Fayetteville: University of Arkansas Press, 1999.

Baker, Liva. *Miranda: Crime, Law, and Politics.* New York: Atheneum, 1983.

Bankston, Carl L., III, and Stephen J. Caldas. *A Troubled Dream: The Promise and Failure of School Desegregation in Louisiana.* Nashville, Tenn.: Vanderbilt University Press, 2002.

Barnett, Bernice McNair. "Race, Gender, and Class in the Personal-Political Struggles of African Americans: Reclaiming Voice." In *Race, Gender, and Class in Sociology: Toward an Inclusive Curriculum,* ed. Jean Ait Amber Belkhir and Bernice McNair Barnett. Washington, D.C.: American Sociological Association, 1999.

Bartley, Abel. "Reading, Writing, and Racism: The Fight to Desegregate the Duval County Public School System." *Journal of Negro History* 86, no. 3 (2001): 336–47.

Battu, Harminder, McDonald Mwale, and Yves Zenou. "Do Oppositional Identities Reduce Employment for Ethnic Minorities?" CEPR Discussion Paper no. 3819 (2003), http://papers.ssrn.com/sol3/papers.cfm?abstract_id=404622.

Baughman, E. Earl, and W. Grant Dahlstrom. *Negro and White Children: A Psychological Study in the Rural South.* New York: Academic, 1968.

Beals, Melba Pattillo. *Warriors Don't Cry.* New York: Pocket, 1994.

Beauboeuf-Lafontant, Tamara. "A Movement Against and Beyond Boundaries: 'Politically Relevant Teaching' Among African American Teachers." *Teachers College Record* 100, no. 4 (1999): 702–23.

Bell, Derrick. "A Model Alternative Desegregation Plan." In *Shades of Brown: New Perspectives on School Desegregation,* ed. Derrick Bell. New York: Teachers College Press, 1980.

———. *Silent Covenants: Brown v. Board of Education and the Unfulfilled Hopes for Racial Reform.* Oxford: Oxford University Press, 2004.

———. "Time for the Teachers: Putting Educators Back into the Brown Remedy." *Journal of Negro Education* 52, no. 3 (1983): 290–301.

Bellamy, Donnie D. "The Education of Blacks in Missouri Prior to 1861." *Journal of Negro History* 59, no. 2 (1974): 143–57.

Berg, William M., and David L. Colton. "Brown and the Distribution of School Resources." *New Directions for Testing and Measurement: Impact of Desegregation* 14 (June 1982): 83–97.

Bergin, David A., and Helen C. Cooks. "High School Students of Color Talk About Accusations of 'Acting White.'" *Urban Review,* 34, no. 2 (2002): 113–34.

Berlin, Ira, Marc Favreau, and Steven F. Miller. *Remembering Slavery: African Americans Talk About Their Personal Experiences of Slavery and Emancipation.* New York: New Press, 1998.

Berry, Tracey. "Inherently Unequal." *Missouri Resources* 17, no. 4 (2000–2001), www.dnr.mo.gov/magazine/2000-01-winter.pdf.

Billger, Sherrilyn M. "Reconstructing School Segregation: On the Efficacy and Equity of Single-Sex Schooling." IZA Discussion Paper no. 2037 (Mar. 2006), ftp://ftp.iza.org/dps/dp2037.pdf.

Billig, Michael, and Henri Tajfel. "Social Categorization and Similarity in Intergroup Behaviour." *European Journal of Social Psychology* 3 (1973): 27–52.

Billingsley, Andrew. *Black Families in White America*. Englewood Cliffs, N.J.: Prentice-Hall, 1968.

Binder, Amy. "Why Do Some Curricular Challenges Work While Others Do Not? The Case of Three Afrocentric Challenges." *Sociology of Education* 73, no. 2 (2000): 69–91.

Bishop, John H., Matthew Bishop, Michael Bishop, Lara Gelbwasser, Shanna Green, Erica Peterson, Anna Rubinsztaj, and Andrew Zuckerman. "Why We Harass Nerds and Freaks: A Formal Theory of Student Culture and Norms." *Journal of School Health* 74, no. 7 (2004): 235–51.

Blaney, Nancy T., Cookie Stephan, David Rosenfield, Elliot Aronson, and Jev Sikes. "Interdependence in the Classroom: A Field Study." *Journal of Educational Psychology* 69, no. 2 (1977): 121–28.

Bloome, David, and Cathy Golden. "Literacy Learning, Classroom Processes, and Race: A Microanalytic Study of Two Desegregated Classrooms." *Journal of Black Studies* 13, no. 2 (1982): 207–26.

Bodenhorn, Howard, and Christopher S. Ruebeck. "The Economics of Identity and the Endogenity of Race." NBER Working Paper 9962 (2003), www.nber.org/papers/w9962.

Bolner, James, and Arnold Vedlitz. "The Affinity of Negro Pupils for Segregated Schools: Obstacle to Desegregation." *Journal of Negro Education* 40, no. 4 (1971): 313–21.

Bolton, Charles C. "Mississippi's School Equalization Program, 1945–1954: 'A Last Gasp to Try to Maintain a Segregated Educational System.'" *Journal of Southern History* 66, no. 4 (2000): 781–814.

Bond, Horace Mann. *The Education of the Negro in the American Social Order*. New York: Octagon, 1966.

Boozer, Michael A., and Stephen E. Cacciola. "Inside the 'Black Box' of Project Star: Estimation of Peer Effects Using Experimental Data." Yale Economic Growth Center Discussion Paper no. 832 (1997), http://papers.ssrn.com/sol3/papers.cfm?abstract_id=277009.

Bowles, Samuel, and Rajiv Sethi. "Social Segregation and the Dynamics of Group Inequality." University of Massachusetts Amherst, Department of Economics, Working Paper 2006-02 (2006), www.columbia.edu/~rs328/GroupInequality.pdf.

Bowman, Lorenzo. "Black and White Attorneys' Perspectives on Race, the Legal System, and Continuing Legal Education: A Critical Race Theory Analysis." Ph.D. diss., University of Georgia, 2004, www.coe.uga.edu/leap/adulted/pdf/bowman_lorenzo_200405_phd.pdf.

Braddock, Jomills Henry, II, and Marvin P. Dawkins. "Ability Grouping, Aspirations, and Attainments: Evidence from the National Educational Longitudinal Study of 1988." *Journal of Negro Education* 62, no. 3 (1993): 324–36.

Brooks, Roy L. *Integration or Separation? A Strategy for Racial Equality.* Cambridge: Harvard University Press, 1996.

Brooks-Gunn, Jeanne, Greg J. Duncan, Pamela Kato Klebanov, and Naomi Sealand. "Do Neighborhoods Influence Child and Adolescent Development?" *American Journal of Sociology* 99, no. 2 (1993): 353–95.

Brown, Ann L., Annemarie Sullivan Palincsar, and Linda Purcell. "Poor Readers: Teach, Don't Label." In *The School Achievement of Minority Children: New Perspectives,* ed. Ulric Neisser. Hillsdale, N.J.: Lawrence Erlbaum, 1986.

Brown, Lionel. "America's Black Male: Disadvantaged from Birth to Death." *Perspectives on Urban Education* 3, no. 2 (2005): 1–16, www.urbanedjournal.org/notes/notes0016.pdf.

Brown, Rupert. *Group Processes: Dynamics Within and Between Groups.* New York: Basil Blackwell, 1988.

Buhs, Eric S., Gary W. Ladd, and Sarah L. Herald. "Peer Exclusion and Victimization: Processes That Mediate the Relation Between Peer Group Rejection and Children's Classroom Engagement and Achievement?" *Journal of Educational Psychology* 98, no. 1 (2006): 1–13.

Bullard, Pamela, and Judith Stoia. *The Hardest Lesson: Personal Accounts of a School Desegregation Crisis.* Boston: Little, Brown, 1980.

Bullock, Henry Allen. *The History of Negro Education in the South From 1619 to the Present.* New York: Praeger, 1967.

Burke, Mary A., and Tim R. Sass. "Classroom Peer Effects and Student Achievement." Working paper (2006), http://garnet.acns.fsu.edu/~tsass/.

Burrell, Brenda Joyce. "Bear Witness: African American Teachers' Perspectives of Their Teaching Practices in Segregated and Desegregated Schools." Ph.D. diss., University of Texas at Austin, 2005, http://dspace.lib.utexas.edu/bitstream/2152/933/1/burrellb20361.pdf.

Burrell, Leon, and Nicholas F. Rayder. "Black and White Students' Attitudes Toward White Counselors." *Journal of Negro Education* 40, no. 1 (1971): 48–52.

Butler, Johnny S. "Black Educators in Louisiana—A Question of Survival." *Journal of Negro Education* 43, no. 1 (1974): 9–24.

Buxton, Thomas H., and Keith W. Prichard. "The Power Erosion Syndrome of the Black Principal." *Integrated Education* 15, no. 3 (May–June 1977): 9–14.

Byers, Bryan, ed. *Readings in Social Psychology: Perspective and Method.* Needham Heights, Mass.: Allyn and Bacon, 1993.

Cagle, Laurence T., and Jerome Beker. "Social Characteristics and Educational Aspirations of Northern, Lower-Class, Predominantly Negro Parents Who Accepted and Declined a School Integration Opportunity." *Journal of Negro Education* 37, no. 4 (1968): 406–17.

Calabrese, Raymond L. "The Public School: A Source of Alienation for Minority Parents." *Journal of Negro Education* 59, no. 2 (1990): 148–54.

Caldas, Stephen J., Roslin Growe, and Carl L. Bankston III. "African American Re-action to Lafayette Parish School Desegregation Order: From Delight to Disen-chantment." *Journal of Negro Education* 71, no. 1–2 (2002): 43–59.

Carbonaro, William. "Tracking, Students' Effort, and Academic Achievement." *Soci-ology of Education* 78 (2005): 27–49.

Card, David, and Alan B. Krueger. "Does School Quality Matter? Returns to Educa-tion and the Characteristics of Public Schools in the United States." *Journal of Po-litical Economy* 100, no. 1 (1992): 1–40.

———. "School Quality and Black-White Relative Earnings: A Direct Assessment." *Quarterly Journal of Economics* 107, no. 1 (1992): 151–200.

Card, David, and Jesse Rothstein. "Racial Segregation and the Black-White Test Score Gap." NBER Working Paper no. 12078 (May 2005), www.nber.org/papers /W12078.

Carithers, Martha W. "School Desegregation and Racial Cleavage, 1954–1970: A Re-view of the Literature." *Journal of Social Issues* 26, no. 4 (1970): 25–47.

Carmichael, Stokely, and Charles V. Hamilton. *Black Power: The Politics of Liberation in America.* New York: Vintage, 1967.

Carneiro, Pedro, James J. Heckman, and Dimitriy V. Masterov. "Labor Market Dis-crimination and Racial Differences in Premarket Factors." *Journal of Law and Eco-nomics* 48 (2005): 1–39.

Carrell, Scott E., Richard L. Fullerton, Robert N. Gilchrist, and James E. West. "Peer and Leadership Effects in Academic and Athletic Performance." Working paper (2 May 2007), www.rand.org/labor/seminars/adp/pdfs/2007_carrell.pdf.

Carter, Alice E. "Segregation and Integration in the Appalachian Coalfields: McDowell County Responds to the *Brown* Decision." *West Virginia History* 54 (1995): 78–104, www.wvculture.org/HISTORY/journal_wvh/wvh54-5.html.

Carter, David G. "Second-Generation School Integration Problems for Blacks." *Jour-nal of Black Studies* 13, no. 2 (1982): 175–88.

Carter, Prudence. "Intersecting Identities: 'Acting White,' Gender, and Academic Achievement." In *Beyond Acting White: Reframing the Debate on Black Student Achievement,* ed. Erin McNamara Horvat and Carla O'Connor. Lanham, Md.: Row-man and Littlefield, 2006.

Carter, Robert L. "The Effects of Segregation and the Consequences of Desegrega-tion: A Social Science Statement." *Journal of Negro Education* 22, no. 1 (1953): 68–76.

Carter, Robert L., and Thurgood Marshall. "The Meaning and Significance of the Supreme Court Decree." *Journal of Negro Education* 24, no. 3 (1955): 397–404.

Cashin, Sheryll D. "American Public Schools Fifty Years After *Brown:* A Separate and Unequal Reality." *Howard Law Journal* 47 (2004): 341.

———. *The Failures of Integration.* New York: Public Affairs, 2004.

Casteel, Clifton A. "Teacher-Student Interactions and Race in Integrated Classrooms." *Journal of Educational Research* 92, no. 2 (1998): 115–20.

Catsambis, Sophia, and Andrew A. Beveridge, "Does Neighborhood Matter? Family,

Neighborhood, and School Influences on Eighth-Grade Mathematics Achievement." *Sociological Focus* 34, no. 4 (2001): 435–57.

Cecelski, David S. *Along Freedom Road: Hyde County, North Carolina, and the Fate of Black Schools in the South.* Chapel Hill: University of North Carolina Press, 1994.

Chafe, William H. *Civilities and Civil Rights: Greensboro, North Carolina, and the Black Struggle for Freedom.* New York: Oxford University Press, 1980.

Charles A. Dana Center, University of Texas at Austin. *Hope for Urban Education: A Study of Nine High-Performing, High-Poverty, Urban Elementary Schools.* Washington, D.C.: U.S. Department of Education, Planning and Evaluation Service, 1999, www.ed.gov/pubs/urbanhope/.

Cheng, Simon, and Brian Starks. "Racial Differences in the Effects of Significant Others on Students' Educational Expectations." *Sociology of Education* 75, no. 4 (2002): 306–27.

Chin, Tiffani, and Meredith Phillips. "The Ubiquity of Oppositional Culture." Working paper (2005).

Clark, Kenneth B., and Mamie P. Clark. "The Development of Consciousness of Self and the Emergence of Racial Identification in Negro Pre-School Children." *Journal of Social Psychology* 10 (1939): 591–99.

———. "Emotional Factors in Racial Identification and Preference in Negro Children." *Journal of Negro Education* 19, no. 3 (1950): 341–50.

Clarke, Nina H., and Lillian B. Brown, *History of the Black Public Schools of Montgomery County, Maryland, 1872–1961.* New York: Vantage, 1978.

Clifton, Rodney A., Raymond P. Perry, Karen Parsonson, and Stella Hryniuk. "Effects of Ethnicity and Sex on Teachers' Expectations of Junior High School Students." *Sociology of Education* 59, no. 1 (1986): 58–67.

Clotfelter, Charles T. *After Brown: The Rise and Retreat of School Desegregation.* Princeton: Princeton University Press, 2004.

Cohen, Ed. "Who's to Blame When Schools Fail?" *Notre Dame Magazine,* Summer 2001, www.nd.edu/~ndmag/sm2001/schools.html.

Cohen, Geoffrey L., et al. "Recursive Processes in Self-Affirmation: Intervening to Close the Minority Achievement Gap." *Science* 324 (17 April 2009): 400–403.

Cohen, Geoffrey L., Julio Garcia, Nancy Apfel, and Allison Master. "Reducing the Racial Achievement Gap: A Social-Psychological Intervention." *Science* 313 (2006): 1307–10.

Cohen, Jere M. "Sources of Peer Group Homogeneity." *Sociology of Education* 50, no. 4 (1977): 227–41.

Coleman, James S. *The Adolescent Society: The Social Life of the Teenager and Its Impact on Education.* New York: Free Press, 1961.

———. *Equality and Achievement in Education.* London: Westview, 1990. Coleman, James S., and Thomas Hoffer. *Public and Private High Schools: The Impact of Communities.* New York: Basic, 1987.

Coleman, James S., Thomas Hoffer, and Sally Kilgore. "Achievement and Segregation in Secondary Schools: A Further Look at Public and Private School Differences." *Sociology of Education* 55, no. 2–3 (1982): 162–82.

Coleman, James S., and Edward L. McDill. "Family and Peer Influences in College Plans of High School Students." *Sociology of Education* 38, no. 2 (1965): 112–26.

Coles, Robert. *Children of Crisis: A Study of Courage and Fear.* New York: Atlantic Monthly Press, 1964.

Collins, Thomas W. "From Courtrooms to Classrooms: Managing School Desegregation in a Deep South High School." In *Desegregated Schools: Appraisals of an American Experiment,* ed. Ray C. Rist. New York: Academic, 1979.

Collins, William J., and Robert A. Margo. "Historical Perspectives on Racial Differences in Schooling in the United States." Vanderbilt University Working Paper no. 03-W13 (2003), www.econ.duke.edu/aeasp/Sloan/Education/Collins_and_Margo_NBER_2003.pdf.

Collins-Eaglin, Jan, and Stuart A. Karabenick. "Devaluing of Academic Success by African-American Students: On 'Acting White' and 'Selling Out.'" Paper presented at Annual Meeting of the American Educational Research Association, Atlanta, Georgia, 12–16 Apr. 1993, http://eric.ed.gov/ERICDocs/data/ericdocs2sql/content_storage_01/0000019b/80/13/1e/01.pdf.

Comminney, Shawn. "The Society for the Propagation of the Gospel in Foreign Parts and Black Education in South Carolina, 1702–1764." *Journal of Negro History* 84, no. 4 (1999): 360–69. Cook, Michael D., and William N. Evans. "Families or Schools? Explaining the Convergence in White and Black Academic Performance." *Journal of Labor Economics* 18, no. 4 (2000): 729–54.

Cook, Philip J., and Jens Ludwig. "The Burden of 'Acting White': Do Black Adolescents Disparage Academic Achievement?" In *The Black-White Test Score Gap,* ed. Christopher Jencks and Meredith Phillips. Washington, D.C.: Brookings Institution Press, 1998.

———. "Weighing the 'Burden of "Acting White"' Are There Race Differences in Attitudes Toward Education?" *Journal of Policy Analysis and Management* 16, no. 2 (1997): 256–78.

Cooley, Jane. "Desegregation and the Achievement Gap: Do Diverse Peers Help?" Working paper (6 May 2009), www.ssc.wisc.edu/~jcooley/CooleyDeseg.pdf.

Cooper, Arnold. *Between Struggle and Hope: Four Black Educators in the South, 1894–1915.* Ames: Iowa State University Press, 1989.

Cooper, Robert. "Detracking Reform in an Urban California High School: Improving the Schooling Experiences of African American Students." *Journal of Negro Education* 65, no. 2 (1996): 190–208.

Corcoran, Sean P., and William N. Evans. "The Role of Inequality in Teacher Quality." In *Steady Gains and Stalled Progress: Inequality and the Black-White Test Score Gap,* ed. Katherine Magnuson and Jane Waldfogel. New York: Russell Sage Foundation, 2008.

Cornelius, Janet Duitsman. *When I Can Read My Title Clear: Literacy, Slavery, and Religion in the Antebellum South.* Columbia: University of South Carolina Press, 1991.

Correspondents of the New York Times. *How Race Is Lived in America.* New York: Times, 2001.

Corwin, Miles. *And Still We Rise: The Trials and Triumphs of Twelve Gifted Inner-City Students*. New York: Perennial, 2000.

Crain, Robert L. *The Politics of School Desegregation*. New York: Anchor, 1969.

———. "School Integration and the Academic Achievement of Negroes." *Sociology of Education* 44, no. 1 (1971): 1–26.

Crain, Robert L., and Rita E. Mahard. "School Racial Composition and Black College Attendance and Achievement Test Performance." *Sociology of Education* 51, no. 2 (1978): 81–101.

Crane, Jonathan. "The Epidemic Theory of Ghettos and Neighborhood Effects on Dropping Out and Teenage Childbearing." *American Journal of Sociology* 96, no. 5 (1991): 1226–59.

Cross, Theodore, and Robert Bruce Slater. "The Alarming Decline in the Academic Performance of African-American Men." *Journal of Blacks in Higher Education* 27 (2000): 82–87.

Cruse, Harold. *Plural but Equal*. New York: William Morrow, 1987.

Curry, Constance. *Silver Rights*. New York: Harcourt Brace, 1995.

Cutler, David M., and Edward L. Glaeser. "Are Ghettos Good or Bad?" *Quarterly Journal of Economics* 112, no. 3 (1997): 827–72.

daCosta, G. A. "Orphans and Outlaws: Some Impacts of Racism." *Multiculturalism* 2, no. 1 (1978): 4–7.

Dales, Ruth J., and James F. Keller. "Self-Concept Scores Among Black and White Culturally Deprived Adolescent Males." *Journal of Negro Education* 41, no. 1 (1972): 31–34.

Darity, William, Jr. "Intergroup Disparity: Why Culture Is Irrelevant." *Review of Black Political Economy* 29, no. 4 (2002): 77–90.

Darkenwald, Gordon G. "Some Effects of the 'Obvious Variable': Teacher's Race and Holding Power with Black Adult Students." *Sociology of Education* 48, no. 4 (1975): 420–31.

Datnow, Amanda, and Robert Cooper. "Peer Networks of African American Students in Independent Schools: Affirming Academic Success and Racial Identity." *Journal of Negro Education* 66, no. 1 (1997): 56–72.

Davis, Allison, and John Dollard. *Children of Bondage: The Personality Development of Negro Youth in the Urban South*. Washington, D.C.: American Council on Education, 1940.

Davis, F. James. *Who Is Black? One Nation's Definition*. University Park: Pennsylvania State University Press, 1991.

Davis, John W. "Protecting the Negro Teacher." *Journal of Negro Education* 25, no. 2 (1956): 182–84.

Davis, Lenwood G. *A History of Beaufort/Queen Street High School, 1928–1968*. Kingston, N.Y.: Tri State Services, 1996.

Davis, Sampson, George Jenkins, and Rameck Hunt, with Lisa Frazier Page. *The Pact: Three Young Men Make a Promise and Fulfill a Dream*. New York: Riverhead, 2002.

Deci, Edward L., Richard Koestner, and Richard M. Ryan. "Extrinsic Rewards and

Intrinsic Motivation in Education: Reconsidered Once Again." *Review of Educational Research* 71, no. 1 (2001): 1–27.

Dee, Thomas S. "Teachers, Race, and Student Achievement in a Randomized Experiment." *Review of Economics and Statistics* 86, no. 1 (2004): 195–210, www.swarthmore.edu/SocSci/tdee1/Research/restato4.pdf.

———. "Teachers and the Gender Gaps in Student Achievement." NBER Working Paper no. 11660 (2005), www.nber.org/papers/W11660 or www.swarthmore.edu/SocSci/tdee1/Research/w11660revised.pdf.

Delpit, Lisa. *Other People's Children: Cultural Conflict in the Classroom.* New York: New Press, 2006.

Dempsey, Van, and George Noblit. "Cultural Ignorance and School Desegregation: A Community Narrative." In *Beyond Desegregation: The Politics of Quality in African American Schooling*, ed. Mwalimu J. Shujaa. Thousand Oaks, Calif.: Corwin, 1996.

Dent, David J. *In Search of Black America.* New York: Simon and Schuster, 2000.

Dent, Tom. *Southern Journey: A Return to the Civil Rights Movement.* Athens: University of Georgia Press, 2001.

Detweiler, John S. "The Negro Teacher and the Fourteenth Amendment." *Journal of Negro Education* 36, no. 4 (1967): 403–9.

Deutsch, Martin, Irwin Katz, and Arthur R. Jensen. *Social Class, Race, and Psychological Development.* New York: Holt, Rinehart, and Winston, 1968.

Diamond, John B. "Are We Barking Up the Wrong Tree? Rethinking Oppositional Culture Explanations for the Black/White Achievement Gap" (1968), http://agi.harvard.edu/events/download.php?id=79.

Dickens, Angelia. "Revisiting Brown v. Board of Education: How Tracking Has Resegregated America's Public Schools." *Columbia Journal of Law and Social Problems* 29 (1996): 469.

Ding, Weili, and Steven F. Lehrer. "Do Peers Affect Student Achievement in China's Secondary Schools?" NBER Working Paper 12305 (June 2006), www.nber.org/papers/w12305.

Doddy, Hurley H. "Desegregation and the Employment of Negro Teachers." *Journal of Negro Education* 24, no. 4 (1955): 405–8.

Doddy, Hurley H., and G. Franklin Edwards. "Apprehensions of Negro Teachers Concerning Desegregation in South Carolina." *Journal of Negro Education* 24, no. 1 (1955): 26–43.

Donelan, Richarde W., Gerald A. Neal, and Deneese L. Jones. "The Promise of Brown and the Reality of Academic Grouping: The Tracks of My Tears." *Journal of Negro Education* 63, no. 3 (1994): 376–87.

Dornbusch, Sanford M. "The Sociology of Adolescence." *Annual Review of Sociology* 15 (1989): 233–59.

Dornbusch, Sanford M., Philip I. Ritter, and Laurence Steinberg. "Community Influences on the Relation of Family Statuses to Adolescent School Performance: Differences Between African Americans and Non-Hispanic Whites." *American Journal of Education* 99, no. 4 (1991): 543–67.

Dougherty, Jack. "From Anecdote to Analysis: Oral Interviews and New Scholarship in Educational History." *Journal of American History* 86, no. 2 (1999): 712–23.

Douglas, Davison M. *Jim Crow Moves North: The Battle over Northern School Segregation, 1865–1954*. New York: Cambridge University Press, 2005.

———. *Reading, Writing, and Race: The Desegregation of the Charlotte Schools*. Chapel Hill: University of North Carolina Press, 1995.

Douglass, Harl R., and Joseph H. Collins. "The Relationship of Certain Factors to Failure Among Superior Pupils in a Junior High School for Negroes." *Journal of Negro Education* 5, no. 4 (1936): 599–601.

Downey, Douglas B., and James W. Ainsworth-Darnell. "The Search for Oppositional Culture Among Black Students." *American Sociological Review* 67 (2002): 156–64.

Downey, Douglas B., and Shana Pribesh. "When Race Matters: Teachers' Evaluations of Students' Classroom Behavior." *Sociology of Education* 77 (2004): 267–82.

Drago, Edmund L. *Initiative, Paternalism, and Race Relations: Charleston's Avery Normal Institute*. Athens: University of Georgia Press, 1990.

Drennen, William M., Jr., and Kojo Jones, Jr. *Red, White, Black, and Blue: A Dual Memoir of Race and Class in Appalachia*. Athens: Ohio University Press, 2004.

Drury, Darrel W. "Black Self-Esteem and Desegregated Schools." *Sociology of Education* 53, no. 2 (1980): 88–103.

Du Bois, W. E. Burghardt. "Does the Negro Need Separate Schools?" *Journal of Negro Education* 4, no. 3 (1935): 328–35.

Due, Tananarive, and Patricia Stephens Due. *Freedom in the Family: A Mother-Daughter Memoir of the Fight for Civil Rights*. New York: Ballantine, 2003.

Dyer, Henry S. "School Factors and Equal Educational Opportunity." In *Equal Educational Opportunity*. Cambridge: Harvard University Press, 1969.

Dyson, Michael Eric. *Is Bill Cosby Right?* New York: Basic Civitas, 2005.

Eckert, Penelope. *Jocks and Burnouts: Social Categories and Identity in the High School*. New York: Teachers College Press, 1989.

Eder, Donna. "Ability Grouping as a Self-Fulfilling Prophecy: A Micro-Analysis of Teacher-Student Interaction." *Sociology of Education* 54, no. 3 (1981): 151–62.

Edwards, Patricia A. "Before and After School Desegregation: African American Parents' Involvement in Schools." In *Beyond Desegregation: The Politics of Quality in African American Schooling*, ed. Mwalimu J. Shujaa. Thousand Oaks, Calif.: Corwin, 1996.

Edwards, William J. *Twenty-Five Years in the Black Belt*. Boston: Cornhill, 1918, http://docsouth.unc.edu/edwards/edwards.html.

Ehrenberg, Ronald G., and Dominic J. Brewer. "Did Teachers' Verbal Ability and Race Matter in the 1960s? *Coleman* Revisited." *Economics of Education Review* 14, no. 1 (1995): 1–21.

Eibl-Eibesfeldt, Irenäus. *Ethology: The Biology of Behavior*. New York: Holt, Rinehart, and Winston, 1970.

Ellemers, Naomi, Cathy van Dyck, Steve Hinkle, and Annelieke Jacobs. "Intergroup Differentiation in Social Context: Identity Needs Versus Audience Constraints." *Social Psychology Quarterly* 63, no. 1 (2000): 60–74.

Ellen, Ingrid Gould, and Margery Austin Turner. "Does Neighborhood Matter? Assessing Recent Evidence." *Housing Policy Debate* 8, no. 4 (1997): 833–66.

Enck, Henry S. "Black Self-Help in the Progressive Era: The 'Northern Campaigns' of Smaller Southern Black Industrial Schools, 1900–1915." *Journal of Negro History* 61, no. 1 (1976): 73–87.

Enomoto, Ernestine K., and David L. Angus. "African American School Attendance in the 19th Century: Education in a Rural Northern Community, 1850–1880." *Journal of Negro Education* 64, no. 1 (1995): 42–51.

Ensign, Jacque. "Subsequent Educational and Professional Attainment of Black and White Students from Two Segregated Schools." *Journal of Negro Education* 71, no. 4 (2002): 331–46.

Entwisle, Doris R., and Karl L. Alexander. "Summer Setback: Race, Poverty, School Composition, and Mathematics Achievement in the First Two Years of School." *American Sociological Review* 57, no. 1 (1992): 72–84.

———. "Winter Setback: The Racial Composition of Schools and Learning to Read." *American Sociological Review* 59, no. 3 (1994): 446–60.

Entwisle, Doris R., and Murray Webster, Jr. "Expectations in Mixed Racial Groups." *Sociology of Education* 47, no. 3 (1974): 301–18.

Epps, Edgar, ed. *Black Students in White Schools.* Worthington, Ohio: Charles A. Jones, 1972.

Epstein, Erwin H. "Social Class, Ethnicity, and Academic Achievement: A Cross-Cultural Approach." *Journal of Negro Education* 41, no. 3 (1972): 202–15.

Eve, Raymond A. "'Adolescent Culture': Convenient Myth or Reality? A Comparison of Students and Their Teachers." *Sociology of Education* 48, no. 2 (1975): 152–67.

Fairclough, Adam. "'Being in the Field of Education and also Being a Negro . . . Seems . . . Tragic': Black Teachers in the Jim Crow South." *Journal of American History* 87, no. 1 (2000): 65–91.

———. *Teaching Equality: Black Schools in the Age of Jim Crow.* Athens: University of Georgia Press, 2001.

Falk, William W. "Mobility Attitudes of Segregated and Desegregated Black Youths." *Journal of Negro Education* 47, no. 2 (1978): 132–42.

Farkas, George. "Racial Disparities and Discrimination in Education: What Do We Know, How Do We Know It, and What Do We Need to Know?" *Teachers College Record* 105, no. 6 (2003): 1119–46.

Farkas, George, Christy Lleras, and Steve Maczuga. "Does Oppositional Culture Exist in Minority and Poverty Peer Groups." *American Sociological Review* 67 (2002): 148–55.

Farmer, G. Lawrence. "Longitudinal Exploration of the Caste Theory of Educational Aspirations." *Children and Schools* 23, no. 3 (2001): 160–70.

Farmer, Harold E. "The Revival of Classical Learning as the Most Potent Force in Negro Progress." *Journal of Negro Education* 9, no. 4 (1940): 591–94.

Fauth, Rebecca C. "The Impacts of Neighborhood Poverty Deconcentration Efforts on Low-Income Children's and Adolescents' Well-Being." *Children, Youth, and Environments* 14, no. 1 (2004): 1–55.

Feld, Scott L., and William C. Carter. "When Desegregation Reduces Interracial Contact: A Class Size Paradox for Weak Ties." *American Journal of Sociology* 103, no. 5 (1998): 1165–86.

Felice, Lawrence G. "Black Student Dropout Behavior: Disengagement from School Rejection and Racial Discrimination." *Journal of Negro Education* 50, no. 4 (1981): 415–24.

Felmlee, Diane, and Donna Eder. "Contextual Effects in the Classroom: The Impact of Ability Groups on Student Attention." *Sociology of Education* 56, no. 2 (1983): 77–87.

Fen, Sing-nan. "Notes on the Education of Negroes in North Carolina During the Civil War." *Journal of Negro Education* 36, no. 1 (1967): 24–31.

Ferguson, Ronald F. "Comment." In *The Black-White Test Score Gap,* ed. Christopher Jencks and Meredith Phillips. Washington, D.C.: Brookings Institution Press, 1998.

———. "A Diagnostic Analysis of Black-White GPA Disparities in Shaker Heights, Ohio." In *Brookings Papers on Educational Policy 2001,* ed. Diane Ravitch. Washington, D.C.: Brookings Institution Press, 2001.

———. "Paying for Public Education: New Evidence on How and Why Money Matters." *Harvard Journal on Legislation* 28 (1991): 488–89.

Figlio, David N. "Names, Expectations, and the Black-White Test Score Gap." NBER Working Paper no. 11195 (2005), www.nber.org/papers/W11195 or http://bear.cba.ufl.edu/figlio/blacknames1.pdf.

Figlio, David N., and Marianne E. Page. "School Choice and the Distributional Effects of Ability Tracking: Does Separation Increase Inequality?" *Journal of Urban Economics* 51 (2002): 497–514.

Finn, Jeremy D., and Kristin E. Voelkl. "School Characteristics Related to Student Engagement." *Journal of Negro Education* 62, no. 3 (1993): 249–68.

Fleming, Cynthia Griggs. "The Plight of Black Educators in Postwar Tennessee, 1865–1920." *Journal of Negro History* 64, no. 4 (1979): 355–64.

Fletcher, Anne C., Nancy E. Darling, Laurence Steinberg, and Sanford M. Dornbusch. "The Company They Keep: Relation of Adolescents' Adjustment and Behavior to Their Friends' Perceptions of Authoritative Parenting in the Social Network." *Developmental Psychology* 31, no. 2 (1995): 300–310.

Foley, Douglas. "Ogbu's Theory of Academic Disengagement: Its Evolution and Its Critics." *Intercultural Education* 15, no. 4 (2004): 385–97.

Ford, Donna Y. "A Challenge for Culturally Diverse Families of Gifted Children: Forced Choices Between Achievement or Affiliation." *Gifted Child Today* 27, no. 3 (2004): 26–29, www.prufrock.com/client/client_pages/GCT_articles/Culturally_Diverse_Families_of_Gifted_Children.cfm.

———. "Desegregating Gifted Education: A Need Unmet." *Journal of Negro Education* 64, no. 1 (1995): 52–62.

———. "Determinants of Underachievement as Perceived by Gifted, Above-Average, and Average Black Students." *Roeper Review* 14, no. 3 (1992): 130–36.

———. "An Investigation of the Paradox of Underachievement Among Gifted Black Students." *Roeper Review* 16, no. 2 (1993): 78–84.

———. "Underachievement Among Gifted and Non-Gifted Black Females." *Journal of Secondary Gifted Education* (Winter 1994–95): 165–75.

Ford, Donna Y., Tarek C. Grantham, and Gilman W. Whiting. "Another Look at the Achievement Gap." *Urban Education* 43, no. 2 (2008): 216–39.

Ford, Donna Y., and J. John Harris III. "The American Achievement Ideology and Achievement Differentials Among Preadolescent Gifted and Nongifted African American Males and Females." *Journal of Negro Education* 61, no. 1 (1992): 45–64.

Ford, Donna Y., J. John Harris III, Cynthia A. Tyson, and Michelle Frazier Trotman. "Beyond Deficit Thinking: Providing Access for Gifted African American Students." *Roeper Review* 24, no. 2 (2002): 52–58.

Ford, Donna Y., and Karen S. Webb. "Desegregation of Gifted Educational Programs: The Impact of Brown on Underachieving Children of Color." *Journal of Negro Education* 63, no. 3 (1994): 358–75.

Ford, Thomas E., and George R. Tonander. "The Role of Differentiation Between Groups and Social Identity in Stereotype Formation." *Social Psychology Quarterly* 61, no. 4 (1998): 372–84.

Fordham, Signithia, and John Ogbu. "Black Students' School Successes: Coping with the Burden of Acting White." *Urban Review* 18, no. 3 (1986): 176–206.

Foster, Kevin Michael. "Coming to Terms: A Discussion of John Ogbu's Cultural-Ecological Theory of Minority Academic Achievement." *Intercultural Education* 15, no. 4 (2004): 369–84.

Foster, Michele. *Black Teachers on Teaching.* New York: New Press, 1997.

Fowler, Lee V. "School Integration: A Case Study of the 1971–1972 School Year at Indian River High School." Ph.D. diss., Virginia Polytechnic Institute and State University, 1997, http://scholar.lib.vt.edu/theses/public/etd-11398-163747/materials/FINAL.PDF.

Frank, Kenneth A., Chandra Muller, and Kathryn Schiller. "The Social Milieus of Adolescent Society: Effects on Adolescents' Academic Effort" (2005), www.econ.msu.edu/HIPI/brownbagpapers/kennethfranko203.pdf.

Frankenberg, Erica. *The Segregation of American Teachers.* Cambridge: Civil Rights Project at Harvard University, 2006, www.civilrightsproject.ucla.edu/research/deseg/segregation_american_teachers12-06.pdf.

Frazier, E. Franklin. *Black Bourgeoisie.* New York: Free Press, 1957. Freedman, David. "African-American Schooling in the South Prior to 1861." *Journal of Negro History* 84, no. 1 (1999): 1–47.

Freeman, Morgan. "Home." In *America Behind the Color Line,* ed. Henry Louis Gates, Jr. New York: Warner, 2004. Freemen, Kassie. "Increasing African Americans' Participation in Higher Education: African American High-School Students' Perspectives." *Journal of Higher Education* 68, no. 5 (1997): 523–50.

Frerichs, Allen H. "Relationship of Self-Esteem of the Disadvantaged to School Success." *Journal of Negro Education* 40, no. 2 (1971): 117–20.

Fries-Britt, Sharon. "Moving Beyond Black Achiever Isolation: Experiences of Gifted Black Collegians." *Journal of Higher Education* 69, no. 5 (1998): 556–76.

Frost, Michelle Bellessa. "Texas Students' College Expectations: Does High School Racial Composition Matter?" Ph.D. diss., Princeton University, 2004, http://theop .princeton.edu/.

Fryer, Roland G. "Acting White." *Education Next,* Jan. 2006, www.educationnext .org/20061/pdf/52.pdf.

———. "A Model of Social Interactions and Endogenous Poverty Traps." NBER Working Paper (May 2006), http://post.economics.harvard.edu/faculty/fryer/ papers/cultural_capital_final.pdf.

Fryer, Roland G., Federico Echenique, and Alex Kaufman. "Is School Segregation Good or Bad?" *American Economic Review* 96, no. 2 (2006): 265–69, http://post .economics.harvard.edu/faculty/fryer/papers/echen_fryer_kaufm.pdf.

Fryer, Roland G., Jr., and Steven D. Levitt. "The Black-White Test Score Gap Through Third Grade." *American Law and Economic Review* 8, no. 2 (2006): 249–81.

———. "Understanding the Black-White Test Score Gap in the First Two Years of School." *Review of Economics and Statistics* 86, no. 2 (2004): 447–64, http://price theory.uchicago.edu/levitt/Papers/FryerLevittUnderstandingTheBlack2004.pdf.

Fryer, Roland G., Jr., and Paul Torelli. "Measuring the Prevalence and Impact of 'Acting White.'" Paper presented at Annual Meeting, Allied Social Science Associations, Boston, Jan. 2006.

Fultz, Michael. "The Displacement of Black Educators Post-Brown: An Overview and Analysis." *History of Education Quarterly* 44 (2004): 11–45.

Futrell, Mary Hatwood. "Preparing Teachers for a New Era 50 Years After the Brown Decision." Speech at the Unite Leadership Development Institute, Nashville, Tenn., 3 Apr. 2004.

Gadsden, Vivian L., and Ralph R. Smith. "African American Males and Fatherhood: Issues in Research and Practice." *Journal of Negro Education* 63, no. 4 (1994): 634–48.

Gamoran, Adam. "Instructional and Institutional Effects of Ability Grouping." *Sociology of Education* 59, no. 4 (1986): 185–98.

———. "The Variable Effects of High School Tracking." *American Sociological Review* 57, no. 6 (1992): 812–28.

Gamoran, Adam, and Robert D. Mare. "Secondary School Tracking and Educational Inequality: Compensation, Reinforcement, or Neutrality?" *American Journal of Sociology* 94, no. 5 (1989): 1146–83.

Garibaldi, Antoine M. "Educating and Motivating African American Males to Succeed." *Journal of Negro Education* 61, no. 1 (1992): 4–11.

———. "Four Decades of Progress . . . and Decline: An Assessment of African American Educational Attainment." *Journal of Negro Education* 66, no. 2 (1997): 105–20.

Garner, Catherine L., and Stephen W. Raudenbush. "Neighborhood Effects on Educational Attainment: A Multilevel Analysis." *Sociology of Education* 64, no. 4 (1991): 251–62.

Gates, Henry Louis, Jr. *America Behind the Color Line*. New York: Warner, 2004.

———. *Colored People: A Memoir*. New York: Vintage, 1994.

Genovese, Eugene D. *Roll, Jordan, Roll: The World the Slaves Made*. New York: Vintage, 1976.

Gerard, Harold B., Terrence D. Jackson, and Edward S. Conolley. "Social Contact in the Desegregated Classroom." In *School Desegregation: A Long-Term Study*, ed. Harold B. Gerard and Norman Miller. New York: Plenum, 1975.

Gerken, Kathryn Clark. "What Have We Been Doing? Black School Psychologists and the Desegregation Issue." *Journal of Negro Education* 47, no. 1 (1978): 81–87.

Gersman, Elinor Mondale. "The Development of Public Education for Blacks in Nineteenth-Century St. Louis, Missouri." *Journal of Negro Education* 41, no. 1 (1972): 35–47.

Gerson, Mark. *In the Classroom: Dispatches from an Inner-City School That Works*. New York: Free Press, 1997.

Gibson, Judith Y. "Mighty Oaks: Five Black Educators." In *A History of African Americans of Delaware and Maryland's Eastern Shore*, ed. Carole Marks. Wilmington: Delaware Heritage Commission, 1998, www.udel.edu/BlackHistory/index.html.

Gill, Peggy B. "Community, Commitment, and African American Education: The Jackson School of Smith County, Texas, 1925–1954." *Journal of African American History* 87 (2002): 256–68.

Gilliam, George H., and the Central Virginia Educational Television Corporation. Interview of George Tremontain (2000), www.vcdh.virginia.edu/HIST604/people.html.

Gilton, Donna L. Letter to the editor, *Journal of Blacks in Higher Education*, no. 31 (2001): 5–6.

Gitomer, Drew H. "Teacher Quality in a Changing Policy Landscape: Improvements in the Teacher Pool." Educational Testing Service Report (2007), www.ets.org/Media/Education_Topics/pdf/TQ_full_report.pdf.

Gladden, Elzee C., and Jessie B. Gladden. "The Dunbar Chronicle: A Case Study." *Journal of Negro Education* 57, no. 3 (1988): 372–93.

Glaeser, Edward L., Giacomo A. M. Ponzetto, and Jesse M. Shapiro. "Strategic Extremism: Why Republicans and Democrats Divide on Religious Values" (2004), www.economics.harvard.edu/hier/2004papers/HIER2044.pdf.

Glenn, Norval D. "Television Watching, Newspaper Reading, and Cohort Differences in Verbal Ability." *Sociology of Education* 67, no. 3 (1994): 216–30.

Goethals, George R. "Peer Effects, Gender, and Intellectual Performance Among Students at a Highly Selective College: A Social Comparison of Abilities Analysis." Working paper (Oct. 2001), www.williams.edu/wpehe/DPs/DP-61.pdf.

Goetz, Judith Preissle, and E. Anne Rowley Breneman. "Desegregation and Black Students' Experiences in Two Rural Southern Elementary Schools." *The Elementary School Journal* 88, no. 5 (1988): 489–502.

Goldfield, David R. *Black, White, and Southern: Race Relations and Southern Culture, 1940 to the Present*. Baton Rouge: Louisiana State University Press, 1990.

Goldhaber, Dan. "Everyone's Doing It, but What Does Teacher Testing Tell Us About Teacher Effectiveness." Urban Institute Working Paper (16 Oct. 2006), www.caldercenter.org/PDF/1001072_everyones_doing.PDF.

Goldhaber, Dan D., and Michael Hansen. "Race, Gender, and Teacher Testing: How Objective a Tool Is Teacher Licensure Testing?" Center on Reinventing Public Education, University of Washington, Working Paper no. 2008-2 (2008), www.crpe .org/cs/crpe/view/csr_pubs/201.

Goldhaber, Michael. "A Mission Unfulfilled: Freedmen's Education in North Carolina, 1865–1870." *Journal of Negro History* 77, no. 4 (1992): 199–210.

Goldsmith, Pat Antonio. "Schools' Racial Mix, Students' Optimism, and the Black-White and Latino-White Achievement Gaps." *Sociology of Education* 77 (Apr. 2004): 121–47.

Gonzales, Nancy A., Ana Mari Cauce, Ruth J. Friedman, and Craig A. Mason, "Family, Peer, and Neighborhood Influences on Academic Achievement Among African-American Adolescents: One-Year Prospective Effects." *American Journal of Community Psychology* 24, no. 3 (1996): 365–87.

Gordon, Robert, Thomas J. Kane, and Douglas O. Staiger. *Identifying Effective Teachers Using Performance on the Job*. Brookings Institution White Paper 2006-01 (Apr. 2006), www.brookings.edu/views/papers/200604hamilton_1.pdf.

Gottlieb, David. "Teaching and Students: The Views of Negro and White Teachers." *Sociology of Education* 37, no. 4 (1964): 345–53.

Granberry, Dorothy. "Black Community Leadership in a Rural Tennessee County, 1865–1903." *Journal of Negro History* 83, no. 4 (1998): 249–57.

Grant, Gerald. *The World We Created at Hamilton High*. Cambridge: Harvard University Press, 1988.

Grantham, Tarek C., and Donna Y. Ford. "A Case Study of the Social Needs of Danisha: An Underachieving Gifted African-American Female." *Roeper Review* 21, no. 2 (1998).

Graybill, Susan W. "Questions of Race and Culture: How They Relate to the Classroom for African American Students." *Clearing House* 70, no. 6 (1997): 311.

Gray-Little, Bernadette, and Robert A. Carels. "The Effect of Racial Dissonance on Academic Self-Esteem and Achievement in Elementary, Junior High, and High School Students." *Journal of Research on Adolescence* 7, no. 2 (1997): 109–31.

Green, Robert L., and Louis J. Hofmann. "A Case Study of the Effects of Educational Deprivation on Southern Rural Negro Children." *Journal of Negro Education* 34, no. 3 (1965): 327–41.

Greenberg, Jack. *Crusaders in the Courts*. New York: Basic, 1994.

Greene, James E., Sr. "A Comparison of the 'School Morale' of White and Negro Students in a Large Southeastern School System." *Journal of Negro Education* 31, no. 2 (1962): 132–38.

———. "Disciplinary Status of White and Negro High School Students in a Large Southeastern School System." *Journal of Negro Education* 31, no. 1 (1962): 25–29.

Greene, Jay P. *Education Myths*. Oxford: Rowman and Littlefield, 2005.

Greene, Jay P., and Marcus A. Winters. "The Boys Left Behind: The Gender Graduation Gap." *National Review,* 19 Apr. 2006.

Greenwald, R. L., L. V. Hedges, and R. D. Laine. "The Effect of School Resources on Student Achievement." *Review of Educational Research* 66, no. 3 (1996): 361–96.

Gregory, Sophfronia Scott. "The Hidden Hurdle: Talented Black Students Find That One of the Most Insidious Obstacles to Achievement Comes from a Surprising Source: Their Own Peers." *Time,* 16 Mar. 2002, p. 44.

Grogger, Jeff. "School Expenditures and Post-Schooling Earnings: Evidence from High School and Beyond." *Review of Economics and Statistics* 78, no. 4 (1996): 628–37.

Guryan, Jonathan. "Desegregation and Black Dropout Rates." *American Economic Review* 94, no. 4 (2004): 919–43.

Hale, Janice E. *Learning While Black: Creating Educational Excellence for African American Children.* Baltimore: Johns Hopkins University Press, 2001.

Hall, Kermit L. "The Constitutional Lessons of the Little Rock Crisis." In *Understanding the Little Rock Crisis: An Exercise in Remembrance and Reconciliation,* ed. Elizabeth Jacoway and C. Fred Williams. Fayetteville: University of Arkansas Press, 1999.

Hall, Morrill M., and Harold W. Gentry. "Isolation of Negro Students in Integrated Public Schools." *Journal of Negro Education* 38, no. 2 (1969): 156–61.

Hallinan, Maureen T. "The Organization of Students for Instruction in the Middle School." *Sociology of Education* 65, no. 2 (1992): 114–27.

———. "Sociological Perspectives on Black-White Inequalities in American Schooling." *Sociology of Education* 74 (2002): 50–70.

Hallinan, Maureen T., and Richard A. Williams. "Students' Characteristics and the Peer-Influence Process." *Sociology of Education* 63, no. 2 (1990): 122–32.

Hamann, Edmund T. "Lessons From the Interpretation/Misinterpretation of John Ogbu's Scholarship." *Intercultural Education* 15, no. 4 (2004): 399–412.

Haney, James E. "The Effects of the Brown Decision on Black Educators." *Journal of Negro Education* 47, no. 1 (1978): 88–95.

Hansen, Suzy. "Another Shade of Black." *Salon,* 2003, http://dir.salon.com/story/books/int/2003/01/14/mcwhorter/print.html.

Hanushek, Eric A. "Black-White Achievement Differences and Governmental Interventions." *AEA Papers and Proceedings: Human Capital: Growth, History, and Policy* 91, no. 2 (2001): 24–28, http://edpro.stanford.edu/hanushek/admin/pages/files/uploads/aer.may2001.pdf.

———. "The Economics of Schooling: Production and Efficiency in Public Schools." *Journal of Economic Literature* 24, no. 3 (1986): 1141–77.

———. "The Failure of Input-Based Schooling Policies." *Economic Journal* 113 (2003): F64–F98.

Hanushek, Eric A., John F. Kain, Jacob M. Markman, and Steven G. Rivkin, "Does Peer Ability Affect Student Achievement?" *Journal of Applied Econometrics* 18, no. 5 (2003): 527–44.

Hanushek, Eric A., John F. Kain, Daniel M. O'Brien, and Steven G. Rivkin. "The Market for Teacher Quality." NBER Working Paper no. 11154 (2005), www.nber .org/papers/w11154 or http://urban.hunter.cuny.edu/RePEc/seminar/quality _nber.pdf.

Hanushek, Eric A., John F. Kain, and Steven G. Rivkin. "New Evidence About *Brown v. Board of Education:* The Complex Effects of School Racial Composition on Achievement." NBER Working Paper no. 8741 (2004), http://edpro.stanford.edu /hanushek/admin/pages/files/uploads/race.pdf.

Hanushek, Eric A., Steven G. Rivkin, and Lori L. Taylor. "Aggregation and the Estimated Effects of School Resources." *Review of Economics and Statistics* 78 (1996): 611–27.

Hanushek, Eric A., and Ludger Wößmann. "Does Educational Tracking Affect Performance and Inequality? Differences-in-Differences Evidence Across Countries." *Economic Journal* 116 (2006): C63–C76.

Harmon, Deborah. "They Won't Teach Me: The Voices of Gifted African American Inner-City Students." *Roeper Review* 24, no. 2 (2002): 68–75.

Harpalani, Vinay. "What Does 'Acting White' Really Mean? Racial Identity Formation and Academic Achievement Among Black Youth." *Perspectives on Urban Education* 1, no. 1 (2002).

Harris, Angel L. "I (Don't) Hate School: Revisiting Oppositional Culture Theory of Blacks' Resistance to Schooling." *Social Forces* 85, no. 2 (Dec. 2006): 797–833.

Harris, Angel L., and Keith Robinson. "Schooling Behaviors or Prior Skills? A Cautionary Tale of Omitted Variable Bias Within Oppositional Culture Theory." *Sociology of Education* 80, no. 2 (Apr. 2007): 139–57.

Harris, Judith Rich. *No Two Alike: Human Nature and Human Individuality.* New York: W. W. Norton, 2006.

Hart, Betty, and Todd R. Risley. *Meaningful Differences in the Everyday Experience of Young American Children.* Baltimore: Brookes, 1995.

Harvard Educational Review. *Equal Educational Opportunity.* Harvard University Press, 1969.

Hauser, Robert M., and Douglas K. Anderson. "Post-High School Plans and Aspirations of Black and White High School Seniors, 1976–1986." *Sociology of Education* 64, no. 4 (1991): 263–77.

Haviland, Laura S. *A Woman's Life-Work, Labors, and Experiences* (1881), www.gutenberg .org/dirs/etext05/wlwrk10.txt.

Hedges, Larry V., and Amy Nowell. "Changes in the Black-White Gap in Achievement Test Scores." *Sociology of Education* 72, no. 2 (1999): 111–35.

Hedrick, James E. "A Case Study in the Desegregation of George Washington High School and Langston High School in Danville, Virginia During the 1970–1971 School Year." Ph.D. diss., Virginia Polytechnic Institute and State University, 2002, http://scholar.lib.vt.edu/theses/available/etd-04042002-203119/unrestricted /1.pdf and http://scholar.lib.vt.edu/theses/available/etd-04042002-203119/ unrestricted/4.pdf.

Hemmings, Annette. "The 'Hidden' Corridor." *High School Journal*, 83, no. 2 (1 Dec. 1999): 1.

Henry, Sue Ellen, and Abe Feuerstein. "'Now We Go to Their School': Desegregation and Its Contemporary Legacy." *Journal of Negro Education* 68, no. 2 (1999): 164–81.

Hermans, Philip. "Applying Ogbu's Theory of Minority Academic Achievement to the Situation of Moroccans in the Low Countries." *Intercultural Education* 15, no. 4 (2004): 431–39.

Herndon, Ruth Wallis. "Literacy Among New England's Transient Poor, 1750–1800." *Journal of Social History* 29, no. 4 (Summer 1996): 963–65.

Hertel, Guido, and Norbert L. Kerr. "Priming In-Group Favoritism: The Impact of Normative Scripts in the Minimal Group Paradigm." *Journal of Experimental Social Psychology* 37 (2001): 316–24.

Hickerson, Nathaniel. "Some Aspects of School Integration in a California High School." *Journal of Negro Education* 34, no. 2 (1965): 130–37.

Hochschild, Jennifer L. *The New American Dilemma: Liberal Democracy and School Desegregation.* New Haven: Yale University Press, 1984.

Hodgkins, Benjamin J., and Robert G. Stakenas. "A Study of Self-Concepts of Negro and White Youth in Segregated Environments." *Journal of Negro Education* 38, no. 4 (1969): 370–77.

Hoel, Jessica, Jeffrey Parker, and Jon Rivenburg. "A Test for Classmate Peer Effects in Higher Education" (2005), http://academic.reed.edu/economics/course_pages/421_f05/Classroom_Peer_Effects_3.pdf.

Hogg, Michael A., and Dominic Abrams. *Social Identifications: A Social Psychology of Intergroup Relations and Group Processes.* New York: Routledge, 1988.

Holliday, Bertha Garrett. "Differential Effects of Children's Self-Perceptions and Teachers' Perceptions on Black Children's Academic Achievement." *Journal of Negro Education* 54, no. 1 (1985): 71–81.

Homel, Michael W. *Down from Equality: Black Chicagoans and the Public Schools, 1920–1941.* Urbana: University of Illinois Press, 1984.

Hooker, Robert W. "Displacement of Black Teachers in the Eleven Southern States." *Afro-American Studies* 2 (1971): 165–80.

Hooks, Bell. *Bone Black: Memories of Girlhood.* New York: Henry Holt, 1996.

———. *Teaching to Transgress: Education as the Practice of Freedom.* New York: Routledge, 1994.

———. *We Real Cool: Black Men and Masculinity.* New York: Routledge, 2004.

Hopkins, Ronnie. *Educating Black Males: Critical Lessons in Schooling, Community, and Power.* Albany: State University of New York Press, 1997.

Hornsby, Alton, Jr. "Black Public Education in Atlanta, Georgia, 1954–1973: From Segregation to Segregation." *Journal of Negro History* 76, no. 1–4 (1991): 21–47.

Horst, Samuel L. *Education for Manhood: The Education of Blacks in Virginia During the Civil War.* Lanham, Md.: University Press of America, 1987.

Horvat, Erin McNamara, and Carla O'Connor, eds. *Beyond Acting White: Reframing the Debate on Black Student Achievement.* Lanham, Md.: Rowman and Littlefield, 2006.

Horvat, Erin McNamara, and Kristine S. Lewis. "Reassessing the 'Burden of "Acting White"': The Importance of Peer Groups in Managing Academic Success." *Sociology of Education* 76 (2003): 265–80.

Houtte, Mieke Van. "Tracking Effects on School Achievement: A Quantitative Explanation in Terms of the Academic Culture of School Staff." *American Journal of Education* 110 (Aug. 2004): 354–88.

Howard, Walter T., and Virginia M. Howard. "Family, Religion, and Education: A Profile of African-American Life in Tampa, Florida, 1900–1930." *Journal of Negro History* 79, no. 1 (1994): 1–17.

Howell, Martha C., and Walter Prevenier. *From Reliable Sources: An Introduction to Historical Methods.* Ithaca: Cornell University Press, 2001.

Howell, William G., and Paul E. Peterson. *The Education Gap: Vouchers and Urban Schools.* Washington, D.C.: Brookings Institution Press, 2002.

Hoxby, Caroline. "Peer Effects in the Classroom: Learning from Gender and Race Variation." NBER Working Paper 7867 (2000), www.nber.org/papers/w7867.

Hoxby, Caroline M., and Andrew Leigh. "Pulled Away or Pushed Out? Explaining the Decline of Teacher Aptitude in the United States." *American Economic Review* 94, no. 2 (2004): 236–40.

Hoxby, Caroline M., and Gretchen Weingarth. "Taking Race Out of the Equation: School Reassignment and the Structure of Peer Effects." Working paper, Harvard University (2006), http://post.economics.harvard.edu/faculty/hoxby/papers/hoxby_weingarth_taking_race.pdf.

Hrabowski, Freeman A., III. "Reflections on America's Academic Achievement Gap: A 50-Year Perspective." The 2004 W. Augustus Low Lecture at the University of Maryland, Baltimore County, www.umbc.edu/AboutUMBC/Welcome/LowLecture-May04.pdf.

Hudson, Mildred J., and Barbara J. Holmes. "Missing Teachers, Impaired Communities: The Unanticipated Consequences of *Brown v. Board of Education* on the African American Teaching Force at the Precollegiate Level." *Journal of Negro Education* 63, no. 3 (1994): 388–93.

Hudson, Winson, and Constance Curry. *Mississippi Harmony: Memoirs of a Freedom Fighter.* New York: Palgrave Macmillan, 2002.

Hughes, George M. "The Success Story of Lee Elementary School: A R.I.S.E. School." *Journal of Negro Education* 57, no. 3 (1988): 267–81.

Hunter-Gault, Charlayne. *In My Place.* New York: Vintage, 1992.

Inbar, Michael, and Chaim Adler. "The Vulnerable Age: A Serendipitous Finding." *Sociology of Education* 49, no. 3 (1976): 193–200.

Inniss, Leslie Baham. "Desegregation Pioneers: Casualties of a Peaceful Process." *International Journal of Contemporary Sociology* 31, no. 2 (1994): 253–72.

——. "Historical Footprints: The Legacy of the School Desegregation Pioneers." In *The Bubbling Cauldron: Race, Ethnicity, and the Urban Crisis,* ed. Michael Peter Smith and Joe R. Feagin. Minneapolis: University of Minneapolis Press, 1995.

Interview with Eleanor Thomas Traynham, 8 Jan. 2003, www.princegeorges.org /Northwestern_history/oral_history_interviews/long_Eleanor_Thomas_Traynham .htm.

Interview with Leo Hamilton by Mary Hebert, 21 Aug. 1993, Tape 453, at Hill Memorial Library at Louisiana State University.

Irvine, Russell W., and Jacqueline Jordan Irvine. "The Impact of the Desegregation Process on the Education of Black Students: Key Variables." *Journal of Negro Education* 52, no. 4 (1983): 410–22.

Jackson-Coppin, Fanny. *Reminiscences of School Life, and Hints on Teaching.* Philadelphia: L. J. Coppin, 1913, http://docsouth.unc.edu/jacksonc/jackson.html.

Jacobson, Jonathan, Cara Olsen, Jennifer King Rice, Stephen Sweetland, and John Ralph. *Educational Achievement and Black-White Inequality.* National Center for Education Statistics, 2001, http://nces.ed.gov/pubs2001/2001061.PDF.

Jacoway, Elizabeth, and C. Fred Williams. *Understanding the Little Rock Crisis: An Exercise in Remembrance and Reconciliation.* Fayetteville: University of Arkansas Press, 1999.

Jaffe, Harry. "Avenging Angel." *Washingtonian,* Aug. 1995.

Jargowsky, Paul A. "Take the Money and Run: Economic Segregation in U.S. Metropolitan Areas." *American Sociological Review* 61, no. 6 (1996): 984–98.

Jencks, Christopher, and Marsha Brown. "The Effects of Desegregation on Student Achievement: Some New Evidence from the Equality of Educational Opportunity Survey." *Sociology of Education* 48, no. 1 (1975): 126–40.

Jencks, Christopher, and Meredith Phillips, eds. *The Black-White Test Score Gap.* Washington, D.C.: Brookings Institution Press, 1998.

Johnson, Charles S. "The Education of the Negro Child." *American Sociological Review* 1, no. 2 (1936): 264–72.

Johnson, David W., Roger Johnson, and Geoffrey Maruyama. "Goal Interdependence and Interpersonal Attraction in Heterogeneous Classrooms: A Metanalysis." In *Groups in Contact: The Psychology of Desegregation,* ed. Norman Miller and Marilynn B. Brewer. New York: Academic, 1984.

Johnson, David W., Roger T. Johnson, Margaret Tiffany, and Brian Zaidman. "Cross-Ethnic Relationships: The Impact of Intergroup Cooperation and Intergroup Competition." *Journal of Educational Research* 78, no. 2 (1984): 75–79.

Johnson, Monica Kirkpatrick, Robert Crosnoe, and Glen H. Elder, Jr. "Students' Attachment and Academic Engagement: The Role of Race and Ethnicity." *Sociology of Education* 74, no. 4 (2001): 318–40.

Johnson, Simon O. "A Study of the Perceptions of Black Administrators Concerning the Role of the Black Principal in Florida During the Period 1973–1978." *Journal of Negro Education* 46, no. 1 (1977): 53–61.

Johnson, Thomas L. *Twenty-Eight Years a Slave, or the Story of My Life in Three Con-*

tinents. Bournemouth: W. Math, 1909, http://docsouth.unc.edu/johnson/johnson
.html.

Jones, Faustine C. "Editorial Comment: Unintended Consequences." *Journal of Negro Education* 49, no. 1 (1980): 1–2.

———. "Ironies of School Desegregation." *Journal of Negro Education* 47, no. 1 (1978): 2–27.

———. *A Traditional Model of Educational Excellence: Dunbar High School of Little Rock, Arkansas*. Washington, D.C.: Howard University Press, 1981.

Jones, Jacqueline. *Soldiers of Light and Love: Northern Teachers and Georgia Blacks, 1965–1873*. Athens: University of Georgia Press, 1992; orig. pub. Chapel Hill: University of North Carolina Press, 1980.

Jordan, Vernon. "Chairman of the Board." In *America Behind the Color Line,* ed. Henry Louis Gates, Jr. New York: Warner, 2004.

Kalekin-Fishman, Deborah. "Diagnosing Inequalities in Schooling: Ogbu's Orientation and Wider Implications." *Intercultural Education* 15, no. 4 (2004): 413–30.

Kao, Grace. "Group Images and Possible Selves Among Adolescents: Linking Stereotypes to Expectations by Race and Ethnicity." *Sociological Forum* 15, no. 3 (2000): 407–30.

Kao, Grace, and Marta Tienda. "Optimism and Achievement: The Educational Performance of Immigrant Youth." *Social Science Quarterly* 76, no. 1 (1995): 1–19.

Kao, Grace, Marta Tienda, and Barbara Schneider. "Racial and Ethnic Variation in Academic Performance." *Research in Sociology of Education and Socialization* 11 (1996): 263–97.

Kaplan, Avi, and Martin L. Maehr. "Enhancing the Motivation of African American Students: An Achievement Goal Theory Perspective." *Journal of Negro Education* 68, no. 1 (1999): 23–41.

Katz, Irwin. "Review of Evidence Relating to Effects of Desegregation on the Intellectual Performance of Negroes." *American Psychologist* 19, no. 6 (1964): 381–99.

Kaufman, Phillip, Marilyn M. McMillen, and Denise Bradby. "Dropout Rates in the United States, 1991." U.S. Department of Education, Office of Educational Research and Improvement, National Center for Education Statistics, http://nces.ed
.gov/pubs92/92129.pdf.

Keane, Michael P., and Kenneth I. Wolpin. "Eliminating Race Differences in School Attainment and Labor Market Success." *Journal of Labor Economics* 18, no. 4 (2000): 614–52.

Kennedy, Eugene. "Correlates of Perceived Popularity Among Peers: A Study of Race and Gender Differences Among Middle School Students." *Journal of Negro Education* 64, no. 2 (1995): 186–95.

———. "A Multilevel Study of Elementary Male Black Students and White Students." *Journal of Educational Research* 92, no. 2 (1992): 105–10.

Kentucky Historical Society. Civil Rights Movement in Kentucky, Interview with John Johnson, www.ket.org/civilrights/bio_jjohnson.htm.

Kilgore, Sally B. "The Organizational Context of Tracking in Schools." *American So-ciological Review* 56, no. 2 (1991): 189–203.

Kinney, David A. "From Nerds to Normals: The Recovery of Identity Among Adolescents from Middle School to High School." *Sociology of Education* 66, no. 1 (1993): 21–40.

Klarman, Michael J. *From Jim Crow to Civil Rights.* Oxford: Oxford University Press, 2004.

Kling, Jeffrey R., Jeffrey B. Liebman, and Lawrence F. Katz. "Experimental Analysis of Neighborhood Effects." *Econometrica* 75 (2007): 83–119.

Kling, Jeffrey R., Jens Ludwig, Lawrence F. Katz. "Youth Criminal Behavior in the Moving to Opportunity Experiment." Princeton University Industrial Relations Section, Working Paper no. 482 (2004), www.irs.princeton.edu/pubs/working_papers.html.

Klopfenstein, Kristin. "Beyond Test Scores: The Impact of Black Teacher Role Models on Rigorous Math Taking." *Contemporary Economic Policy* 23, no. 3 (2005): 416–28.

Kluger, Richard. *Simple Justice.* New York: Alfred A. Knopf, 2004.

Klugh, Elgin L. "Reclaiming Segregation-Era, African American Schoolhouses: Building on Symbols of Past Cooperation." *Journal of Negro Education* 74 (Summer 2005): 246–59.

Knight, James H., Kinnard P. White, and Luther R. Taff. "The Effect of School Desegregation, Sex of Student, and Socioeconomic Status on the Interpersonal Values of Southern Negro Students." *Journal of Negro Education* 41, no. 1 (1972): 4–11.

Kosof, Anna. *Living in Two Worlds: The Immigrant Children's Experience.* New York: Twenty-First Century, 1996.

Kremer, Michael, and Dan M. Levy. "Peer Effects from Alcohol Use Among College Students," NBER Working Paper 9876 (July 2003), www.ssc.wisc.edu/econ/Durlauf/networkweb1/London/kramer.pdf.

Kuncel, Nathan R., Marcus Credé, and Lisa L. Thomas. "The Validity of Self—Reported Grade Point Averages, Class Ranks, and Test Scores: A Meta-Analysis and Review of the Literature." *Review of Educational Research* 75, no. 1 (2005): 63–82.

Kunjufu, Jawanza. *To Be Popular or Smart: The Black Peer Group.* Chicago: African American Images, 1988.

———. *Black Students, Middle Class Teachers.* Chicago: African American Images, 2002.

Kuran, Timur. "Ethnic Norms and Their Transformation Through Reputational Cascades." *Journal of Legal Studies* 27 (1998): 623–59.

Kurzban, Robert, John Tooby, and Leda Cosmides. "Can Race Be Erased? Coalitional Computation and Social Categorization." *Proceedings of the National Academy of Sciences* 98, no. 26 (2001): 15387–92.

Kvaraceus, William C., John S. Gibson, Franklin Patterson, Bradbury Seasholes, and Jean D. Grambs. *Negro Self-Concept: Implications for School and Citizenship.* New York: McGraw-Hill, 1965.

Ladd, Gary W. *Children's Peer Relations and Social Competence.* New Haven: Yale University Press, 2005.

Ladino, Robyn Duff. *Desegregating Texas Schools: Eisenhower, Shivers, and the Crisis at Mansfield High*. Austin: University of Texas Press, 1996.

Ladson-Billings, Gloria. *The Dreamkeepers: Successful Teachers of African American Children*. San Francisco: Jossey-Bass, 1994.

———. "Landing on the Wrong Note: The Price We Paid For *Brown*." *Educational Researcher* 33, no. 7 (2004): 3–13.

LaFree, Gary, and Richard Arum. "The Impact of Racially Inclusive Schooling on Adult Incarceration Rates Among U.S. Cohorts of African Americans and Whites Since 1930." *Criminology* 44, no. 1 (2006): 73–103.

Laird, J., S. Lew, M. DeBell, and C. Chapman. "Dropout Rates in the United States: 2002 and 2003." NCES 2006062, U.S. Department of Education. Washington, D.C.: National Center for Education Statistics, 2006, http://nces.ed.gov/pubs 2006/2006062.pdf.

Lake, Robin J., and Paul T. Hill, eds. *Hopes, Fears, and Reality: A Balanced Look at American Charter Schools in 2005*. National Charter School Research Project, Center on Reinventing Public Education, University of Washington, 2005.

Lankford, Hamilton, Susanna Loeb, and James Wyckoff. "Teacher Sorting and the Plight of Urban Schools: A Descriptive Analysis." *Educational Evaluation and Policy Analysis* 24, no. 1 (2002): 37–62.

Lareau, Annette. "Invisible Inequality: Social Class and Childrearing in Black Families and White Families." *American Sociological Review* 67, no. 5 (2002): 747–76.

Lazear, Edward. "Educational Production." *Quarterly Journal of Economics*, 116, no. 3 (2001): 777–803.

Leake, Donald O., and Christine J. Faltz. "Do We Need to Desegregate All of Our Black Schools?" *Educational Policy* 7, no. 3 (1993): 370–87.

Leloudis, James L. *Schooling the New South: Pedagogy, Self, and Society in North Carolina, 1880–1920*. Chapel Hill: University of North Carolina Press, 1996.

Levin, Jessica, Jennifer Mulhern, and Joan Schunck. "Unintended Consequences: The Case for Reforming the Staffing Rules in Urban Teachers Union Contracts." The New Teacher Project Report, www.tntp.org/newreport/TNTP%20Unintended %20Consequences.pdf.

Levine, Daniel U. "Differences Between Segregated and Desegregated Settings." *Journal of Negro Education* 39, no. 2 (1970): 139–47.

Levinsohn, Florence H., and Benjamin D. Wright, eds. *School Desegregation: Shadow and Substance*. Chicago: University of Chicago Press, 1976.

Lewis, Earl. *In Their Own Interests: Race, Class, and Power in Twentieth-Century Norfolk, Virginia*. Berkeley: University of California Press, 1991.

Lincoln, C. Eric. *Coming Through the Fire: Surviving Race and Place in America*. Durham: Duke University Press, 1996.

Littlefield, Valinda W. "A Yearly Contract With Everybody and His Brother: Durham County, North Carolina, Black Female Public School Teachers, 1885–1927." *Journal of Negro History* 79, no. 1 (1994): 37–53.

Litwack, Leon F. *Trouble in Mind: Black Southerners in the Age of Jim Crow*. New York: Knopf, 1998.

Loeb, Susanna, and John Bound. "The Effect of Measured School Inputs on Academic Achievement: Evidence from the 1920s, 1930s, and 1940s Birth Cohorts." *Review of Economics and Statistics* 78, no. 4 (1996): 653–64.

Lubinski, David, and Lloyd G. Humphreys. "Incorporating General Intelligence into Epidemiology and the Social Sciences." *Intelligence* 24, no. 1 (1997): 159–201.

Lucas, Samuel R., and Mark Berends. "Race and Track Assignment in Public School." Presentation at the International Sociological Association Research Committee Number 28 Meeting, Tokyo, Japan, March 2003, http://web.iss.u-tokyo.ac.jp/~rc28/rc28hand.pdf.

Lucas, Samuel R., and Adam Gamoran. "Tracking and the Achievement Gap." In *Bridging the Achievement Gap,* ed. John E. Chubb and Tom Loveless. Washington, D.C.: Brookings Institution Press, 2002.

Lucas, Samuel R., and Aaron D. Good. "Race, Class, and Tournament Track Mobility." *Sociology of Education* 74, no. 2 (2001): 139–56.

Lucker, G. William, David Rosenfield, Jev Sikes, and Elliot Aronson. "Performance in the Interdependent Classroom: A Field Study." *American Educational Research Journal* 13, no. 2 (1976): 115–23.

Ludwig, Jens. "The Great Unknown." *Education Next* (Summer 2003): 79–82, www.educationnext.org/20033/pdf/79.pdf.

Mabee, Carleton. *Black Education in New York State from Colonial to Modern Times.* Syracuse: Syracuse University Press, 1979.

McArdle, C. G., and N. F. Young. "Classroom Discussion of Racial Identity or How Can We Make It Without 'Acting White'?" *American Journal of Orthopsychiatry* 40, no. 1 (1970): 135–41.

McCaul, Robert L. *The Black Struggle for Public Schooling in Nineteenth-Century Illinois.* Carbondale: Southern Illinois University Press, 1987.

McCormick, J. Scott. "The Julius Rosenwald Fund." *Journal of Negro Education* 3, no. 4 (1934): 605–26.

McCullough-Garrett, Alice. "Reclaiming the African American Vision for Teaching: Toward an Educational Conversation." *Journal of Negro Education* 62, no. 4 (1993): 433–40.

McDonough, Molly. "Making Brown Real: A North Carolina Family Fought Threats and Intimidation After Suing to Integrate Schools." *ABA Journal* 90 (2004): 45.

Mack, Kenneth W. "Rethinking Civil Rights Lawyering and Politics in the Era Before Brown." *Yale Law Journal* 115 (2005): 256–354.

MacLeod, Jay. *Ain't No Makin' It: Aspirations and Attainment in a Low-Income Neighborhood.* Boulder, Colo.: Westview, 1987.

McPartland, James. "The Relative Influence of School and of Classroom Desegregation on the Academic Achievement of Ninth-Grade Negro Students." *Journal of Social Issues* 25, no. 3 (1967): 93–102.

McPherson, Miller, Lynn Smith-Lovin, and James Cook. "Birds of a Feather: Homophily in Social Networks." *Annual Review of Sociology* 27 (2001): 415–44.

McWhorter, John. *Authentically Black: Essays for the Black Silent Majority.* New York: Gotham, 2003.

———. "The End of Blackness: Returning the Souls of Black Folk to Their Rightful Owners." *Journal of Blacks in Higher Education* 43 (Spring 2004): 130–32.

———. *Losing the Race: Self-Sabotage in Black America.* New York: Free Press, 2001.

———. "Why the Black-White Test Gap Exists." *American Experiment Quarterly* (Spring 2002): 45–56.

———. *Winning the Race: Beyond the Crisis in Black America.* New York: Gotham, 2006.

Manor-Bullock, Rochelle, Christine Look, and David N. Dixon. "Is Giftedness Socially Stigmatizing? The Impact of High Achievement on Social Interactions." *Journal of Education of the Gifted* 18, no. 3 (1995): 319–38.

Manski, Charles F. "Identification of Endogenous Social Effects: The Reflection Problem." *Review of Economic Studies* 60, no. 3 (July 1993): 531–42.

Marcus, Geoffrey, Susan Gross, and Carol Seefeldt. "Black and White Students' Perceptions of Teacher Treatment." *Journal of Educational Research* 84, no. 6 (1991): 363–67.

Marsh, Herbert W., and Kit-Tai Hau. "Big-Fish-Little-Pond Effect on Academic Self-Concept: A Cross-Cultural (26-Country) Test of the Negative Effects of Academically Selective Schools." *American Psychologist* 58, no. 5 (2003): 364–76.

Marshall, Thurgood. "An Evaluation of Recent Efforts to Achieve Racial Integration in Education Through Resort to the Courts." *Journal of Negro Education* 21, no. 3 (1952): 316–27.

Massey, Douglas. "American Apartheid: Segregation and the Making of the Underclass." *American Journal of Sociology* 96, no. 2 (1990): 329–57.

Mays, Nebraska. "Behavioral Expectations of Negro and White Teachers on Recently Desegregated Public School Faculties." *Journal of Negro Education* 32, no. 3 (1963): 218–26.

Mehan, Hugh, Irene Villanueva, Lea Hubbard, and Angela Lintz. *Constructing School Success: The Consequences of Untracking Low-Achieving Students.* Cambridge: Cambridge University Press, 1996.

Meier, Kenneth J., Joseph Stewart, Jr., and Robert E. England. *Race, Class, and Education: The Politics of Second-Generation Discrimination.* Madison: University of Wisconsin Press, 1989.

Meltzer, Milton, ed. *In Their Own Words: A History of the American Negro, 1865–1916.* New York: Thomas Y. Crowell, 1965.

Metz, Mary Haywood. *Classrooms and Corridors: The Crisis of Authority in Desegregated Secondary Schools.* Berkeley: University of California Press, 1978.

———. "Desegregation as Necessity and Challenge." *Journal of Negro Education* 63, no. 1 (1994): 64–76.

Mickelson, Roslyn Arlin. "The Academic Consequences of Desegregation and Segregation: Evidence from the Charlotte-Mecklenburg Schools." *North Carolina Law Review* 81 (2003): 1513–62.

———. "The Attitude-Achievement Paradox Among Black Adolescents." *Sociology of Education* 63, no. 1 (1990): 44–61.

———. "Subverting Swann: First-and Second-Generation Segregation in the Charlotte-Mecklenburg Schools." *American Educational Research Journal* 38, no. 2 (2001): 215–52.

———. "When Are Racial Disparities in Education the Result of Racial Discrimination? A Social Science Perspective." *Teachers College Record* 105, no. 6 (2003): 1052–86.

Mickelson, Roslyn Arlin, and Anthony D. Greene. "Connecting Pieces of the Puzzle: Gender Differences in Black Middle School Students' Achievement." *Journal of Negro Education* 75, no. 1 (2006): 34–48.

Mickelson, Roslyn Arlin, and Damien Heath. "The Effects of Segregation on African American High School Seniors' Academic Achievement." *Journal of Negro Education* 68, no. 4 (1999): 566–86.

Mickelson, Roslyn Arlin, and Anne E. Velasco. "Bring It On! Diverse Responses to 'Acting White' Among Academically Able Black Adolescents." In *Beyond Acting White: Reframing the Debate on Black Student Achievement,* ed. Erin McNamara Horvat and Carla O'Connor. Lanham, Md.: Rowman and Littlefield, 2006.

Mickett, Carol A. "History Speaks: Visions and Voices of Kansas City's Past." Charles N. Kimball Lecture, University of Missouri at Kansas City, 22 Oct. 2002, p. 13, web2.umkc.edu/whmckc/PUBLICATIONS/KIMBALL/CNKPDF/Mickett10-22-2002.pdf.

Mishel, Lawrence, and Richard Rothstein, eds. *The Class Size Debate.* Washington, D.C.: Economic Policy Institute, 2002.

Mitchell, Jason P., C. Neil Macrae, and Mahzarin R. Banaji. "Dissociable Medial Prefrontal Contributions to Judgments of Similar and Dissimilar Others." *Neuron* 50 (18 May 2006): 655–63.

Modlin, Carolyn Carter. "The Desegregation of Southampton County, Virginia, Schools, 1954–1970." Ph.D. diss., Virginia Polytechnic Institute and State University, 1998, http://scholar.lib.vt.edu/theses/available/etd-121098-154942 /unrestricted/DISSERTATION.PDF.

Moody, James. "Race, School Integration, and Friendship Segregation in America." *American Journal of Sociology* 107, no. 3 (2001): 679–716.

Moore, Julie Anne. "The Influence of Past School Achievement on Emerging Beliefs About Education and Ethnicity." Ph.D. diss., University of North Carolina, 2003.

Morgan, Albert T. *Yazoo; or, On the Picket Line of Freedom in the South.* Columbia: University of South Carolina Press, 2000 [orig. pub. 1884].

Morgan, Stephen L. "Trends in Black-White Differences in Educational Expectations, 1980–1992." *Sociology of Education* 69, no. 4 (1996): 308–19.

Morland, J. Kenneth. "The Tragedy of Public Schools: Prince Edward County, Virginia." A Report for the Virginia Advisory Committee to the United States Commission on Civil Rights, 1964.

Morris, Jerome E. "African American Students and Gifted Education: The Politics of Race and Culture." *Roeper Review* 24, no. 2 (2002): 59–62.

———. "Can Anything Good Come From Nazareth? Race, Class, and African American Schooling and Community in the Urban South and Midwest." *American Educational Research Journal* 41, no. 1 (2004): 69–112.

———. "A 'Communally Bonded' School for African American Students, Families, and a Community." *Phi Delta Kappan* 84, no. 3 (2002): 230.

———. "Forgotten Voices of Black Educators: Critical Race Perspectives on the Implementation of a Desegregation Plan." *Educational Policy* 15, no. 4 (2001): 575–600.

———. "A Pillar of Strength: An African American School's Communal Bonds with Families and Community Since *Brown.*" *Urban Education* 33, no. 5 (1999): 584–605.

Morris, Vivian Gunn, and David L. Morris. *Creating Caring and Nurturing Educational Environments for African-American Children.* Westport, Conn.: Bergin and Garvey, 2000.

———. *The Price They Paid: Desegregation in an African American Community.* New York: Teachers College Press, 2002.

Mosteller, Frederick, and Daniel P. Moynihan, eds. *On Equality of Educational Opportunity.* New York: Vintage, 1972.

Moton, Robert Russa. *Finding a Way Out: An Autobiography.* Garden City, N.Y.: Doubleday, 1921, http://docsouth.unc.edu/moton/moton.html.

Myers, John B. "The Education of the Alabama Freedmen During Presidential Reconstruction, 1865–1867." *Journal of Negro Education* 40, no. 2 (1971): 163–71.

National Center of Education Statistics. *Disparities in Public School District Spending, 1989–1990* (1995), http://nces.ed.gov/pubs95/web/95300.asp.

Natriello, Gary, Aaron M. Pallas, and Karl Alexander. "On the Right Track? Curriculum and Academic Achievement." *Sociology of Education* 62, no. 2 (1989): 109–18.

Neal, Derek A. "Black-White Inequality in the United States." In *New Palgrave Dictionary of Economics.* New York: Palgrave Macmillan, 2005.

Neal, Derek A., and William R. Johnson. "The Role of Premarket Factors in Black-White Wage Differences." *Journal of Political Economy* 104, no. 5 (1996): 869–95.

Neal-Barnett, Angela M. "Being Black: New Thoughts on the Old Phenomenon of Acting White." In *Forging Links: African American Children, Clinical Developmental Perspectives,* ed. Angela M. Neal-Barnett, Josefina M. Contreras, and Kathryn A. Kerns. Westport, Conn.: Praeger, 2001.

Neisser, Ulric. *The School Achievement of Minority Children: New Perspectives.* Hillsdale, N.J.: Lawrence Erlbaum, 1986.

Newby, Robert G., and David B. Tyack. "Victims Without 'Crimes': Some Historical Perspectives on Black Education." *Journal of Negro Education* 40, no. 3 (1971): 192–206.

Newmark, Kathryn G., and Veronique De Rugy. "Hope After Katrina." *Education Next* 6, no. 4 (Fall 2006): 12–21.

Nichols, Joe D., and Janet White. "Impact of Peer Networks on Achievement of High School Algebra Students." *Journal of Educational Research* 94, no. 5 (2001): 267–73.

Nicholsonne, Mary R. "Strides Toward Excellence: The Harford Heights Model." *Journal of Negro Education* 57, no. 3 (1988): 282–91.

Nier, Jason A., Samuel L. Gaertner, John F. Dovidio, Brenda S. Banker, Christine M. Ward, and Mary C. Rust. "Changing Interracial Evaluations and Behavior: The Effects of a Common Group Identity." *Group Processes and Intergroup Relations* 4, no. 4 (2001): 299–316.

Noblit, George W. *Particularities: Collected Essays on Ethnography and Education*. New York: Peter Lang, 1999.

———. "Patience and Prudence in a Southern High School: Managing the Political Economy of Desegregated Education." In *Desegregated Schools: Appraisals of an American Experiment*, ed. Ray C. Rist. New York: Academic, 1979.

Noblit, George W., and Van O. Dempsey. *The Social Construction of Virtue: The Moral Life of Schools*. Albany: State University of New York Press, 1996.

Noguera, Pedro A. "Responding to the Crisis Confronting California's Black Male Youth: Providing Support Without Furthering Marginalization." *Journal of Negro Education* 65, no. 2 (1996): 219–36.

Norwood, Kimberly Jade. "The Virulence of *Blackthink* and How Its Threat of Ostracism Shackles Those Deemed Not *Black Enough*." *Kentucky Law Journal* 93 (2004–5): 143–98.

"Note. Teaching Inequality: The Problem of Public School Tracking." *Harvard Law Review* 102 (1989): 1318.

Oakes, Jeannie. *Keeping Track: How Schools Structure Inequality*. 2nd ed. New Haven: Yale University Press, 2005.

Ogbu, John U. "Collective Identity and the Burden of 'Acting White' in Black History, Community, and Education." *Urban Review* 36, no. 1 (2004): 1–35.

———. "The Consequences of the American Caste System." In *The School Achievement of Minority Children: New Perspectives*, ed. Ulric Neisser. Hillsdale, N.J.: Lawrence Erlbaum, 1986.

———. "Minority Education in Comparative Perspective." *Journal of Negro Education* 59, no. 1 (1990): 45–57.

Ogbu, John U., and Astrid Davis. *Black American Students in an Affluent Suburb: A Study of Academic Disengagement*. Mahwah, N.J.: Lawrence Erlbaum, 2003.

Orfield, Gary, Susan E. Eaton, and the Harvard Project on School Desegregation. *Dismantling Desegregation: The Quiet Reversal of Brown v. Board of Education*. New York: New Press, 1996.

Ornstein, Allan C. *Education and Social Inquiry*. Itasca, Ill.: F. E. Peacock, 1978.

Osborne, Jason W. "Unraveling Underachievement Among African American Boys from an Identification with Academics Perspective." *Journal of Negro Education* 68, no. 4 (2001): 555–65.

Overman, Henry G., and Alex Heath. "The Influence of Neighbourhood Effects on Education Decisions in a Nationally Funded Education System." Working Paper, Centre for Economic Performance, London School of Economics and Political Science (2000), http://158.143.49.27/~overman/research/neighbourhoods.pdf.

Oyserman, Daphna, Markus Kemmelmeier, Stephanie Fryberg, Hezi Brosh, and Tamera Hart-Johnson. "Racial-Ethnic Self-Schemas." *Social Psychology Quarterly* 66, no. 4 (2003): 333–47.

Pajares, Frank. "Toward a Positive Psychology of Academic Motivation." *Journal of Educational Research* 95, no. 1 (2001): 27–35.

Paley, Vivian Gussin. *Kwanzaa and Me: A Teacher's Story.* Cambridge: Harvard University Press, 1995.

Pallas, Aaron M., Doris R. Entwisle, Karl L. Alexander, and M. Francis Stluka. "Ability-Group Effects: Instructional, Social, or Institutional?" *Sociology of Education* 67, no. 1 (1994): 27–46.

Parrish, C. H. "Desegregation in Public Education—A Critical Summary." *Journal of Negro Education* 24, no. 3 (1955): 382–87.

Parrish, William E. *A History of Missouri,* vol. 3: *1860–1875.* Columbia: University of Missouri Press, 1973.

Passow, A. Harry, ed. *Education in Depressed Areas.* New York: Teachers College Press, 1963.

Patchen, Martin. *Black-White Contact in Schools: Its Social and Academic Effects.* West Lafayette, Ind.: Purdue University Press, 1982.

Patchen, Martin, Gerhard Hofmann, and William R. Brown. "Academic Performance of Black High School Students Under Different Conditions of Contact with White Peers." *Sociology of Education* 53, no. 1 (1980): 33–51.

Patterson, James T. *Brown v. Board of Education: A Civil Rights Milestone and Its Troubled Legacy.* Oxford: Oxford University Press, 2001.

Perry, Theresa, Claude Steele, and Asa G. Hilliard III. *Young, Gifted, and Black: Promoting High Achievement Among African-American Students.* Boston: Beacon Press, 2003.

Peske, Heather G., and Kati Haycock. "Teaching Inequality: How Poor and Minority Students Are Shortchanged on Teacher Quality." Report by the Education Trust, 2006.

Petrie, Phil W. "The Triumph of Excellence." *New Crisis,* Mar.–Apr. 2000.

Petroni, Frank A., Ernest A. Hirsch, and C. Lillian Petroni. *2, 4, 6, 8: When You Gonna Integrate?* New York: Behavioral, 1970.

Philipsen, Maike. "Values-Spoken and Values-Lived: Female African Americans' Educational Experiences in Rural North Carolina." *Journal of Negro Education* 62, no. 4 (1993): 419–26.

———. *Values-Spoken and Values-Lived: Race and the Cultural Consequences of a School Closing.* Cresskill, N.J.: Hampton, 1999.

Piper, Adrian. *Out of Order, Out of Sight,* vol. 1: *Selected Essays in Meta-Art, 1968–1992.* Cambridge: MIT Press, 1996.

Pitts, Winfred E. *A Victory of Sorts: Desegregation in a Southern Community.* Lanham, Md.: University Press of America, 2003.

Polite, Vernon C. "If Only We Knew Then What We Know Now: Foiled Opportunities to Learn in Suburbia." *Journal of Negro Education* 62, no. 3 (1993): 337–54.

Posner, Eric. *Law and Social Norms.* Cambridge: Harvard University Press, 2000.

Pottebaum, Sheila M., Timothy Z. Keith, and Stewart W. Ehly. "Is There a Causal Relation Between Self-Concept and Academic Achievement?" *Journal of Educational Research* 79, no. 3 (1986): 140–44.

Powell, Gloria J. *Black Monday's Children: A Study of the Effects of School Desegregation on Self-Concepts of Southern Children.* New York: Appleton-Century-Crofts, 1973.

Powell, Tracie. "A Different World." *Atlanta Magazine,* Jan. 2007, p. 52.

Pribesh, Shana, and Douglas B. Downey. "Why Are Residential and School Moves Associated with Poor School Performance?" *Demography* 36, no. 4 (1999): 521–34.

Proctor, Samuel DeWitt. *The Substance of Things Hoped For: A Memoir of African-American Faith.* New York: G. P. Putnam's Sons, 1995.

Puma, Michael J. "The 'Prospects' Study of Educational Growth and Opportunity: Implications for Policy and Practice." Paper presented at Annual Meeting of American Educational Research Association, Apr. 1999.

———. "The Prospects Study and Desegregation." *Journal of Negro Education* 66, no. 3 (1997): 330–35.

Quillian, Lincoln. "Migration Patterns and the Growth of High-Poverty Neighborhoods, 1970–1990." *American Journal of Sociology* 105, no. 1 (1999): 1–37.

Rabinowitz, Howard N. *Race Relations in the Urban South, 1865–1890.* Urbana: University of Illinois Press, 1980.

Ramsey, Sonya. "'We Will Be Ready Whenever They Are': African American Teachers' Responses to the Brown Decision and Public School Integration in Nashville, Tennessee, 1954–1966." *Journal of African American History* 90 (2005): 29.

Randolph, Adah Ward. "Building upon Cultural Capital: Thomas Jefferson Ferguson and the Albany Enterprise Academy in Southeast Ohio, 1863–1886." *Journal of African American History* 87 (2002): 182–95.

Reardon, Sean F. "Sources of Educational Inequality: The Growth of Racial/Ethnic and Socioeconomic Test Score Gaps in Kindergarten and First Grade." Working draft (2003), www.pop.psu.edu/general/pubs/working_papers/psu-pri/wp0305 R.pdf.

Rech, Janice F., and Dorothy Jo Stevens. "Variables Related to Mathematics Achievement Among Black Students." *Journal of Educational Research* 89, no. 6 (1996): 346–50.

Remsberg, Charles and Bonnie. "Chicago Voices: Tales Told Out of School." In *Our Children's Burden: Studies of Desegregation in Nine American Communities,* ed. Raymond W. Mack. New York: Vintage, 1968.

Rhine, W. Ray, and Leilani M. Spencer. "Effects of Follow Through on School Fearfulness Among Black Children." *Journal of Negro Education* 44, no. 4 (1975): 446–53.

Richardson, Joe M. "Francis L. Cardozo: Black Educator During Reconstruction." *Journal of Negro Education* 48, no. 1 (1979): 73–83.

———. "The Freedmen's Bureau and Negro Education in Florida." *Journal of Negro Education* 31, no. 4 (1962): 460–67.

———. "The Negro in Post Civil-War Tennessee: A Report by a Northern Mission-ary." *Journal of Negro Education* 34, no. 4 (1965): 419–24.

Richeson, Jennifer A., and Clemlyn-Ann Pollydore. "Affective Reactions of African American Students to Stereotypical and Counterstereotypical Images of Blacks in the Media." *Journal of Black Psychology* 28, no. 3 (2002): 261–75.

Rist, Ray C., ed. *Desegregated Schools: Appraisals of an American Experiment.* New York: Academic, 1979.

Rivkin, Steven G. "Residential Segregation and School Integration." *Sociology of Education* 67, no. 4 (1994): 279–92.

———. "School Desegregation, Academic Attainment, and Earnings." *Journal of Human Resources* 35, no. 2 (2000): 333–46.

Rivkin, Steven G., Eric A. Hanushek, and John F. Kain. "Teachers, Schools, and Academic Achievement." *Econometrica* 73, no. 2 (2005): 417–58.

Roach, Ronald. "A Rich, but Disappearing Legacy: Remembering Black Boarding Schools; A Tradition Obscured by Desegregation's Impact." *Black Issues in Higher Education,* 14 Aug. 2003.

Robertson, Donald, and James Symons. "Do Peer Groups Matter? Peer Group Versus Schooling Effect on Academic Achievement." *Economica* 70 (2003): 31–53.

Rodgers, Frederick A. *The Black High School and Its Community.* Lexington, Mass.: Lexington, 1975).

Rodgers, Harrell R., Jr., and Charles S. Bullock III. *Coercion to Compliance.* Lexington, Mass.: Lexington, 1976.

———. *Law and Social Change: Civil Rights Laws and Their Consequences.* New York: McGraw-Hill, 1972.

———. "School Desegregation: A Policy Analysis." *Journal of Black Studies* 2, no. 4 (1972): 409–37.

———. "School Desegregation: Successes and Failures." *Journal of Negro Education* 43, no. 2 (1974): 139–54.

Roff, Merrill, S. B. Sells, and Mary M. Golden. *Social Adjustment and Personality Development in Children.* Minneapolis: University of Minnesota Press, 1972.

Roscigno, Vincent J., and James W. Ainsworth-Darnell. "Race, Cultural Capital, and Educational Resources: Persistent Inequalities and Achievement Returns." *Sociology of Education* 72, no. 3 (1999): 158–78.

Rosenberg, Gerald. *The Hollow Hope: Can Courts Bring About Social Change?* Chicago: University of Chicago Press, 1991.

Rosenberg, Morris, and Roberta G. Simmons. *Black and White Self-Esteem: The Urban School Child.* Washington, D.C.: American Sociological Association, 1971.

Rosenthal, Jonas O. "Negro Teachers' Attitudes Toward Desegregation." *Journal of Negro Education* 26, no. 1 (1957): 63–71.

Rosenthal, Robert. "Covert Communication in Classrooms, Clinics, Courtrooms, and Cubicles." *American Psychologist* 57, no. 11 (2002): 838–49.

Rosenthal, Robert, and Lenore Jacobson. *Pygmalion in the Classroom: Teacher Expec-*

tation and Pupils' Intellectual Development. 2nd ed. Norwalk, Conn.: Crown House, 1992.

Rossell, Christine H., and Willis D. Hawley, eds. *The Consequences of School Desegregation.* Philadelphia: Temple University Press, 1983.

Roswal, Glenn M., et al. "Effects of Collaborative Peer Tutoring on Urban Seventh Graders." *Journal of Educational Research* 88, no. 5 (1995): 275–79.

Rowan, Brian, and Andrew W. Miracle, Jr. "Systems of Ability Grouping and the Stratification of Achievement in Elementary Schools." *Sociology of Education* 56, no. 3 (1983): 133–44.

Rowley, Stephanie J., and Julie A. Moore. "Racial Identity in Context for the Gifted African American Student." *Roeper Review* 24, no. 2 (2002): 63–67.

Roy, Beth. *Bitters in the Honey: Tales of Hope and Disappointment Across Divides of Race and Time.* Fayetteville: University of Arkansas Press, 1999.

Ryabov, Igor. "Educational Achievement of Adolescents: Does Peer Network Segregation Matter?" Paper submitted to the annual meeting of the Population Association of America (2005), http://paa2005.princeton.edu/download.aspx?submission Id=50170.

Ryabov, Igor, and Franklin Goza. "Peer Social Capital and the Educational Progress of Minority Adolescents." Paper submitted to the annual meeting of the Population Association of America (2007), http://paa2007.princeton.edu:80/abstractViewer .aspx?submissionId=70476.

Ryan, Allison. "The Peer Group as a Context for the Development of Young Adolescent Motivation and Achievement." *Child Development* 72, no. 4 (2001): 1135–50.

Ryan, James. "Schools, Race, and Money." *Yale Law Journal* 109 (1999): 249.

Sacerdote, Bruce. "Peer Effects with Random Assignment: Results for Dartmouth Roommates." *Quarterly Journal of Economics* 116, no. 2 (2001): 681–704.

Sackett, Paul, Chaitra Hardison, and Michael Cullen. "On Interpreting Stereotype Threat as Accounting for African American–White Differences in Cognitive Tests." *American Psychologist* 59 (2004): 7–13.

St. John, Nancy H. *School Desegregation Outcomes for Children.* New York: Wiley, 1975.

St. John, Nancy H., and Ralph G. Lewis. "Contribution of Cross-Racial Friendship to Minority Group Achievement in Desegregated Classrooms." *Sociometry* 37, no. 1 (1974): 79–91.

———. "Race and the Social Structure of the Elementary Classroom." *Sociology of Education* 48, no. 3 (1975): 346–68.

Sampson, William A., and Ben Williams. "School Desegregation: The Non-Traditional Sociological Perspective." *Journal of Negro Education* 47, no. 1 (1978): 72–80.

Samuels, Shirley C. "An Investigation into the Self Concepts of Lower- and Middle-Class Black and White Kindergarten Children." *Journal of Negro Education* 42, no. 4 (1973): 467–72.

Sanbonmatsu, Lisa, Jeffrey R. Kling, Greg J. Duncan, and Jeanne Brooks-Gunn.

"Neighborhoods and Academic Achievement: Results from the Moving to Opportunity Experiment." *Journal of Human Resources* 41 (2006): 649–91.

Sanders, Mavis G. "Overcoming Obstacles: Academic Achievement as a Response to Racism and Discrimination." *Journal of Negro Education* 66, no. 1 (1997): 83–93.

Savage, Carter Julian. "Cultural Capital and African American Agency: The Economic Struggle for Effective Education for African Americans in Franklin, Tennessee, 1890–1967." *Journal of African American History* 87 (2002): 206–35.

Scates, Douglas E. "Cincinnati Colored Teachers Set a Standard." *Journal of Negro Education* 7, no. 2 (1938): 144–46.

Scherer, Jacqueline, and Edward J. Slawski. "Color, Class, and Social Control in an Urban Desegregated School." In *Desegregated Schools: Appraisals of an American Experiment,* ed. Ray C. Rist. New York: Academic, 1979.

Schofield, Janet Ward. *Black and White in School: Trust, Tension, or Tolerance.* New York: Teachers College Press, 1989.

Schofield, Janet Ward, and H. Andrew Sagar. "Desegregation, School Practices, and Student Race Relations." In *The Consequences of School Desegregation,* ed. Christine H. Rossell and Willis D. Hawley. Philadelphia: Temple University Press, 1983.

———. "Peer Interaction Patterns in an Integrated Middle School." *Sociometry* 40, no. 2 (1977): 130–38.

———. "The Social Context of Learning in an Interracial School." In *Desegregated Schools: Appraisals of an American Experiment,* ed. Ray C. Rist. New York: Academic, 1979.

Scott, Daryl Michael. *Contempt and Pity: Social Policy and the Image of the Damaged Black Psyche, 1880–1996.* Chapel Hill: University of North Carolina Press, 1997.

Scott, Hugh J. "Views of Black School Superintendents on School Desegregation." *Journal of Negro Education* 52, no. 4 (1983): 378–82.

Scott-Jones, Diane. "Mother-as-Teacher in the Families of High- and Low-Achieving Low-Income Black First-Graders." *Journal of Negro Education* 56, no. 1 (1987): 21–34.

Shagaloff, June. "A Review of Public School Desegregation in the North and West." *Journal of Educational Sociology* 36, no. 6 (1963): 292–96.

Shapiro, Jenessa R., and Steven L. Neuberg. "From Stereotype Threat to Stereotype Threats: Implications of a Multi-Threat Framework for Causes, Moderators, Mediators, Consequences, and Interventions." *Personality and Social Psychology Review* 11 (2007): 107.

Shavit, Yossi. "Segregation, Tracking, and the Educational Attainment of Minorites: Arabs and Oriental Jews in Israel." *American Sociological Review* 55, no. 1 (1990): 115–26.

Sherer, Robert G. *Subordination or Liberation? The Development and Conflicting Theories of Black Education in Nineteenth-Century Alabama.* Tuscaloosa: University of Alabama Press, 1977.

Sherif, Muzafer. "Superordinate Goals in the Reduction of Intergroup Conflict." *American Journal of Sociology* 63 (1958): 349–56.

Shipler, David K. *A Country of Strangers.* New York: Alfred A. Knopf, 1997.

Shircliffe, Barbara. *The Best of That World: Historically Black High Schools and the Crisis of Desegregation in a Southern Metropolis.* Cresskill, N.J.: Hampton, 2006.

———. "'We Got the Best of That World': A Case for the Study of Nostalgia in the Oral History of School Segregation." *Oral History Review* 2, no. 28 (2001): 59.

Shujaa, Mwalimu J., ed. *Beyond Desegregation: The Politics of Quality in African American Schooling.* Thousand Oaks, Calif.: Corwin, 1996.

Simmons, Robert G. "Blacks and High Self-Esteem: A Puzzle." *Social Psychology* 41, no. 1 (1978): 54–57.

Simms, Ruth P. "The Savannah Story: Education and Desegregation." In *Our Children's Burden: Studies of Desegregation in Nine American Communities,* ed. Raymond W. Mack. New York: Vintage, 1968.

Simon, Bernd, and Thomas F. Pettigrew. "Social Identity and Perceived Group Homogeneity: Evidence for the Ingroup Homogeneity Effect." *European Journal of Social Psychology* 20 (1990): 269–86.

Simon, Rita J., and Rhonda M. Roorda. *In Their Own Voices: Transracial Adoptees Tell Their Stories.* New York: Columbia University Press, 2000.

Sims, Edith R. "Successful Programs, Policies, and Practices Employed at Corliss High School." *Journal of Negro Education* 57, no. 3 (1988): 394–407.

Singh, Kusum, Clare Vaught, and Ethel W. Mitchell. "Single-Sex Classes and Academic Achievement in Two Inner-City Schools." *Journal of Negro Education* 67, no. 2 (1998): 157–67.

Singleton, William Henry. *Recollections of My Slavery Days.* Raleigh: North Carolina Department of Cultural Resources, 1999.

Sizemore, Barbara A. "Educational Research and Desegregation: Significance for the Black Community." *Journal of Negro Education* 47, no. 1 (1978): 58–68.

———. "The Madison Elementary School: A Turnaround Case." *Journal of Negro Education* 57, no. 3 (1988): 243–66.

———. "Pitfalls and Promises of Effective Schools Research." *Journal of Negro Education* 54, no. 3 (1985): 269–88.

Skinner, David. "Home Is Where the Heart Is: Can Cory Booker Save Newark's Schools?" *Education Next* 6, no. 4 (Fall 2006): 23–29.

Smith, C. Calvin. *Educating the Masses: The Unfolding History of Black School Administrators in Arkansas, 1900–2000.* Fayetteville: University of Arkansas Press, 2003.

Smith, Charles Lee. *The History of Education in North Carolina.* Government Printing Office, 1888, http://docsouth.unc.edu/true/smith/smith.html.

Smith, John W., and Bette M. Smith. "Desegregation in the South and the Demise of the Black Educator." *Journal of Social and Behavioral Sciences* 20, no. 1 (1974): 33–40.

Smith, Marshall S. "Equality of Educational Opportunity: The Basic Findings Reconsidered." In *On Equality of Educational Opportunity,* ed. Federick Mosteller and Daniel P. Moynihan. New York: Vintage, 1972.

Smith, Michael Peter, and Joe R. Feagin, eds. *The Bubbling Cauldron: Race, Ethnicity, and the Urban Crisis.* Minneapolis: University of Minnesota Press, 1995.

Smith, Paul M., Jr. "The Role of the Guidance Counselor in the Desegregation Process." *Journal of Negro Education* 40, no. 4 (1971): 347–51.

Smrekar, Claire, James W. Guthrie, Debra E. Owens, and Pearl G. Sims. "March Toward Excellence: School Success and Minority Student Achievement in Department of Defense Schools." A Report to the National Educational Goals Panel, 2001.

Solomon, R. Patrick. *Black Resistance in High School: Forging a Separatist Culture.* Albany: State University of New York Press, 1992.

Solorzano, Daniel G. "An Exploratory Analysis of the Effects of Race, Class, and Gender on Student and Parent Mobility Aspirations." *Journal of Negro Education* 61, no. 1 (1992): 30–44.

Sowell, Thomas. "Assumptions Versus History in Ethnic Education." *Teachers College Record* 83, no. 1 (1981): 40.

———. *Black Rednecks and White Liberals.* New York: Encounter, 2005.

———. *Education: Assumptions Versus History: Collected Papers.* Stanford, Calif.: Hoover Institution Press, 1986.

———. *Inside American Education: The Decline, The Deception, The Dogmas.* New York: Free Press, 1993.

Span, Christopher M. "'I Must Learn Now or Not at All': Social and Cultural Capital in the Educational Initiatives of Formerly Enslaved African Americans in Mississippi, 1862–1869." *Journal of African American History* 87 (2002): 196–205.

Spence, A. Michael. "Signaling in Retrospect and the Informational Structure of Market." *American Economic Review* 92, no. 3 (2002): 434–59.

Spilerman, Seymour. "Raising Academic Motivation in Lower Class Adolescents: A Convergence of Two Research Traditions." *Sociology of Education* 44, no. 1 (1971): 103–18.

Spruill, Albert W. "The Negro Teacher in the Process of Desegregation of Schools." *Journal of Negro Education* 29, no. 1 (1960): 80–84.

Stanfield, John H. "Urban Public School Desegregation: The Reproduction of Normative White Domination." *Journal of Negro Education* 51, no. 2 (1982): 90–100.

Stanovich, Keith E. "Matthew Effects in Reading: Some Consequences of Individual Differences in the Acquisition of Literacy." *Reading Research Quarterly* 21, no. 4 (Autumn 1986): 360–407.

Stearns, Charles. *The Black Man of the South and the Rebels; or, the Characteristics of the Former, and the Recent Outrages of the Latter.* Orig. pub. 1872; reprint, New York: Kraus, 1969.

Stedman, Lawrence C. "An Assessment of the Contemporary Debate over U.S. Achievement." In *Brookings Papers on Education Policy 1998,* ed. Diane Ravitch. Washington, D.C.: Brookings Institution Press, 1998.

Steinberg, Laurence. *Beyond the Classroom: Why School Reform Has Failed and What Parents Need To Do.* New York: Touchstone, 1996.

Steinberg, Laurence, Sanford M. Dornbusch, and B. Bradford Brown. "Ethnic Differences in Adolescent Achievement: An Ecological Perspective." *American Psychologist* 47, no. 6 (1992): 723–29.

Stevenson, Harold W., and James W. Stigler. *The Learning Gap: Why Our Schools Are Failing and What We Can Learn from Japanese and Chinese Education.* New York: Touchstone, 1992.

Stiefel, Leanna, Amy Ellen Schwartz, and Ingrid Gould Ellen. "Disentangling the Racial Test Score Gap: Probing the Evidence in a Large Urban School District." *Journal of Policy Analysis and Management* 26, no. 1 (2007): 7–30, http://cpr .maxwell.syr.edu/efap/Jerry_Miner/Stiefel.pdf.

Stringfield, Sam, and Rebecca Herman. "Research on Effective Instruction for At-Risk Students: Implications for the St. Louis Public Schools." *Journal of Negro Education* 66, no. 3 (1997): 258–88.

Tajfel, Henri. "Experiments in Intergroup Discrimination." *Scientific American* 223 (1970): 96–102.

Tajfel, Henri, M. G. Billig, and R. P. Bundy. "Social Categorization and Intergroup Behaviour." *European Journal of Social Psychology* 1, no. 2 (1971): 149–77.

Taulbert, Clifton L. *When We Were Colored.* New York: Penguin, 1989.

Taylor, Dalmas A., and Beatrice F. Moriarty. "Ingroup Bias as a Function of Competition and Race." *Journal of Conflict Resolution* 31, no. 1 (1987): 192–99.

Taylor, Kay Ann. "Mary S. Peake and Charlotte L. Forten: Black Teachers During the Civil War and Reconstruction." *Journal of Negro Education* 74, no. 2 (2005): 122–34.

Taylor, Lottie L., and Joan R. Pinard. "Success Against the Odds: Effective Education of Inner-City Youth in a New York City Public High School." *Journal of Negro Education* 57, no. 3 (1988): 347–61.

Taylor, Susie King. *Reminiscenses of My Life: A Black Woman's Civil War Memoirs.* Orig. pub. 1902; reprint, New York: Wiener, 1988.

Tettegah, Sharon. "The Racial Consciousness Attitudes of White Prospective Teachers and Their Perceptions of the Teachability of Students from Different Racial/Ethnic Backgrounds: Findings from a California Study." *Journal of Negro Education* 65, no. 2 (1996): 151–63.

Thernstrom, Abigail, and Stephan Thernstrom. *No Excuses: Closing the Racial Gap in Learning.* New York: Simon and Schuster, 2003.

Thomas-El, Salome, with Cecil Murphey. *I Choose to Stay: A Black Teacher Refuses to Desert the Inner City.* New York: Kensington, 2003.

Thompson, Chas. H. "The Negro Teacher and Desegregation of the Public Schools." *Journal of Negro Education* 22, no. 2 (1953): 95–101.

———. "Negro Teachers and the Elimination of Segregated Schools." *Journal of Negro Education* 20, no. 2 (1951): 135–39.

Tillman, Linda C. "(Un)Intended Consequences? The Impact of the *Brown v. Board of Education* Decision on the Employment Status of Black Educators." *Education and Urban Society* 6, no. 3 (2004): 280–303.

Tobin, Joseph J., David Y. H. Wu, and Dana H. Davidson. *Preschool in Three Cultures: Japan, China, and the United States.* New Haven: Yale University Press, 1989.

Townsend, Brenda L. "The Disproportionate Discipline of African American Learners: Reducing School Suspensions and Expulsions." *Exceptional Children* 66, no. 3 (2000): 381.

Travis, Cheryl B., and Sharon E. Anthony. "Some Psychological Consequences of Integration." *Journal of Negro Education* 47, no. 2 (1978): 151–58.

Trent, William T. "Outcomes of School Desegregation: Findings from Longitudinal Research." *Journal of Negro Education* 66, no. 3 (1997): 255–57.

———. "Why the Gap Between Black and White Performance in School? A Report on the Effects of Race on Student Achievement in the St. Louis Public Schools." *Journal of Negro Education* 66, no. 3 (1997): 320–29.

Tristano, Richard M. "Holy Family Parish: The Genesis of an African-American Catholic Community in Natchez, Mississippi." *Journal of Negro History* 83, no. 4 (1998): 258–83.

Trotter, John Rhodes. "Academic Attitudes of High Achieving and Low Achieving Academically Able Black Male Adolescents." *Journal of Negro Education* 50, no. 1 (1981): 54–62.

Trouilloud, David O., Philippe G. Sarrazin, Thomas J. Martinek, and Emma Guillet. "The Influence of Teacher Expectations on Student Achievement in Physical Education Classes: Pygmalion Revisited." *European Journal of Social Psychology* 32 (2002): 591–607.

Troyna, B. "Differential Commitment to Ethnic Identity by Black Youth in Britain." *New Community* 7, no. 3 (1978): 406–14.

Turner, J. C., R. J. Brown, and H. Tajfel, "Social Comparison and Group Interest in Ingroup Favouritism." *European Journal of Social Psychology* 9 (1979): 187–204.

Turner, Kara Miles. "'Getting It Straight': Southern Black School Patrons and the Struggle for Equal Education in the Pre- and Post-Civil Rights Eras." *Journal of Negro Education* 72, no. 2 (2003): 217–28.

Tyack, David, and Larry Cuban. *Tinkering Toward Utopia: A Century of Public School Reform.* Cambridge: Harvard University Press, 1995.

Tyson, Karolyn. "The Making of a 'Burden': Tracing the Development of a 'Burden of Acting White' in Schools." In *Beyond Acting White: Reframing the Debate on Black Student Achievement,* ed. Erin McNamara Horvat and Carla O'Connor. Lanham, Md.: Rowman and Littlefield, 2006.

———. "Notes from the Back of the Room: Problems and Paradoxes in the Schooling of Young Black Students." *Sociology of Education* 76, no. 4 (2003): 326–43.

———. "Weighing In: Elementary-Age Students and the Debate on Attitudes Toward School Among Black Students." *Social Forces* 80, no. 4 (2002): 1157–89.

Tyson, Karolyn, William Darity, Jr., and Domini R. Castellino. "It's Not 'a Black Thing': Understanding the Burden of Acting White and Other Dilemmas of High Achievement." *American Sociological Review* 70 (2005): 582–605.

Tyson, Timothy B. *Blood Done Sign My Name.* New York: Crown, 2004.

Unified Committee for Afro-American Contributions. *In Relentless Pursuit of an Education: African American Stories from a Century of Segregation, 1865–1967.* Lexington Park, Md.: Unified Committee for Afro-American Contributions, 2006, www.ucaonline.org.

U.S. Department of Education, National Center for Education Statistics. *A First Look at the Literacy of America's Adults in the Twenty-first Century.* NCES 2006-470 (2006), http://nces.ed.gov/NAAL/PDF/2006470.PDF.

U.S. Department of Education, Office of the Deputy Secretary, Planning and Evaluation Service. *The Longitudinal Evaluation of School Change and Performance in Title I Schools.* 2 vols. (2001), www.ed.gov/offices/OUS/PES/esed/lescp_vol1.pdf, and www.ed.gov/offices/OUS/PES/esed/lescp_vol2.pdf.

U.S. Department of Education, Office of Planning, Evaluation, and Policy Development, Policy and Program Studies Service. *Single-Sex Versus Secondary Schooling: A Systematic Review* (2005), www.ed.gov/rschstat/eval/other/single-sex/single-sex.pdf.

U.S. Department of Education, Office of the Under Secretary, Planning and Evaluation Service. *Promising Results, Continuing Challenges: The Final Report of the National Assessment of Title I* (1999), www.ed.gov/rschstat/eval/disadv/promisingresults/natirpt.pdf.

U.S. Department of Health and Human Services, Office of the Assistant Secretary for Planning and Evaluation. *Trends in the Well-Being of America's Children and Youth, 2000,* http://aspe.hhs.gov/HSP/ootrends/contents.htm#SD.

University of North Carolina, Oral History Interview with Fran Jackson, 23 Mar. 2001, Interview K-0208, Southern Oral History Program Collection (no. 4007), http://docsouth.unc.edu/sohp/K-0208/K-0208.xml.

Vandel, Deborah Lowe, and Sheri E. Hembree. "Peer Social Status and Friendship: Independent Contributors to Children's Social and Academic Adjustment." *Merrill-Palmer Quarterly* 40, no. 4 (1994): 461–77.

Vanfossen, Beth E., James D. Jones, and Joan Z. Spade. "Curriculum Tracking and Status Maintenance." *Sociology of Education* 60, no. 2 (1987): 104–22.

Vaughan, Graham M., Henri Tajfel, and Jennifer Williams. "Bias in Reward Allocation in an Intergroup and an Interpersonal Context." *Social Psychology Quarterly* 44, no. 1 (1981): 37–42.

Vaughn, William Preston. *Schools for All: The Blacks and Public Education in the South, 1865–1877.* Lexington: University of Kentucky Press, 1974.

Vigdor, Jacob, and Thomas Nechyba. "Peer Effects in North Carolina Public Schools" (2004), www.ksg.harvard.edu/pepg/PDF/events/Munich/PEPG-04-20Nechyba.pdf.

Virginia Black History Archives. Interview with Helene Ruby Hinton Lovell, 4 Mar. 1992, www.library.vcu.edu/jbc/speccoll/vbha/school/lovell.html.

Virginia Black History Archives. Interview with James E. Washington, 1992, www.library.vcu.edu/jbc/speccoll/vbha/school/washj.html.

Wade-Gayles, Gloria. *Pushed Back to Strength.* New York: Avon, 1993.

Walberg, Herbert J., and Andrew T. Kopan. *Rethinking Urban Education*. Jossey-Bass, 1972.

Walker, Vanessa Siddle. "African American Teaching in the South, 1940–1960." *American Educational Research Journal* 38, no. 4 (2001): 751–79.

———. *Their Highest Potential: An African American School Community in the Segregated South*. Chapel Hill: University of North Carolina Press, 1996.

———. "Valued Segregated Schools for African American Children in the South, 1935–1969: A Review of Common Themes and Characteristics." *Review of Educational Research* 70, no. 3 (2000): 253–85.

Walker, Vanessa Siddle, and Ulysses Byas. "The Architects of Black Schooling in the Segregated South: The Case of One Principal Leader." *Journal of Curriculum and Supervision* 19, no. 1 (2003): 54–72.

Washington, Carrie Smith Johnson. "A Study of Former Negro High School Students, Teachers, and Administrators in the Piedmont Area of North Carolina." Ph.D. diss., East Tennessee State University, 2002, http:////etd-submit.etsu.edu/etd/theses/available/etd-0531102-163233/unrestricted/Washington062302.pdf.

Webber, Thomas L. *Deep Like the Rivers: Education in the Slave Quarter Community, 1831–1865*. New York: W. W. Norton, 1978.

Weis, Tracey. "Teaching *Brown*: Reflections on Pedagogical Challenges and Opportunities." *History of Education Quarterly* 44 (2004).

Wellman, Barry. "I Am a Student." *Sociology of Education* 44, no. 4 (1971): 422–37.

Wells, Amy Stuart, and Robert L. Crain. *Stepping Over the Color Line: African-American Students in White Suburban Schools*. New Haven: Yale University Press, 1997.

Wentzel, Kathryn R., and Kathryn Caldwell. "Friendships, Peer Acceptance, and Group Membership: Relations to Academic Achievement in Middle School." *Child Development* 68, no. 6 (1997): 1198–1209.

Wheelock, Anne. "Chattanooga's Paideia Schools: A Single Track for All—And It's Working." *Journal of Negro Education* 63, no. 1 (1994): 77–92.

White, Forrest R. *Pride and Prejudice: School Desegregation and Urban Renewal in Norfolk, 1950–1959*. Westport, Conn.: Praeger, 1992.

White, Kinnard, and James H. Knight. "School Desegregation, Socioeconomic Status, Sex, and the Aspirations of Southern Negro Adolescents." *Journal of Negro Education* 42, no. 1 (1973): 71–78.

White, Monica A. "Paradise Lost? Teachers' Perspectives on the Use of Cultural Capital in the Segregated Schools of New Orleans, Louisiana." *Journal of African American History* 87 (2002): 269–81.

Wilkins Center for Human Relations and Social Justice, University of Minnesota. "Analysis of the 1996 Minnesota Basic Standards Test Data" (Mar. 1997), www.hhh.umn.edu/img/assets/9680/96tstrpt.pdf.

Wilkinson, Doris Y. "Integration Dilemmas in a Racist Culture." *Society* 33, no. 3 (1996): 27–31.

Williams, Heather Andrea. "'Clothing Themselves in Intelligence': The Freedpeople,

Schooling, and Northern Teachers, 1861–1871." *Journal of African American History* 87 (2002): 372–89.

———. *Self-Taught: African American Education in Slavery and Freedom*. Chapel Hill: University of North Carolina Press, 2007.

Williams, Juan. *My Soul Looks Back in Wonder: Voices of the Civil Rights Experience*. New York: Sterling, 2005.

Williams, Robin M., Jr. *Strangers Next Door: Ethnic Relations in American Communities*. Englewood Cliffs, N.J.: Prentice-Hall, 1964.

Williams, T., M. Kirst, E. Haertel, et al. "Similar Students, Different Results: Why Do Some Schools Do Better? A Large-Scale Survey of California Elementary Schools Serving Low-Income Students." Mountain View, Calif.: EdSource, 2005, www.edsource.org/pdf/SimStuo5.pdf.

Willis, Paul. *Learning to Labor: Working-Class Kids Get Working-Class Jobs*. New York: Columbia University Press, 1981.

Wilson, Anna Victoria, and William E. Segall. *Oh, Do I Remember! Experiences of Teachers During the Desegregation of Austin's Schools, 1964–1971*. Albany: State University of New York Press, 2001.

Wilson, Kenneth L. "The Effect of Integration and Class on Black Educational Attainment." *Sociology of Education* 52, no. 2 (1979): 84–98.

Wilson, William Julius. *The Truly Disadvantaged: The Inner City, the Underclass, and Public Policy*. Chicago: University of Chicago Press, 1987.

Wolff, Max. "Segregation in the Schools of Gary, Indiana." *Journal of Educational Sociology* 36, no. 6 (1963): 251–61.

Wolters, Raymond. *The Burden of Brown: Thirty Years of School Desegregation*. Knoxville: University of Tennessee Press, 1984.

Woodson, Carter G. *The Education of the Negro Prior to 1861*. Kessinger Reprints, 1919.

———. *The Mis-Education of the Negro*. Trenton, N.J.: Africa World Press, 1990 [orig. pub. 1933].

Woodward, C. Vann. "Strange Career Critics: Long May They Persevere." *Journal of American History* 75, no. 3 (1988): 857–68.

Worchel, Stephen, Danny Axsom, Frances Ferris, Gary Samaha, and Susan Schweizer. "Determinants of the Effect of Intergroup Cooperation on Intergroup Attraction." *Journal of Conflict Resolution* 22, no. 3 (1978): 429–39.

Wright, Elizabeth. "The Greatest School Under the Sun." *Issues and Views* (Winter 1994), www.issues-views.com/index.php/sect/1000/article/1017.

Wright, George C. "Growing Up Segregated." In *Understanding the Little Rock Crisis: An Exercise in Remembrance and Reconciliation*, ed. Elizabeth Jacoway and C. Fred Williams. Fayetteville: University of Arkansas Press, 1999.

Wright, Nathan, Jr. *Black Power and Urban Unrest*. New York: Hawthorn, 1967.

X, Malcolm. *By Any Means Necessary: Speeches, Interviews, and a Letter*, ed. George Breitman. New York: Pathfinder, 1970.

Yan, Wenfan. "Successful African American Students: The Role of Parental Involvement." *Journal of Negro Education* 68, no. 1 (1999): 5–22.

Yeakey, C. C., G. S. Johnston, and J. A. Adkison. "In Pursuit of Equity: A Review of Research on Minorities and Women in Educational Administration." *Educational Administration Quarterly* 22, no. 3 (1986): 122.

Yinger, J. Milton. *A Minority Group in American Society.* New York: McGraw-Hill, 1965.

Young, Rufus, Jr. "A Process for Developing More Effective Urban Schools: A Case Study of Stowe Middle School." *Journal of Negro Education* 57, no. 3 (1988): 307–34.

Zimmerman, David J. "Peer Effects in Academic Outcomes: Evidence from a Natural Experiment." *Review of Economics and Statistics* 85, no. 1 (2003): 15–23.

Zirkel, Sabrina. "Is There a Place for Me? Role Models and Academic Identity Among White Students and Students of Color." *Teachers College Record* 104 (2002): 357–76.

———. "What Will You Think of Me? Racial Integration, Peer Relationships, and Achievement Among White Students and Students of Color." *Journal of Social Issues* 60, no. 1 (2004): 57–74.

Zweigenhaft, Richard L., and G. William Domhoff. *Blacks in the White Establishment? A Study of Race and Class in America.* New Haven: Yale University Press, 1991.